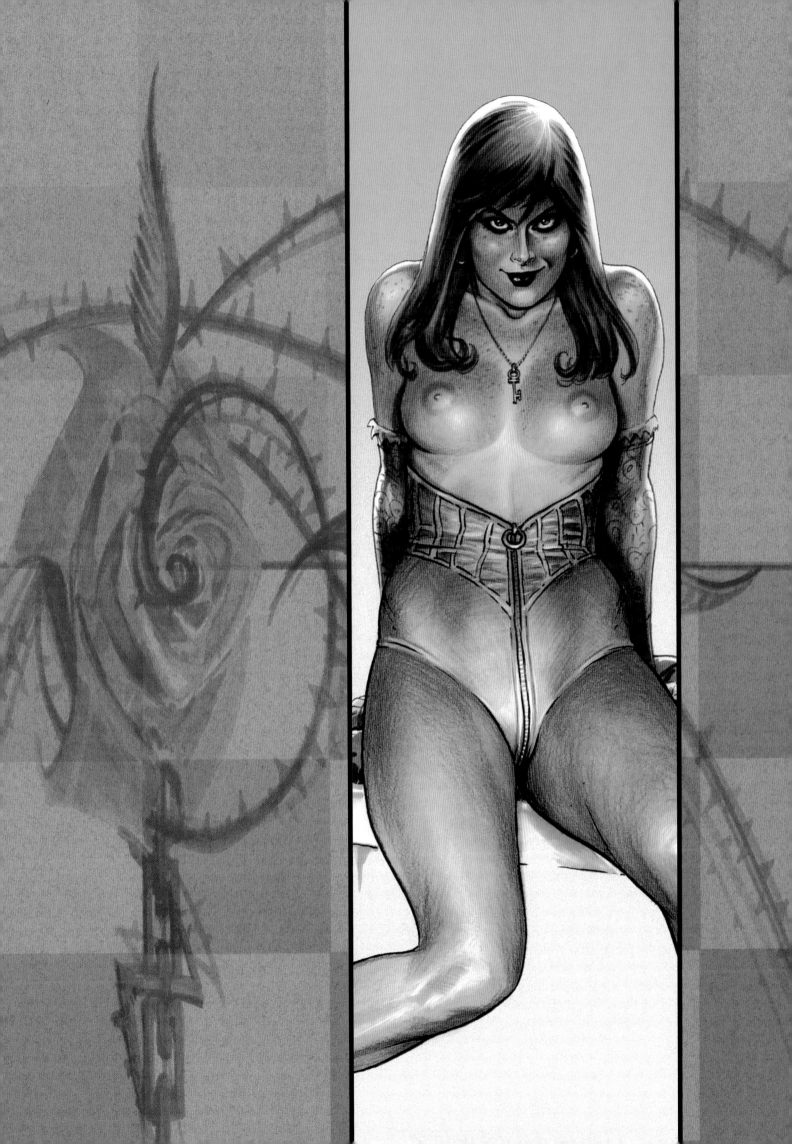

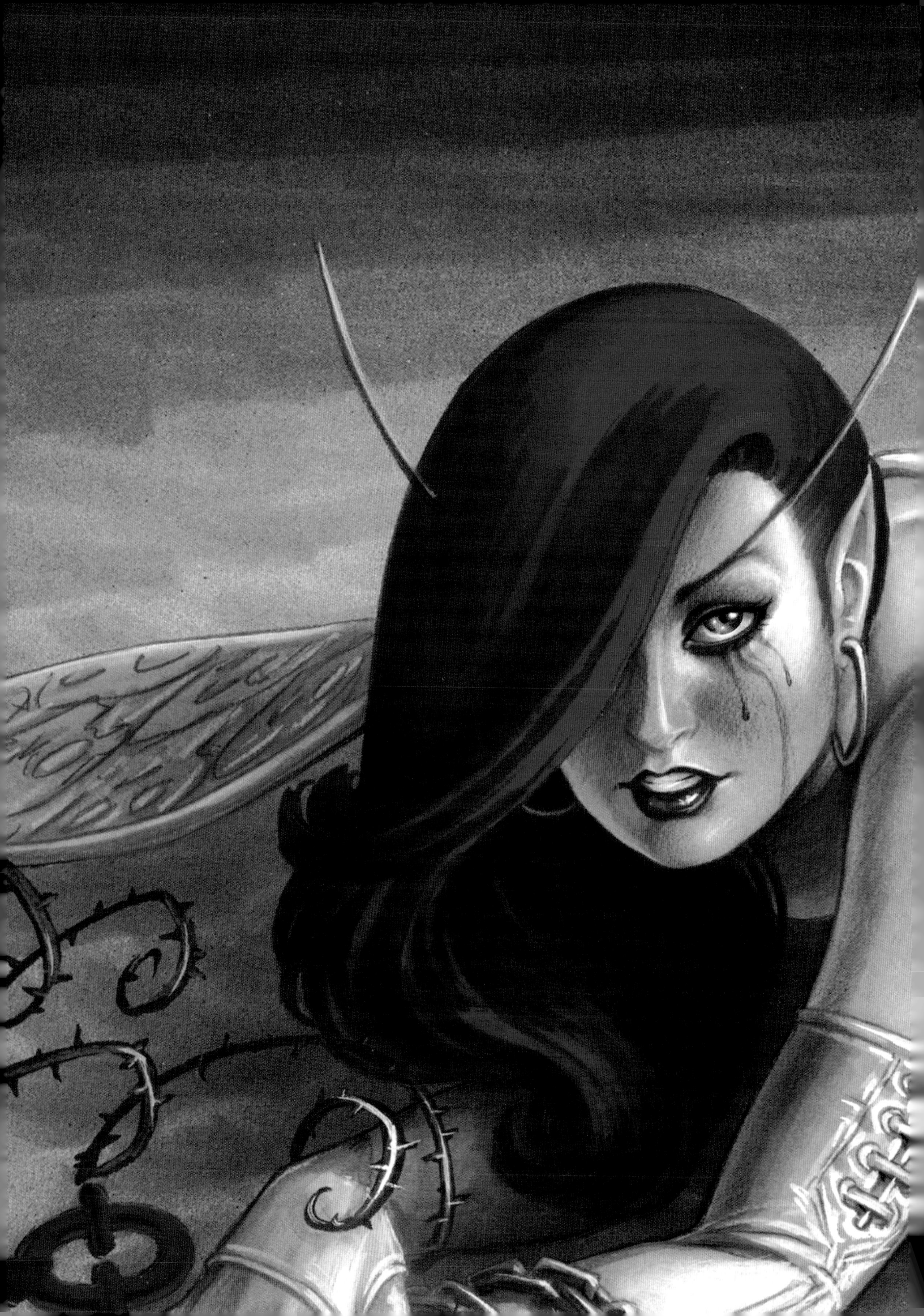

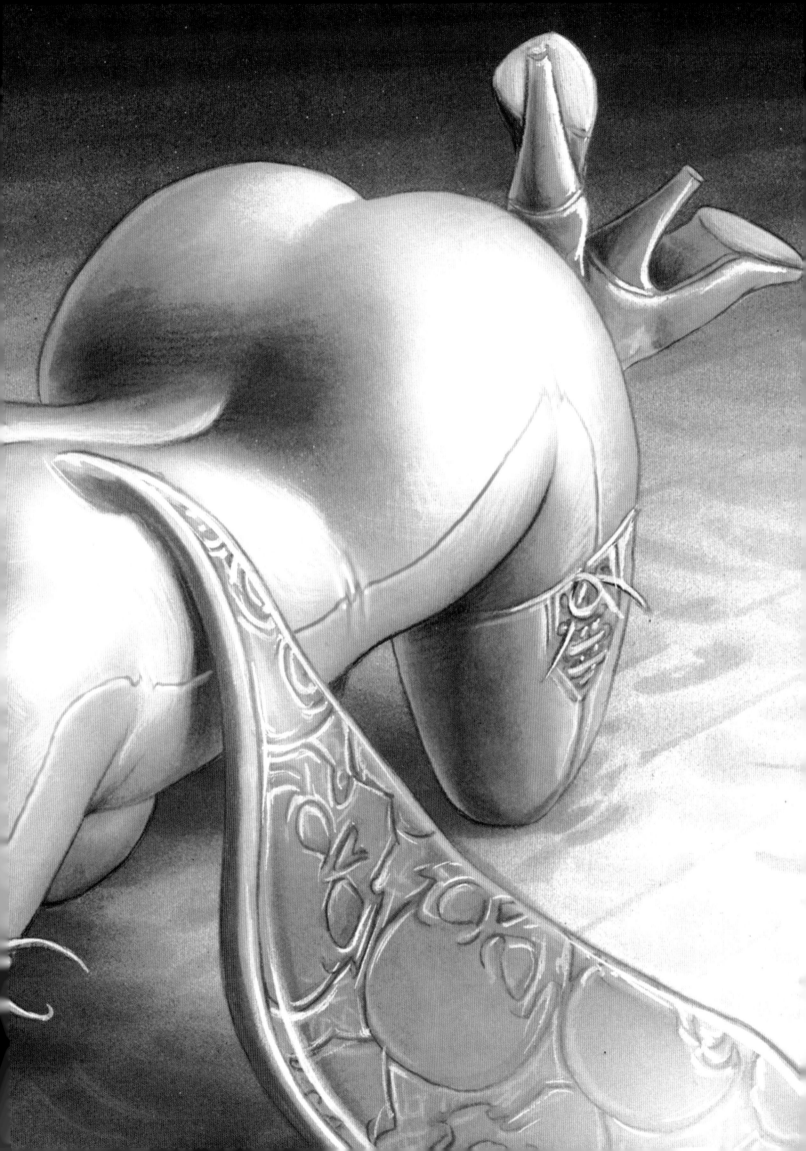

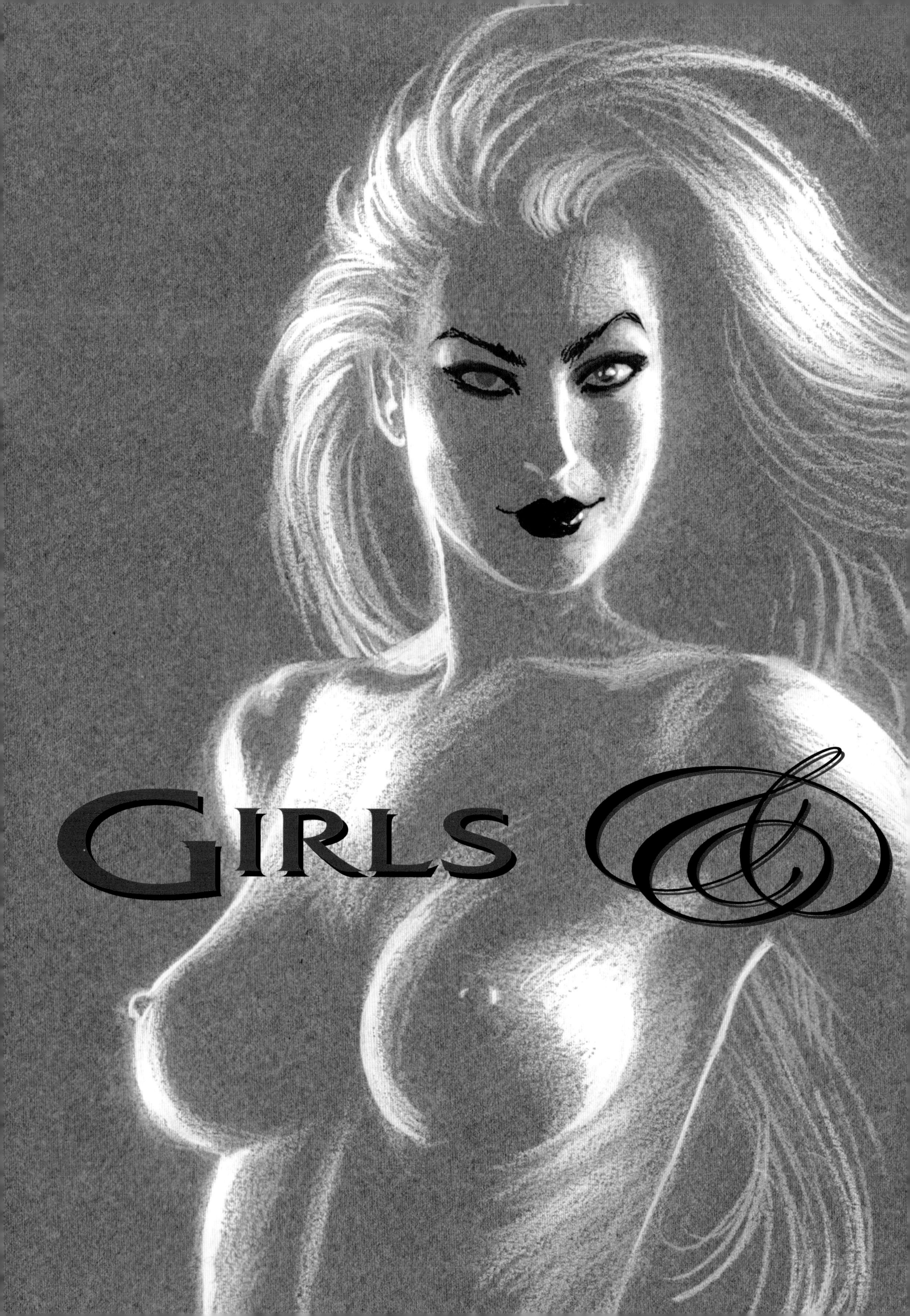
GIRLS &

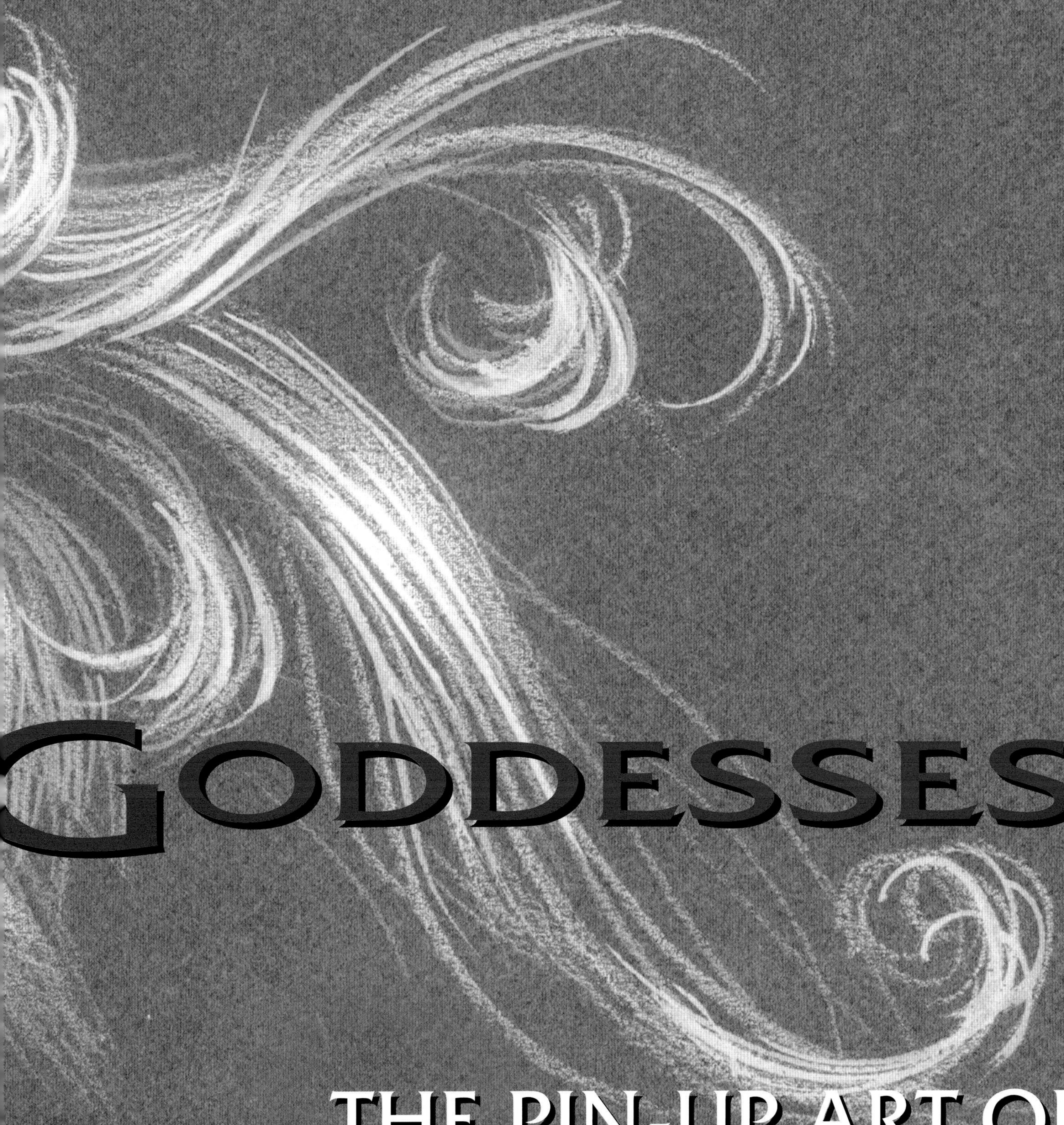

GODDESSES

THE PIN-UP ART OF JOSEPH MICHAEL LINSNER

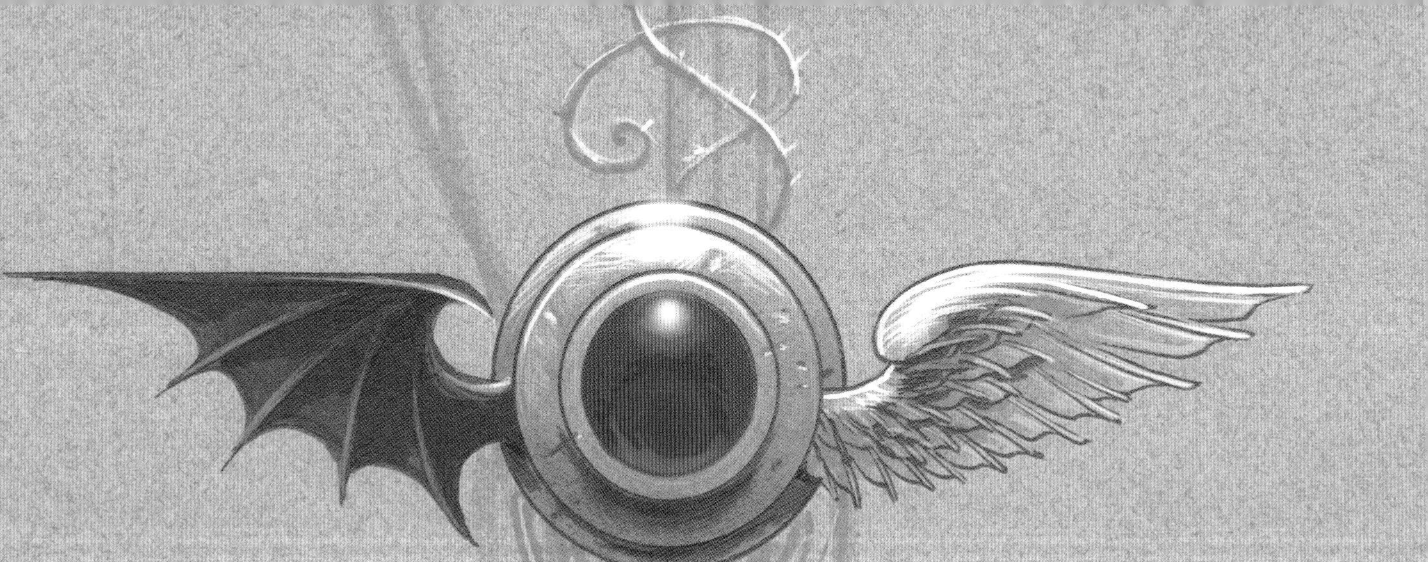

Dedication

I would like to dedicate this book to all of the beautiful ladies who have posed for me over the years. You have all been an inspiration.

JML

For Linsner.com

Eva Hopkins	*Office Goddess* www.lunamusestudios.com
Zeke Feldhaus	*Point Man*
Greg Hinkle	*Webmaster*
Jeff Eckleberry	*Production* www.eckleberry.com

Image Comics, Inc.

Erik Larsen	*Publisher*
Todd McFarlane	*President*
Marc Silvestri	*CEO*
Jim Valentino	*Vice-President*
Eric Stephenson	*Executive Director*
Mark Haven Britt	*Director of Marketing*
Thao Le	*Accounts Manager*
Rosemary Cao	*Accounting Assistant*
Traci Hui	*Administrative Assistant*
Joe Keatinge	*Traffic Manager*
Allen Hui	*Production Manager*
Jonathan Chan	*Production Artist*
Drew Gill	*Production Artist*
Chris Giarrusso	*Production Artist*

www.imagecomics.com

LINSNER: GIRLS & GODDESSES Vol. 1. Published by Image Comics, Inc. Office of publication: 1942 University Avenue, Suite 305, Berkeley, California 94704.

Introduction
by Eva Hopkins

Art has been part of my life since I was a wee little tyke. For
it, I have to thank my parents. My mom would occasionally
take me out of Catholic school, uniform & all, to New York City.
We would go see big exhibits like Picasso or the huge one right
after they opened up King Tut's Tomb. Mom also took me to a
great little bookshop where I came across my first comic books.
Wonder Woman was my favorite. The TV show was really big at
the time, & I had a deep interest in mythology. Since she was both
goddess & superhero, Wonder Woman covered all the bases.

My father accidentally exposed me to a different sort of art.
I used to bring him his morning coffee on the weekends. I suppose I was around seven or eight years old the day I walked in
with his coffee, & saw him stuffing something into his sock drawer,
definitely trying to be stealthy about it. I acted as if I hadn't
noticed, but that drawer of his dresser now needed to be
explored.

One day, my dad had gone off to work, I was home sick with
a tummy bug & my mother was happily busy doing something in
the kitchen. I crept carefully from my room down the hallway to
my dad's room, turned the doorknob, & slipped inside, shutting
the door quietly behind me.

Feeling very adventurous indeed, I slunk over to the dresser,
found the sock drawer, & opened it. I began to poke through the
pairs of socks with my chubby, childish fingers. My hands finally
came in contact with something smooth towards the bottom of
the socks - something smooth & cool - something glossy. I pulled
it out.

I was staring at my first-ever pin-up girl, on the cover of a
Playboy magazine. This would be an even better story if I could
remember which one it was. The model had fluffy hair, big eyes,
perfectly lipsticked lips - & she was mostly naked..! Yes, I'd seen
painted nudity, on walls of museums, but I somehow sensed that
this woman was even more naked than those artworks; that the
purpose of the cover photo was different than the adulation
expressed by the paintings. It was a huge thrill. I didn't really
connect it with sex, of course - that weird, abstract birds & the
bees talk didn't click in any way with what I was observing. I
thought she was very beautiful, & there was something delightful
about being able to see her.

After flipping through the magazine for a few moments, I
noticed that not all the (wow! naked!) women were pho-
tographed. There were drawings of women in various states of
dress & undress. Some were simple drawings used to illustrate
an article; others were cartoons with captions below them that I
didn't quite understand. But all of the women were beautiful -
long-legged, busty, pretty eyes, great mouths.

Once discovered, of course, such a font of knowledge could
not go ignored. I thought about them a lot, but I didn't get to
peep at the magazines often. Eventually, the inevitable happened
- I got caught.

I hadn't heard my father come up the stairs. He opened the
door to his room to find me carefully scrutinizing a brunette
centerfold. A lesser man would have screamed at me, or acted
edgy & flustered. Not my dad, who was older, fifty-something at
the time. Though obviously annoyed, Dad said only, "Don't
invade my privacy; you know you shouldn't be looking at those.
Please put them away." He paused as he turned to leave the
room. "If you have anything you need to ask me, you can. But
don't poke around my things; I don't snoop in your room." He
closed the door quietly. My face was red! I put the magazines
back neatly, covered them with socks, slammed the drawer shut
& fled the scene of the crime. Neither of us brought it up again.

As a teenager, I had frequent free rein in my mother's used
bookshop. I would pick a book to while away time in between
waiting on customers. Often this was fantasy fiction, but sometimes I'd take a book from the art section, crack it open, &
spend the afternoon ogling new art. It was during that time I
became more familiar with pin-up art. I particularly liked the
paintings of Vargas - all the lines were curvier, longer & more
graceful than they could have possibly been in reality. They were
gorgeous but unattainable, it seemed, impossibly lovely - which is
perhaps why I loved looking at them so much. There was no
expectation to be that woman so I could enjoy the fantasy. Being
a child of the 80's, I got into Patrick Nagel as well, but Vargas
remained my favorite for many years.

My early love of comic books returned while I was in college
in the early 90's. I worked at a comic store for a brief period of
time, & got to read great things like "Maus" & "Love &
Rockets". New kinds of stories were being told. Perhaps stories
I would like to tell. I started doing a couple of comic strips for
the college paper, & kept busy writing short stories & drawing
while attending school.

From about 1990 on, various pals of mine would appear at
parties & concerts wearing tee shirts done by the same artist,

one Joseph Michael Linsner. Suddenly this iconic image of a woman - with red hair over one eye & wearing black lingerie - was everywhere. Someone handed me one of the comic books - Cry For Dawn #3, if memory serves. I found the artwork stunning. Cry For Dawn, with its very dark subject matter & seemingly misogynistic themes, blew my mind. It was over-the-top - sensory overload. My friends all agreed, & they couldn't get enough of it.

I met Joe soon after being exposed to his comic books. We met at a party thrown by a mutual friend. I was immediately struck by how different he was than I'd expected him to be. He was polite, charming & funny. He talked about Shakespeare, movies & art with ease. I talked to Joe about his art, which was laden with madonna/whore imagery. "Do you not like women, or something?" I asked Joe.

Just like I can't recall the exact Playboy cover that made such a strong impact on me, I don't remember word for word what Joe said, on that porch in North Jersey, July 1993. But the tone of it stayed with me. Again, it was not what I had expected.

Joe didn't hate women. Joe adored women. Joe had women up so high on a pedestal, that you got the idea that he thought they all were goddesses; that each & every one had some little spark of magic, that only he (or someone very like him) could truly appreciate. When he told me his mom had been letting him hang Playboy centerfolds since he was thirteen or so, it explained a lot. Un-hung-up parents, thankfully, usually equals un-hung-up child.

Later, I complimented his mom about it, that I thought it was cool she let her young son have his Playmates. "Sure," she responded very matter-of-factly. "Hey, what's not to like?"

Over the course of the next few years, Joe & I became closer friends. I wound up going to work for him in 1996. There was a period of time where I would come upon Joe drawing, usually a cover painting, & I'd observe the clothing - skintight skull lace; bikinis; shiny red leather. He went through a phase we both referred to as the spray-on clothes year. We had long conversations about how hypocritical America is; how the model in his painting was nude all but for some color, & a drawn-in neckline & sleeves. One day, exasperated by the old discussion, I replied sharply - "Well, why don't you do what you really want, & just draw them naked?" "I should," he said thoughtfully.

That's definitely not the moment that this book was born. Joe has been ogling women for most of his life. But Joe has mentioned that specific chat to me more than once; I secretly like to imagine it helped push him over the edge, to where we are now.

Joe's work has attained that rare thing in pin-up art; he has a distinct vision, his own voice. A Linsner Girl looks different than a Vargas girl, a Stevens girl, an Olivia Girl, a Hughes Girl

or a Cho Girl. Joe can draw a beautiful girl - the cover of book you are holding is an exquisite example of that. He took main muse, a gorgeous woman, & brought his own polish to painting of her. When Joe does this, I feel his work is just strong as my early pin-up idols. But (excuse my obvious bias think his work goes beyond them.

Before you disagree, consider what Joe does when he pai a woman; he elevates her in his mind beyond even the status goddess - she is all that is beauty. I have seen him take a pho he's shot of a model. She could be a gorgeous classic model ty Plenty of lovely ladies have posed for Joe. But sometimes subject is a more ordinary girl, but she has a particular impish to her grin. Or shift of the hip. Or heavenly look in her eyes. manages to find what is lovely, what is goddess-like, in women many types, shapes & sizes.

Joe emphasizes the positive, but there is an air of real about his paintings. Bodies in his pin-up pieces do things t bodies actually do in real life. Breasts slump softly downwa when a model is in repose; skin by the hip bunches gently wh a leg is raised; the curves of some figures have been touch lightly by gravity. His women have short hair, long hair, sometim even freckles. Even the skinniest of skinny women have pro little feminine curves, indicating the hips, belly, thighs & bu Joe's paintings of women reveal images I feel are attainable based in reality. It's a healthy version of pin-up art & one I proud to have been involved with for over ten years. It wa great honor to me when Joe did not one, but two, portraits myself. I felt like a real pin-up girl. Anytime I see someone w is glimpsing a painting Joe has done of her, seeing it for the fi time, it's amazing. I know the model now sees herself with n eyes, that she appreciates her own charms more than before. is a powerful gift.

I know I am not alone in this feeling. About half of Jose Michael Linsner's many fans are women. The main reason fem fans give for their keen appreciation of Joe's art is the fact th his women look realistic.

Over the years, it's been a joy to be a part of Joe's fantas adventures, chasing the muse - goddess-like, feminine beauty - the way. From the dark & gothic world of his indie cult creatic the Goddess Dawn, to comics cover artist for just about ever one, to a very popular pinup artist, Joe has taken each phase his career in graceful stride. I predict that as he keeps bringing images of heaven, Joe will will keep getting closer to that mu up on high in his mind, & we will continue to see more & mo of the Linsner Girl.

More beauty in a world that is frequently not beautiful - quote Momma Linsner, "Hey, what's not to like?"

Eva Hopkins
February 16, 2007

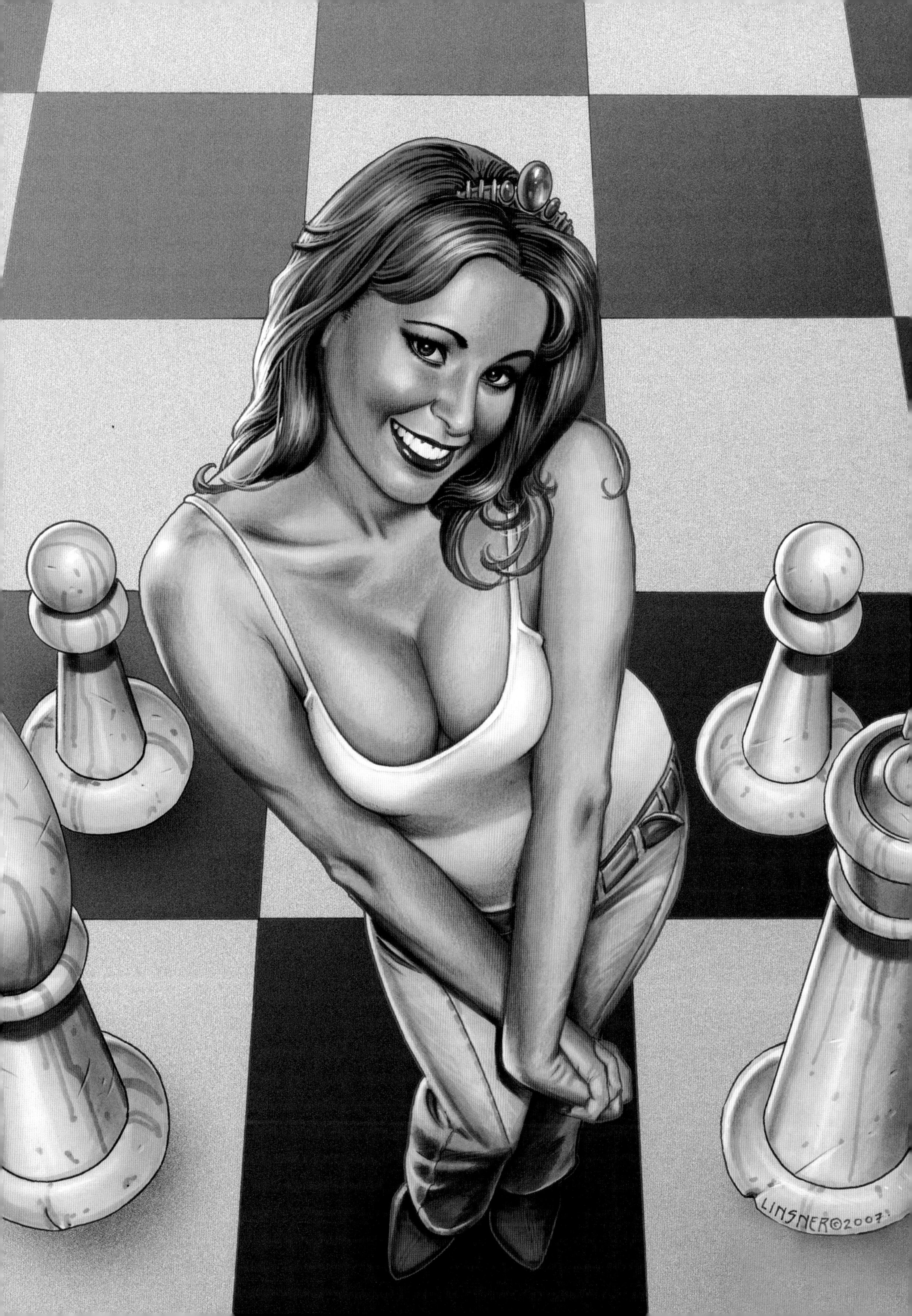
LINSNER©2007

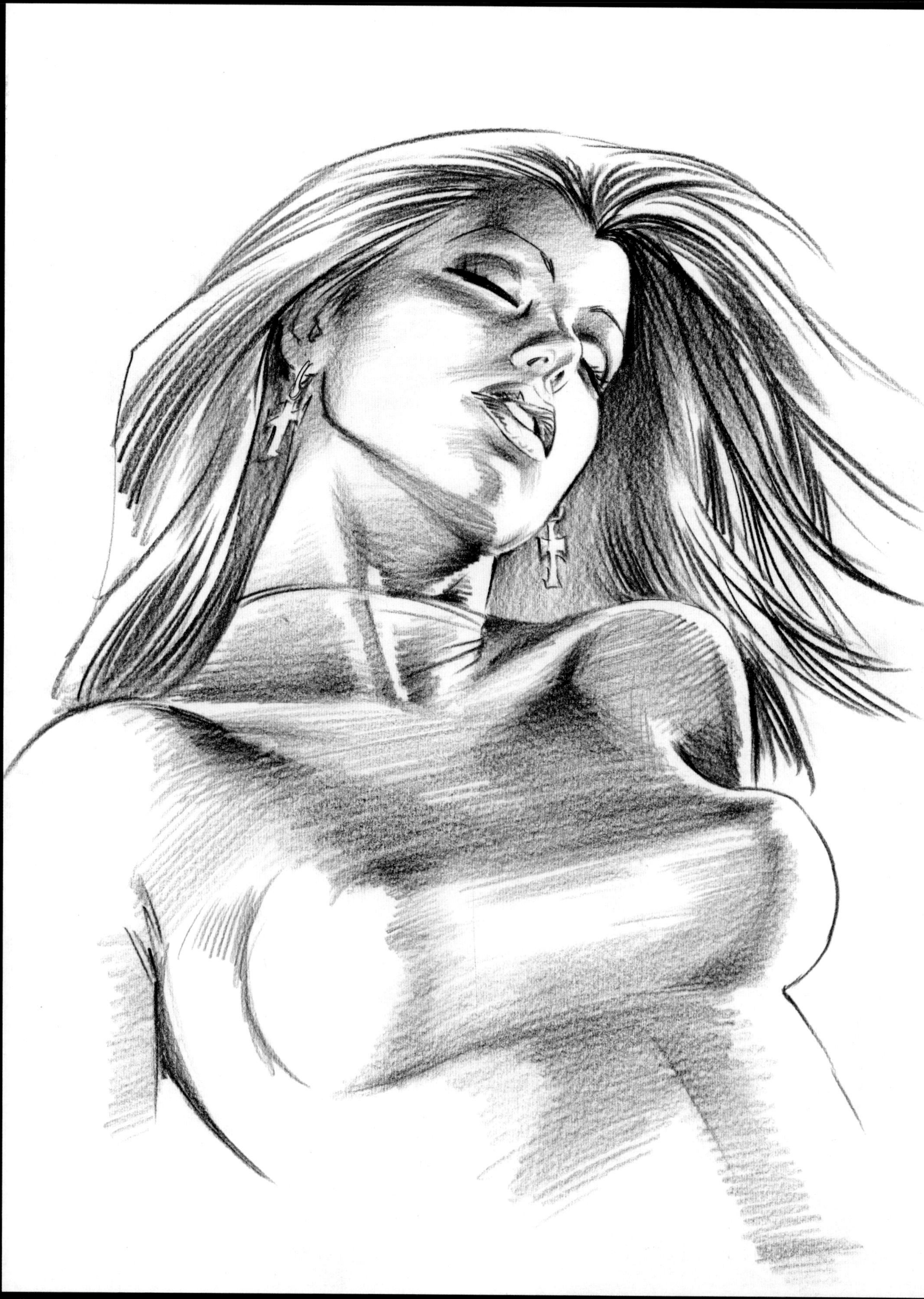

Ivory

the Queen
(Page 9)

Dark Beauty

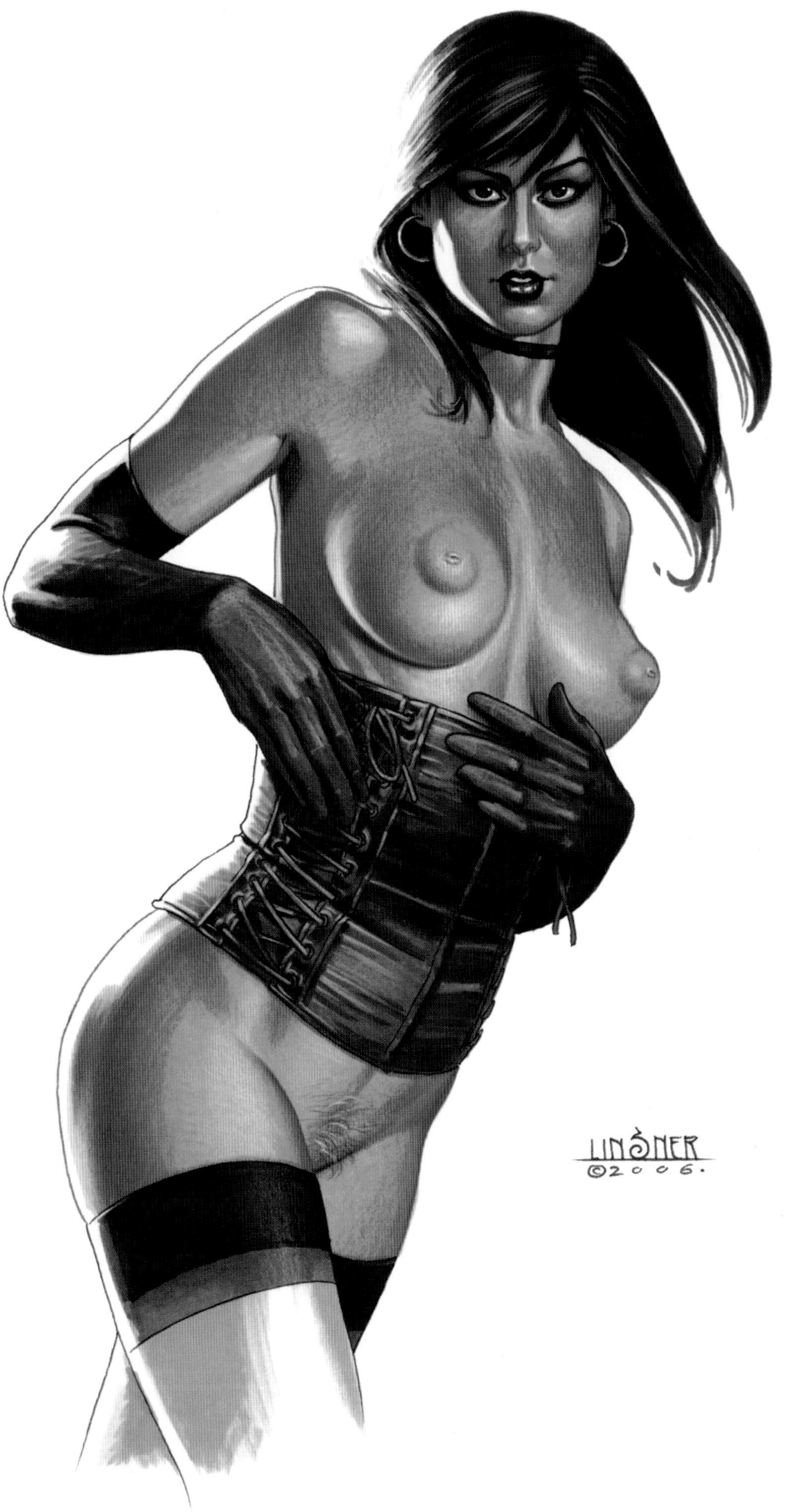
LINSNER
©2006.

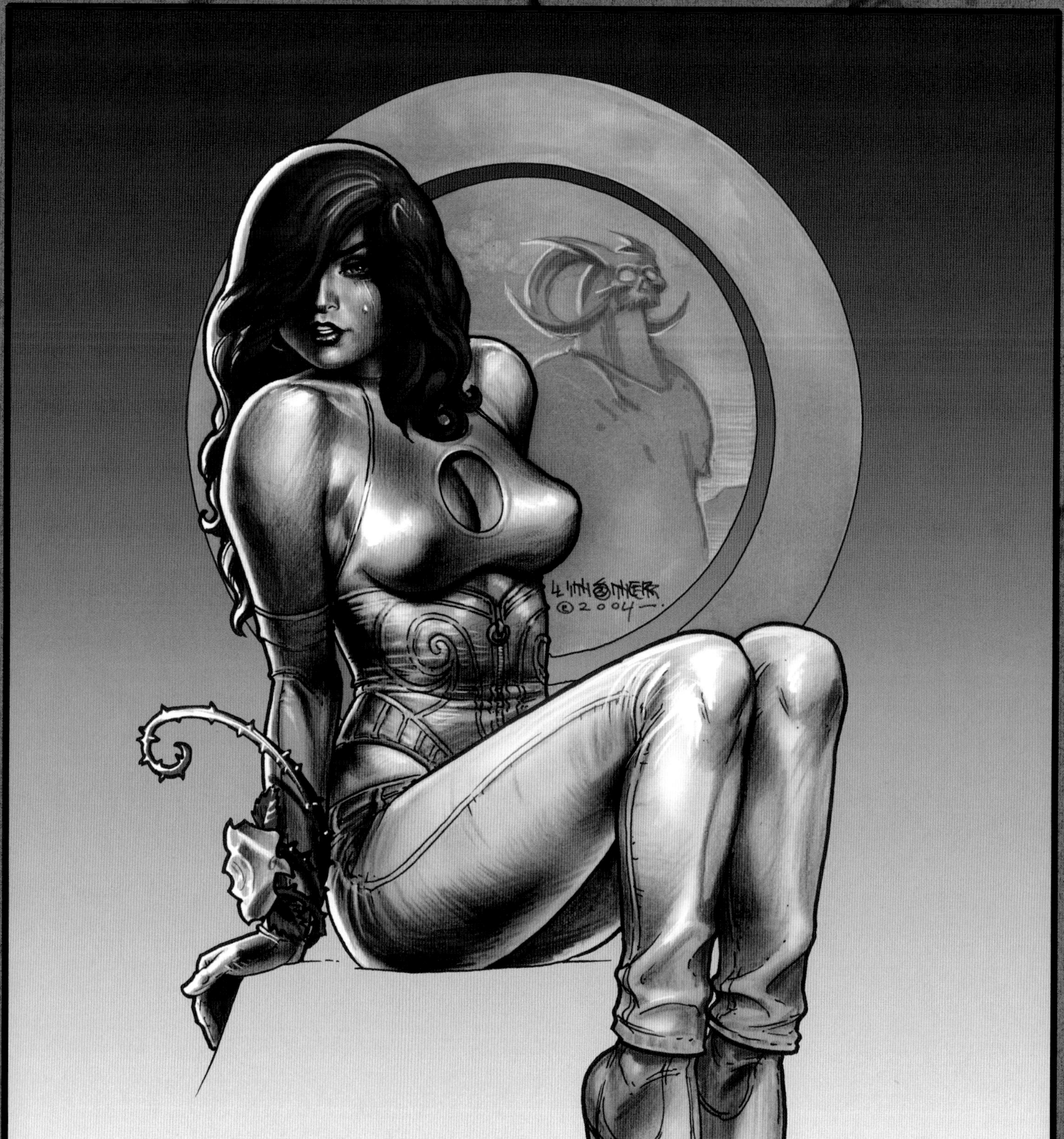

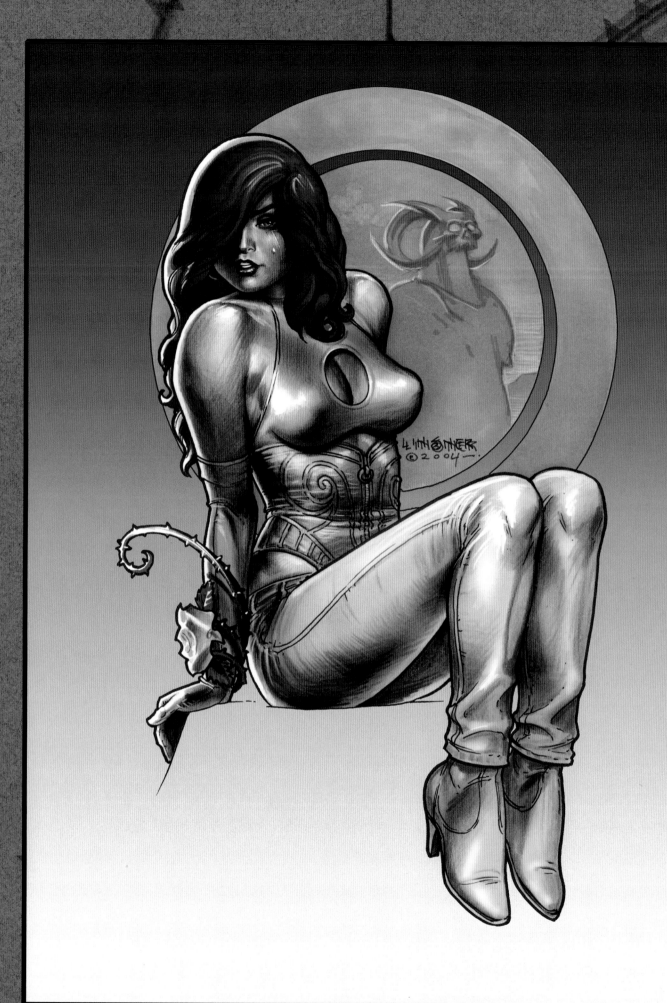

Periwinkle Death

Suzi Blue

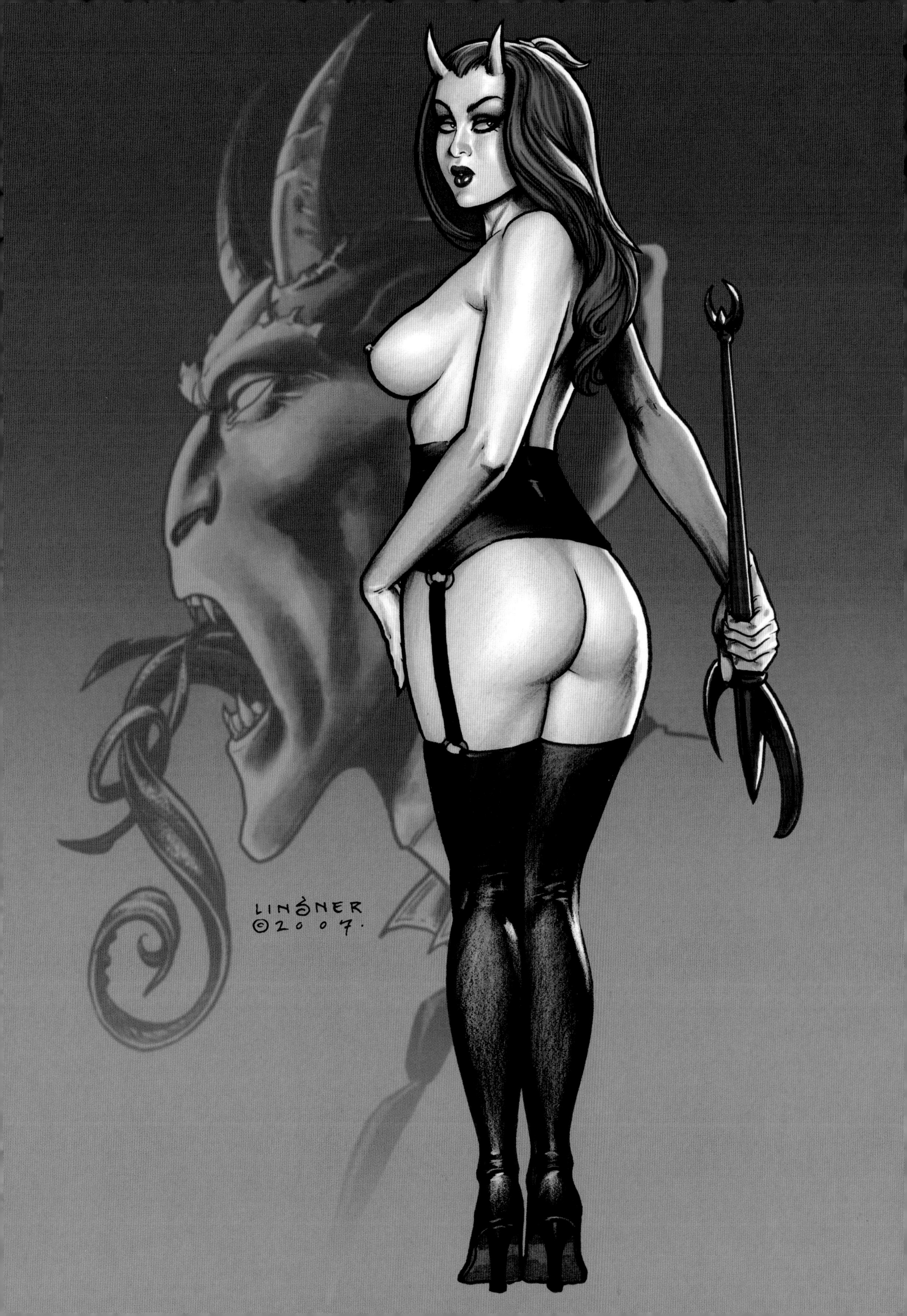
LINSNER
©2007.

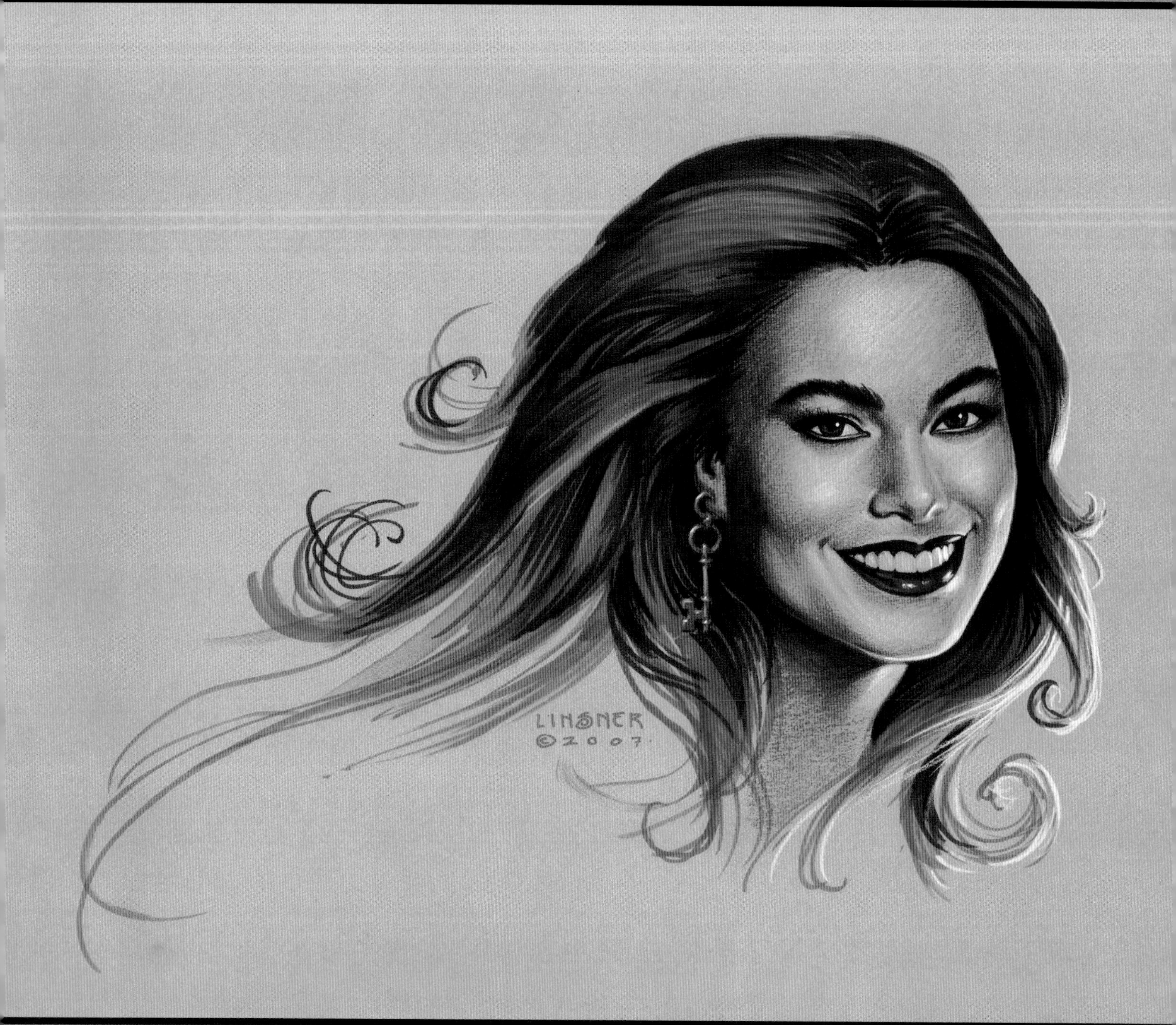
LINSNER
©2007

Sophia

Open Me First

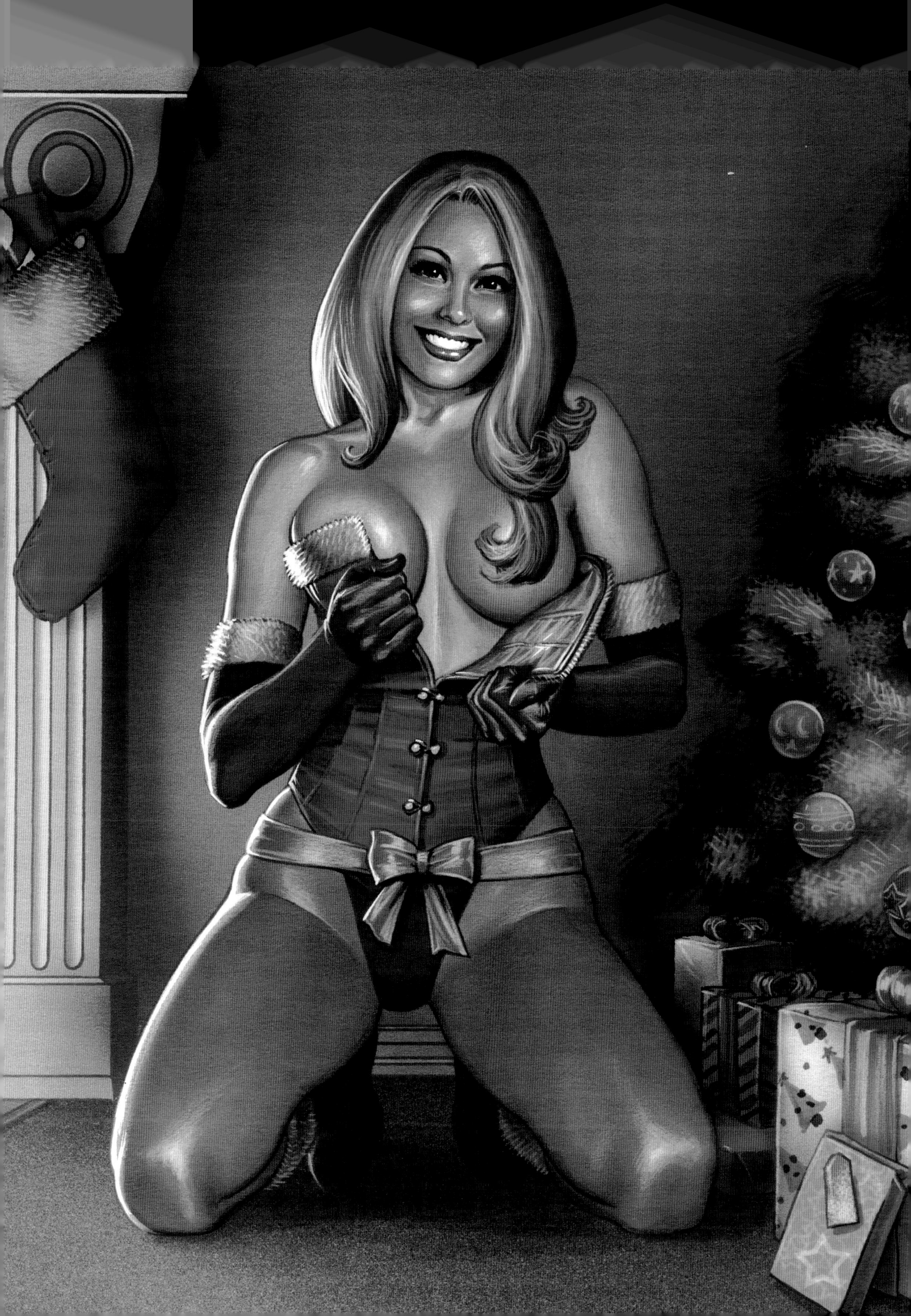

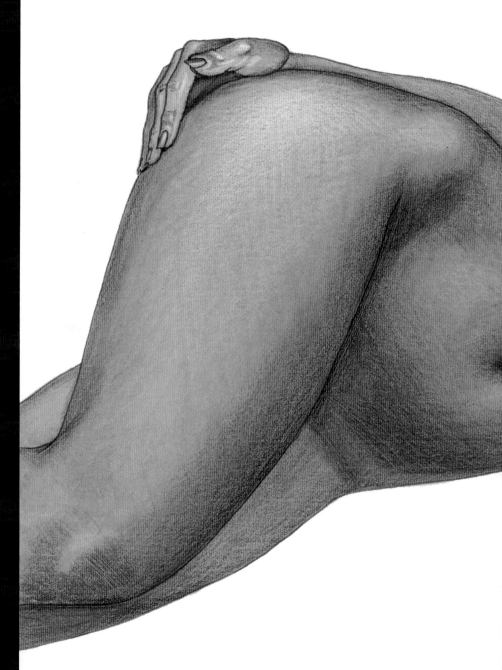

Ashleigh

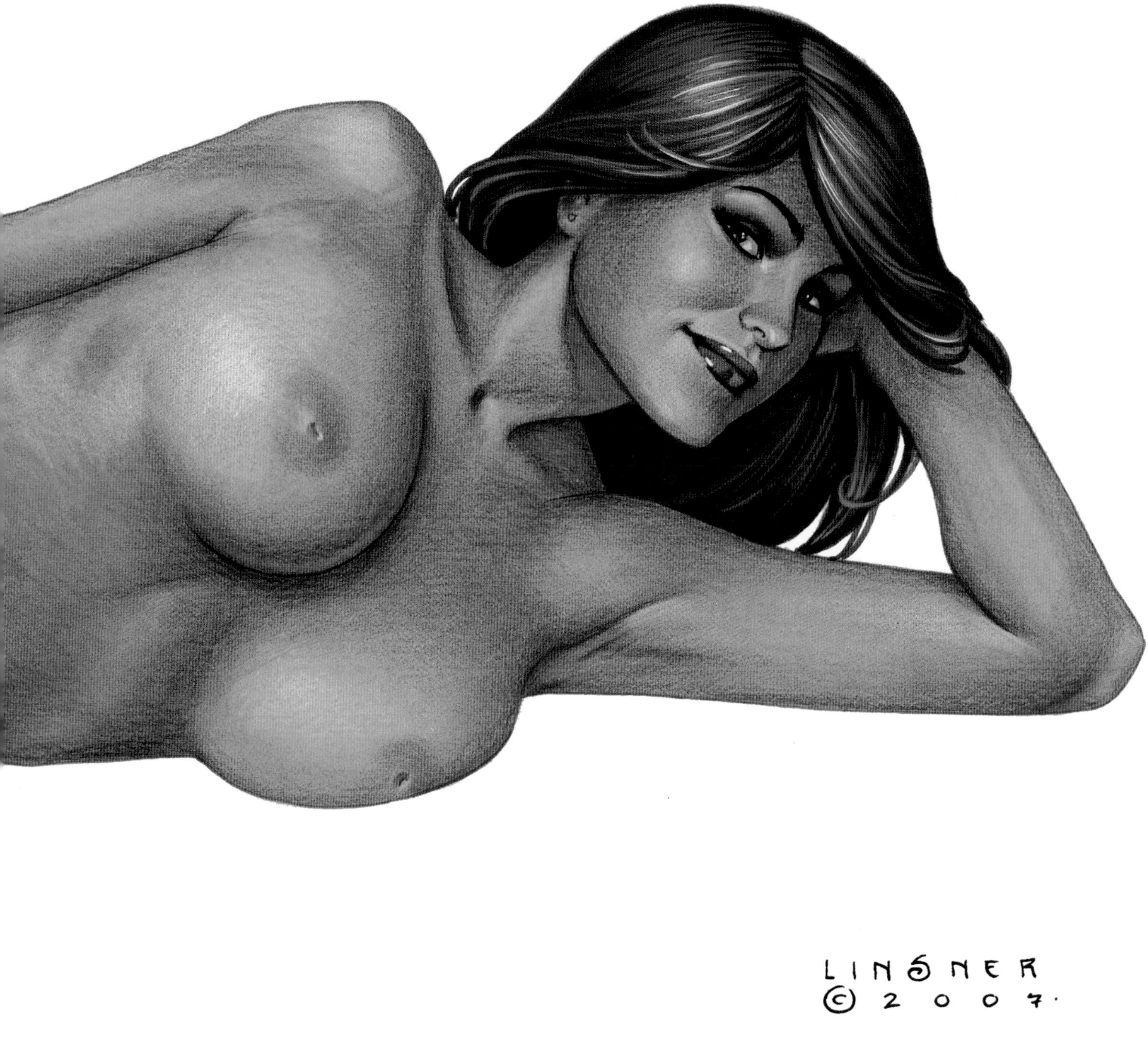
LINSNER
©2007.

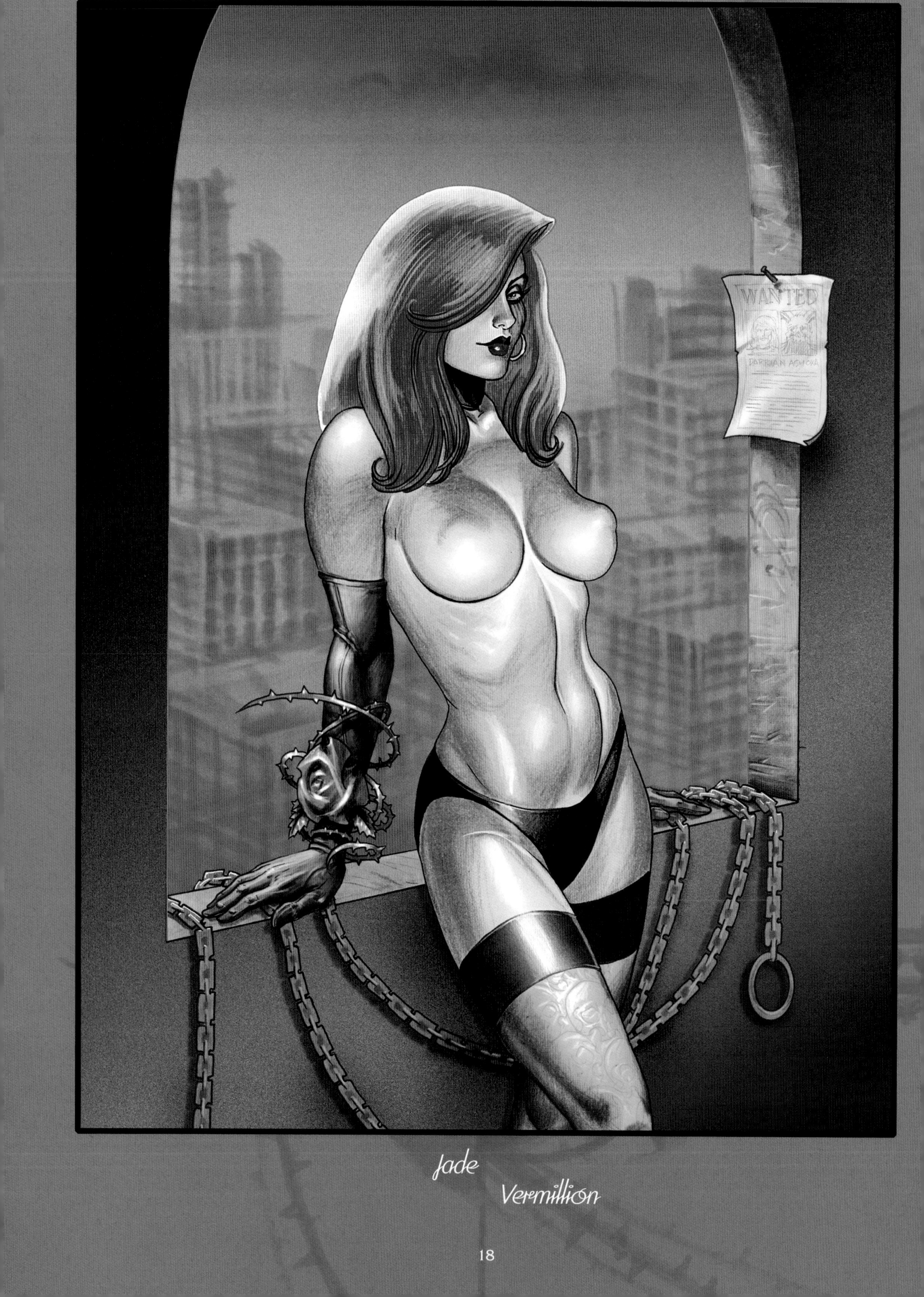
WANTED

Jade Vermillion

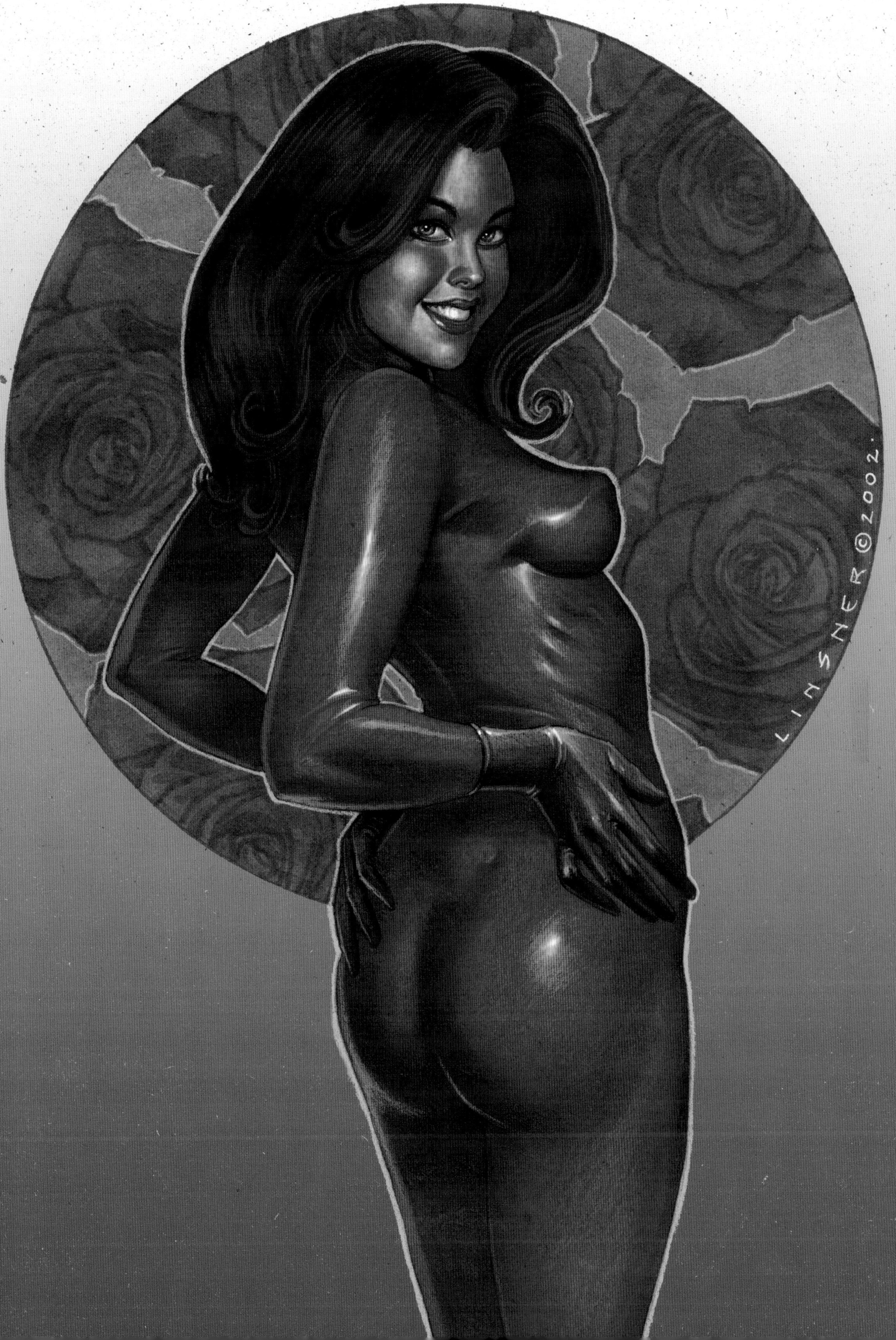
LINSNER ©2002.

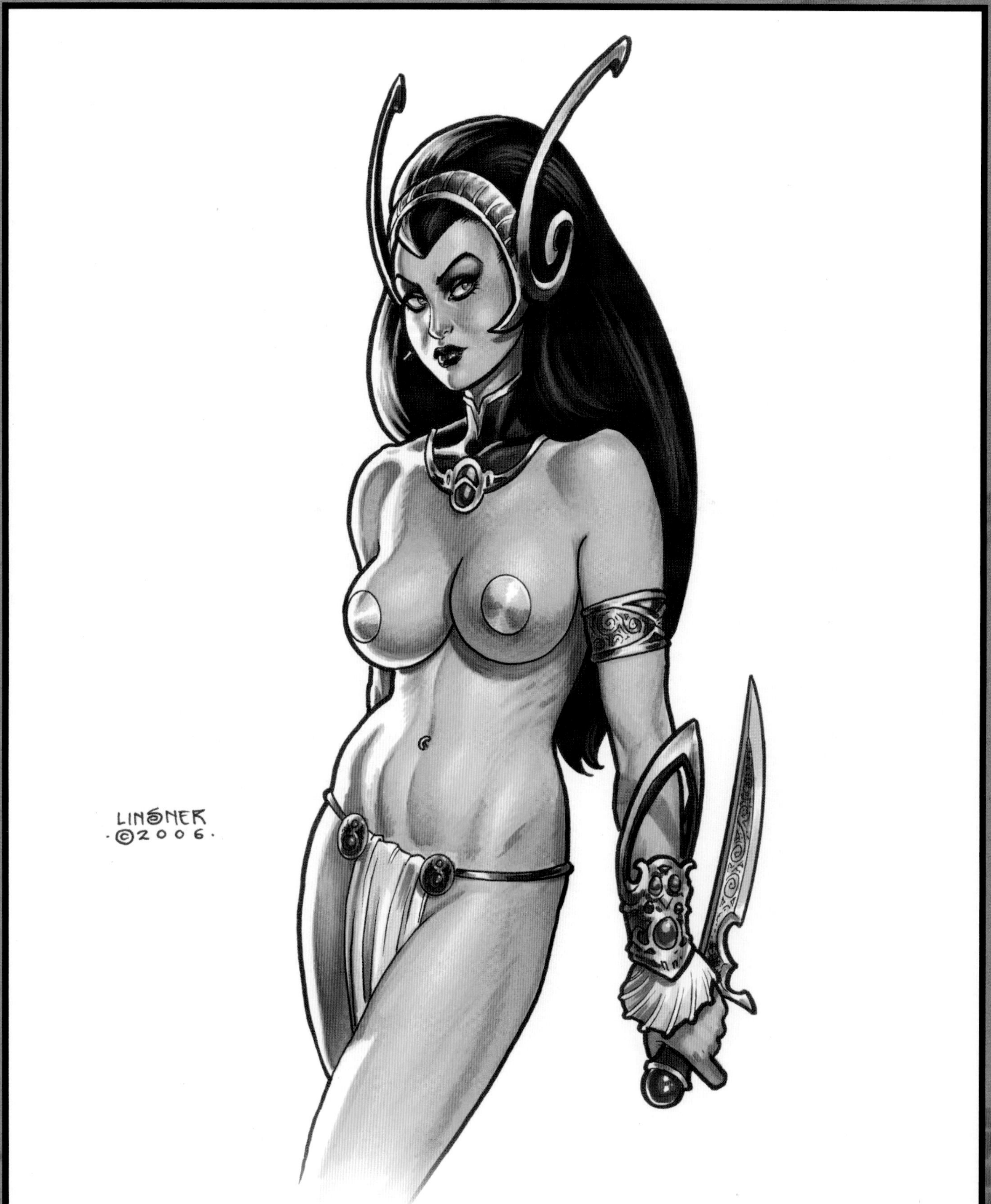
LINSNER
·©2006·

Deadly Dejah
Burgundy

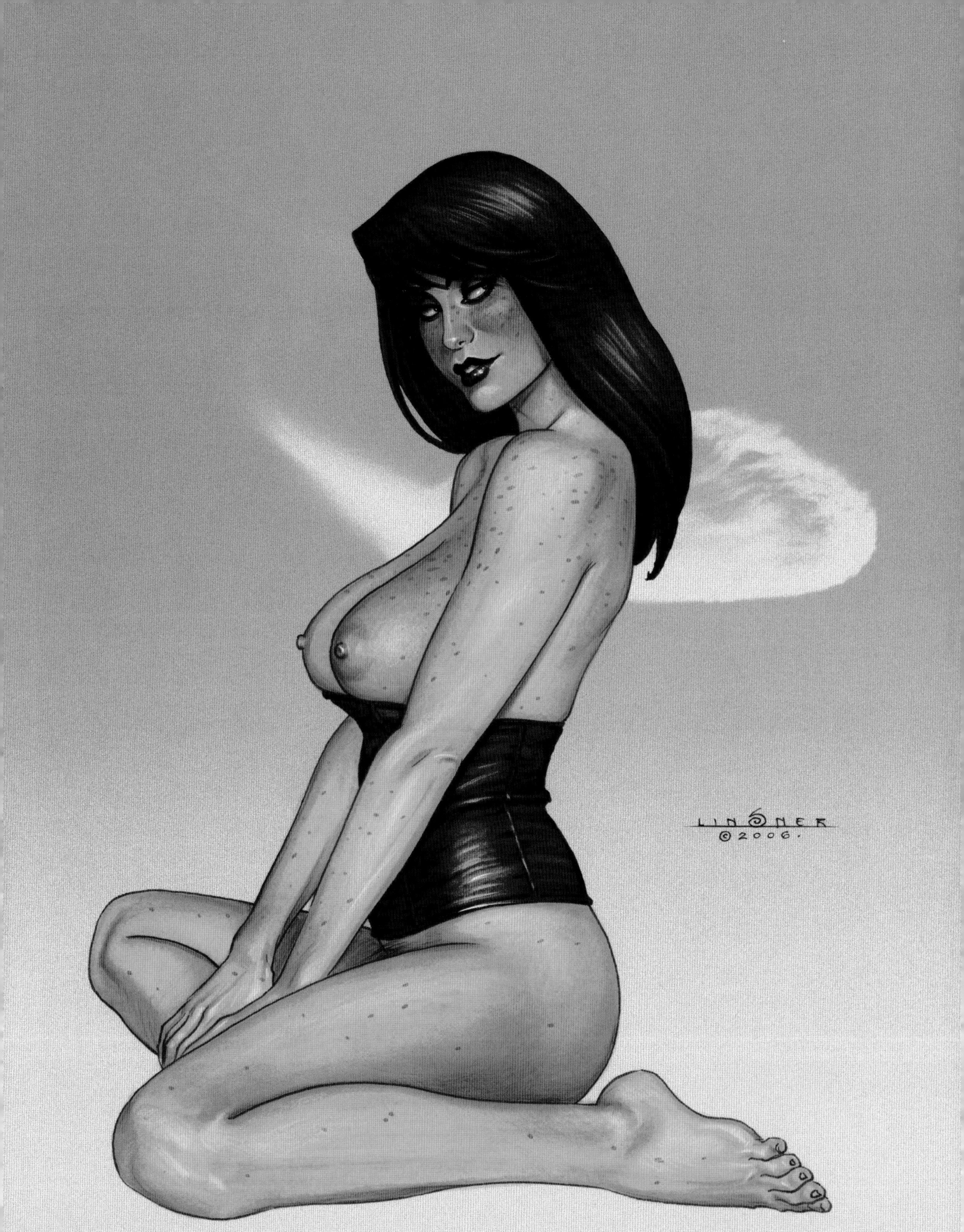
LINSNER
©2006.

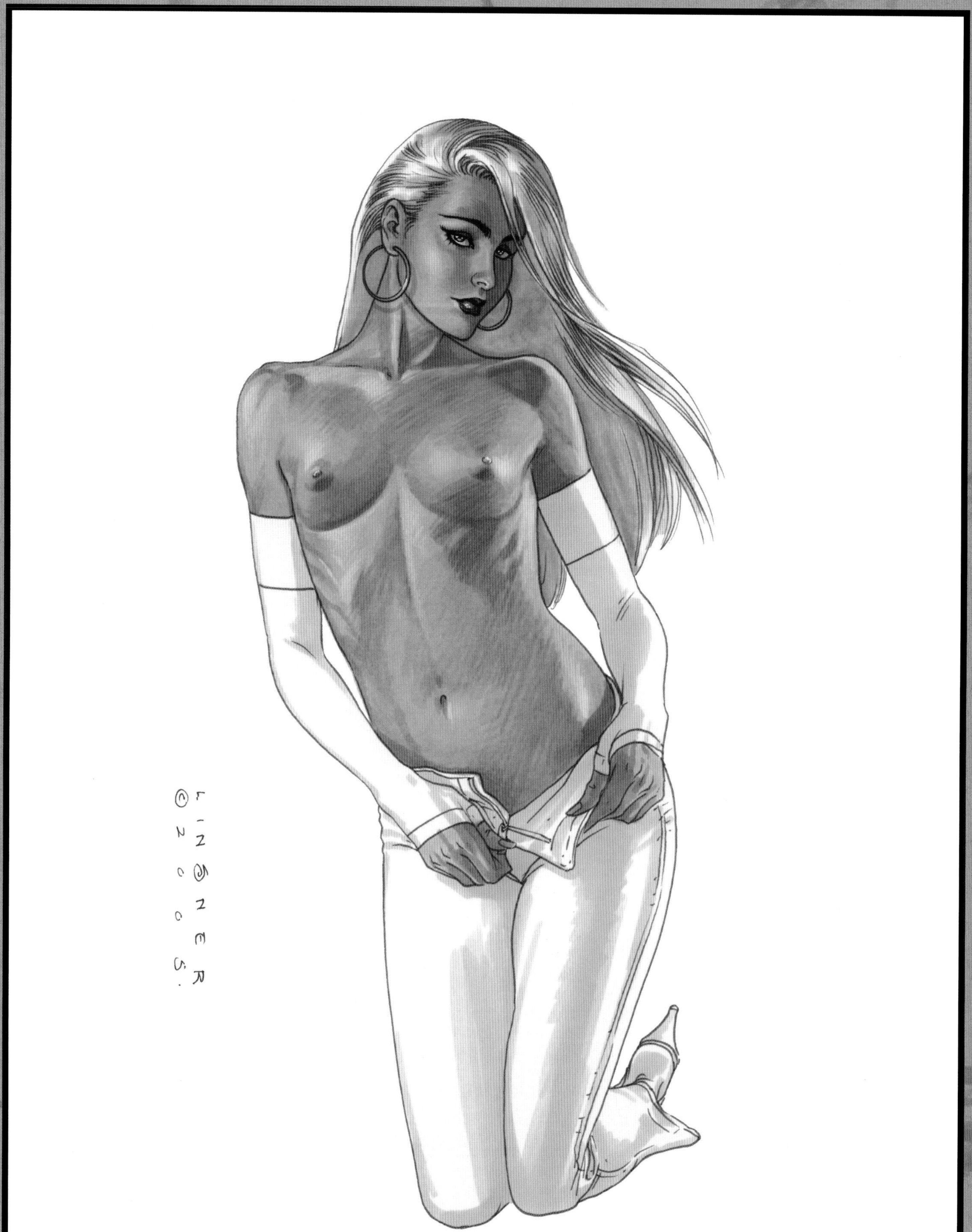
LINSNER
©2005.

Blondie
Misty

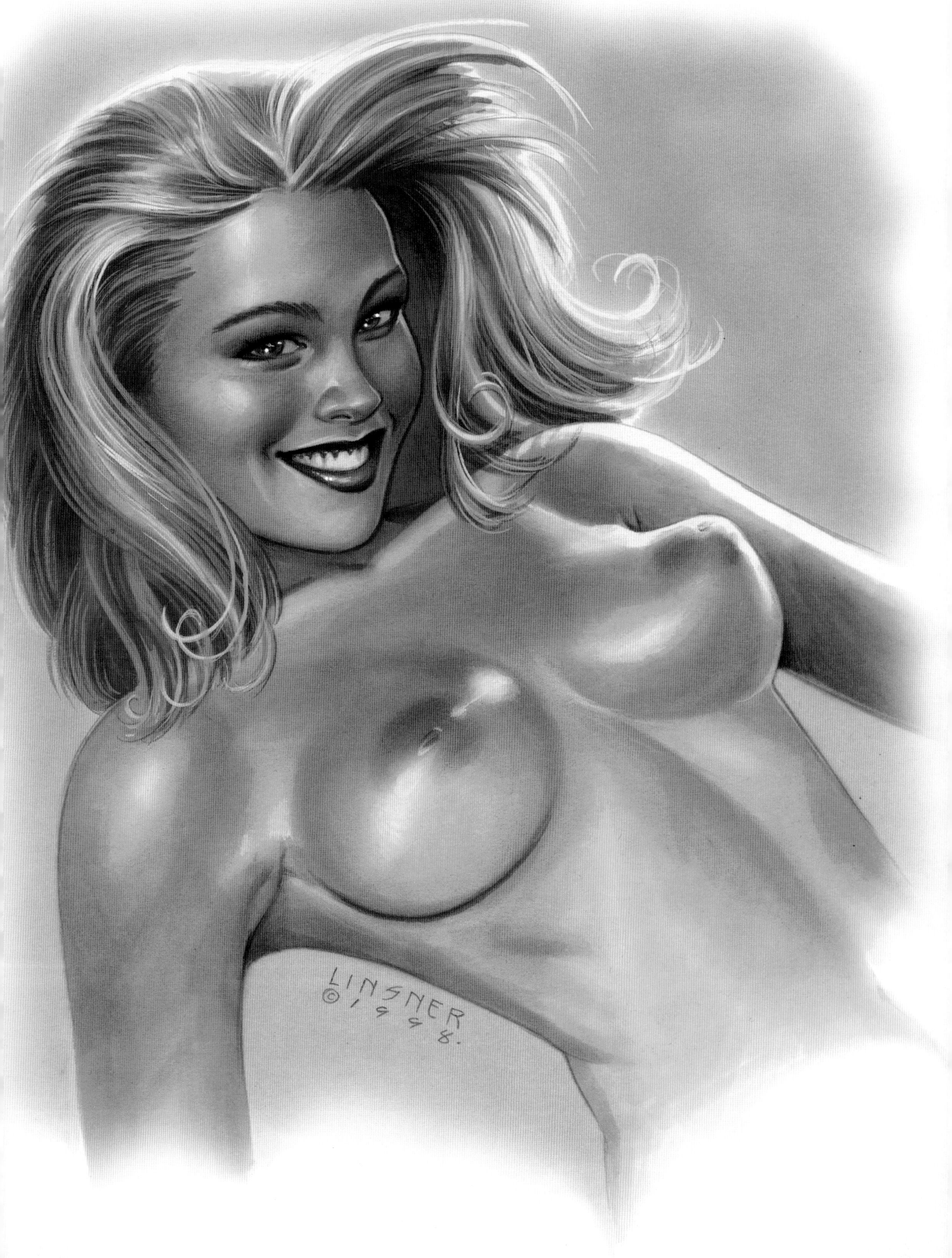
LINSNER
©1998.

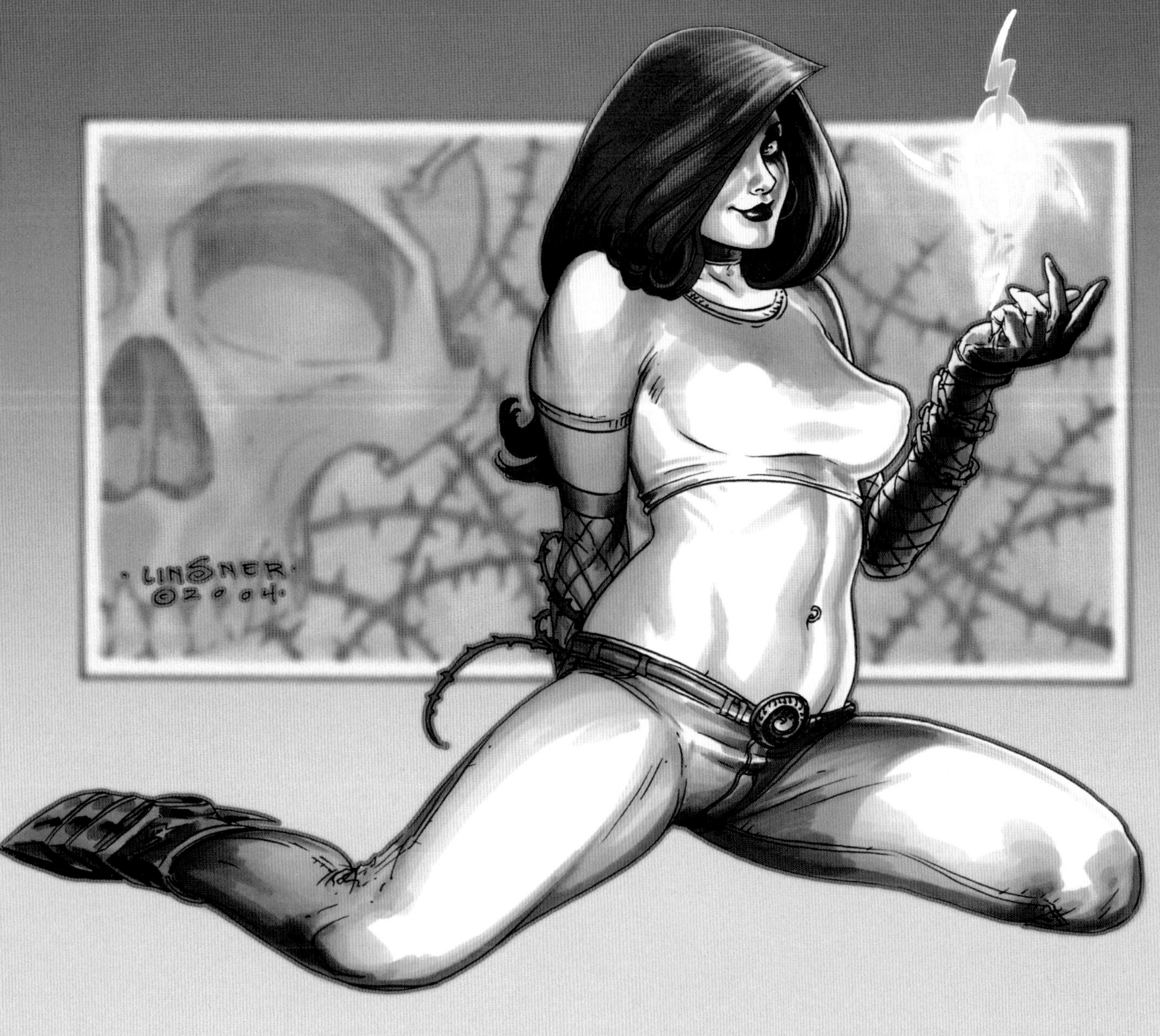
LINSNER
©2004

Golden Halo

Peek-A-Boo

DAWN is my Goddess figure, whose epic and surreal saga is told in a series of three graphic novels, with a fourth to come. Her sexy attire is simply an updated version of what a modern-day fertility goddess might wear. All the aspects of her appearance - the hair hiding one eye, the roses & chains, & most of all, her three tears - symbolize essential parts of her character. The chains of heaven, the roses of hell, the mystery that all women embody, and the tears that she earned gaining knowledge of the world.

Steadily growing in worldwide popularity since her first publication in 1989, Dawn has become something of a cult phenomenon. So many women connect with Dawn, that there is an annual **Dawn Look-a-Like Contest** each year held at the über-fantasy convention **Dragon*Con** *(www.dragoncon.org).* I feel like one very lucky man -- how many artists get an annual contest devoted to their work, and get the thrill of seeing their character brought to life by beautiful women of all shapes and sizes? I draw Dawn many different ways, all depending upon my mood -- she has no totally fixed look. I suppose that allows different women to see themselves reflected in her. I am still trying to figure it all out.

The Dawn Look-a-Like Contest is now in its 10th year; Dawn is almost in her 20th. *My personal Goddess has been very good to me.*

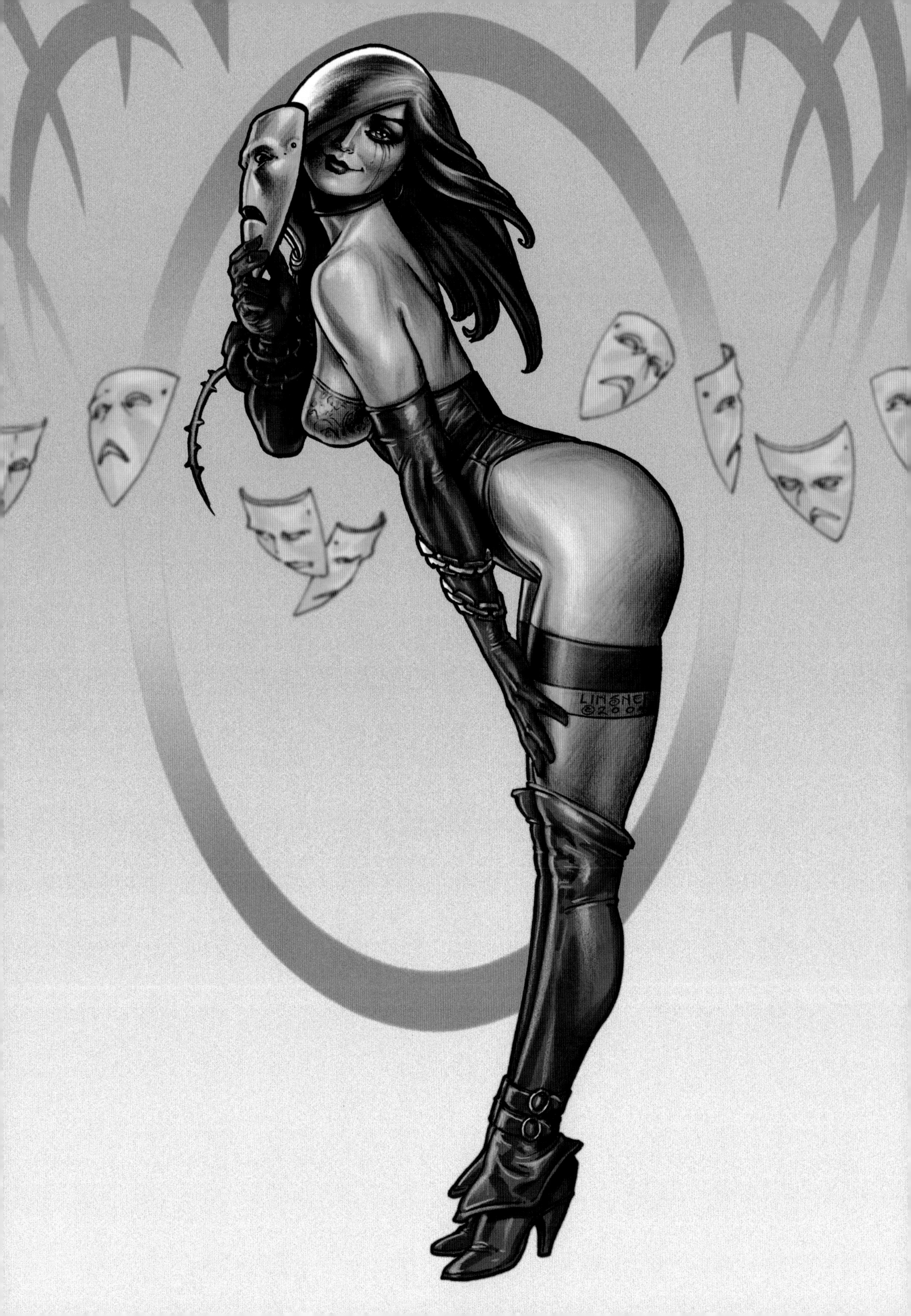

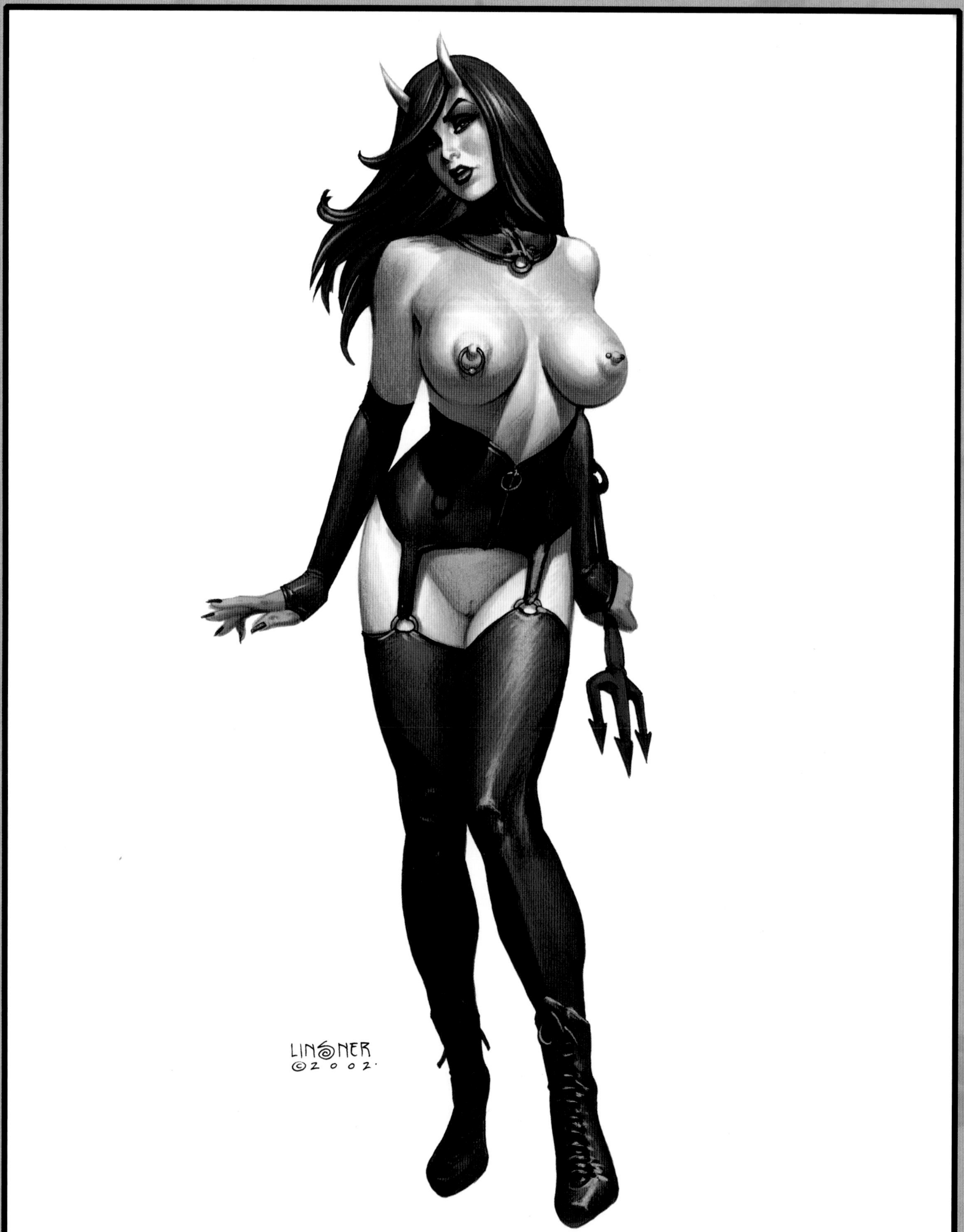
LINSNER
©2002.

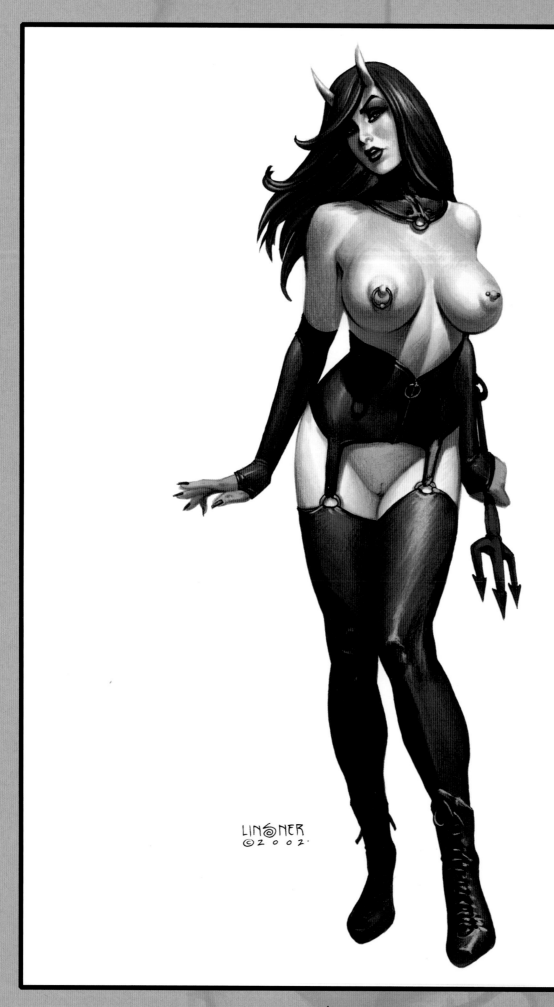

Purple Suzi
Fire Angel

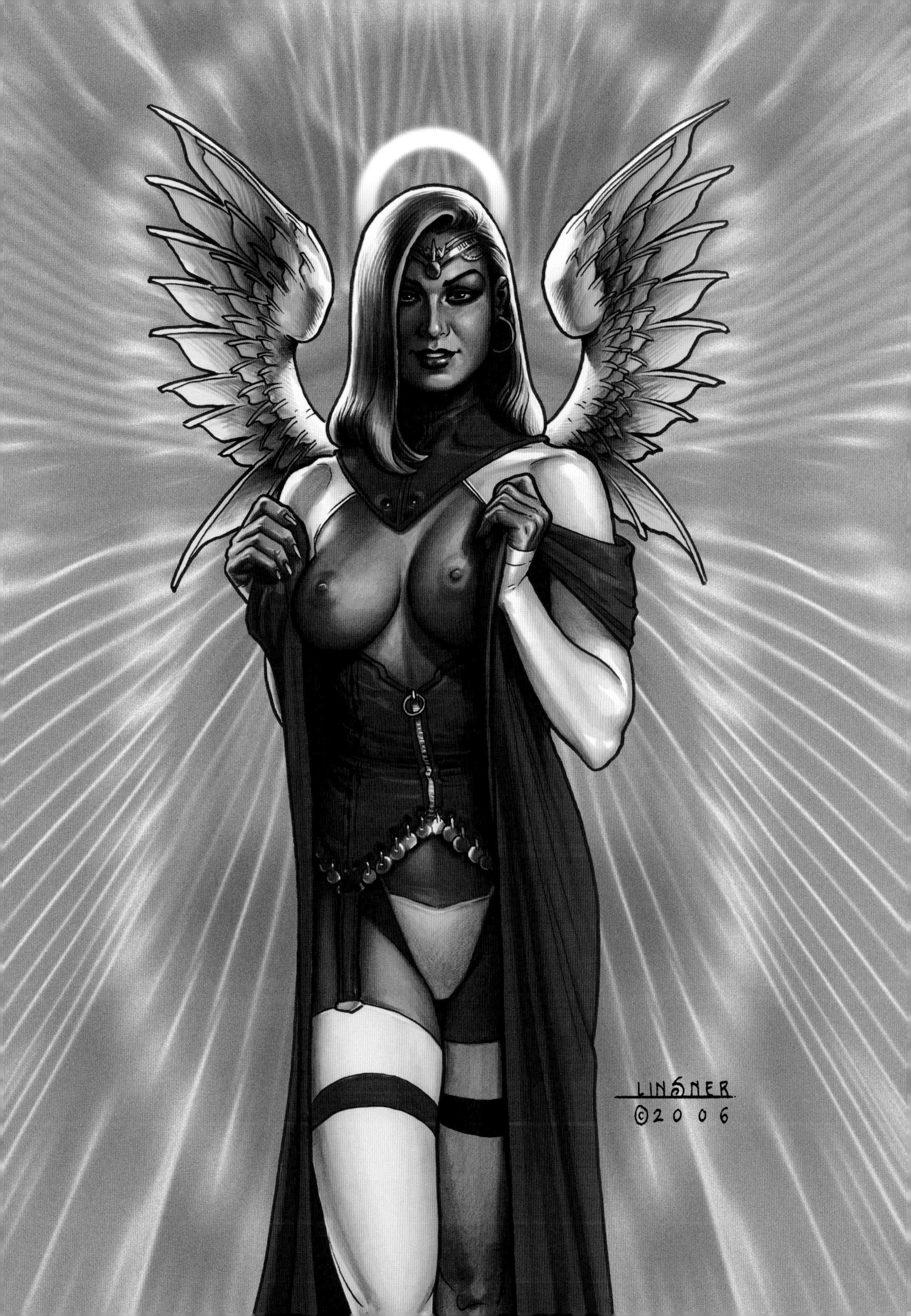
LINSNER
©2006

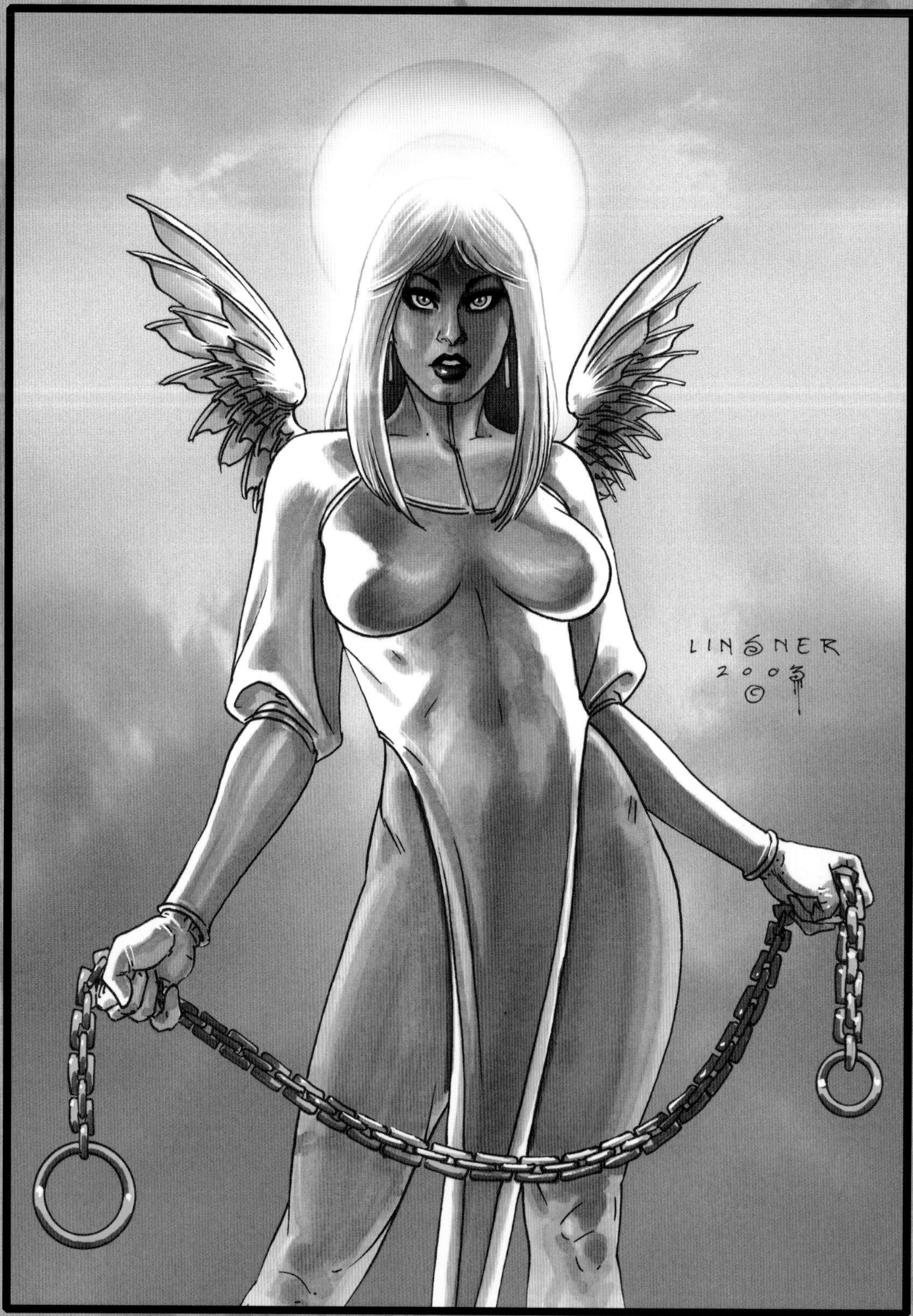
LINSNER
2003
©

Chained Angel

Suzi Red

The Good vs. Evil Auction *(the secret origin of **Sinful Suzi**)*

"I asked Joe do two art pieces, one Good & one Evil, to put up for sale on eBay. I was pretty sure the 'bad girl' would sell first. **Good**, though sexy, took the full auction time to meet her price. ***Evil** sold in under two hours*. So we put up another one, Evil Babe #2, & then when she sold immediately as well, Evil Babe #3. It was around then that Joe realized the "Evil" was actually the embodiment of a character he'd been working on - **Sinful Suzi**, a sexy demoness he hopes to get to after he wraps up work on **Dark Ivory**. I am still amused to this day how much more quickly people snapped up Evil over Good."

- **Eva Hopkins**, longtime Linsner collaborator & art assistant

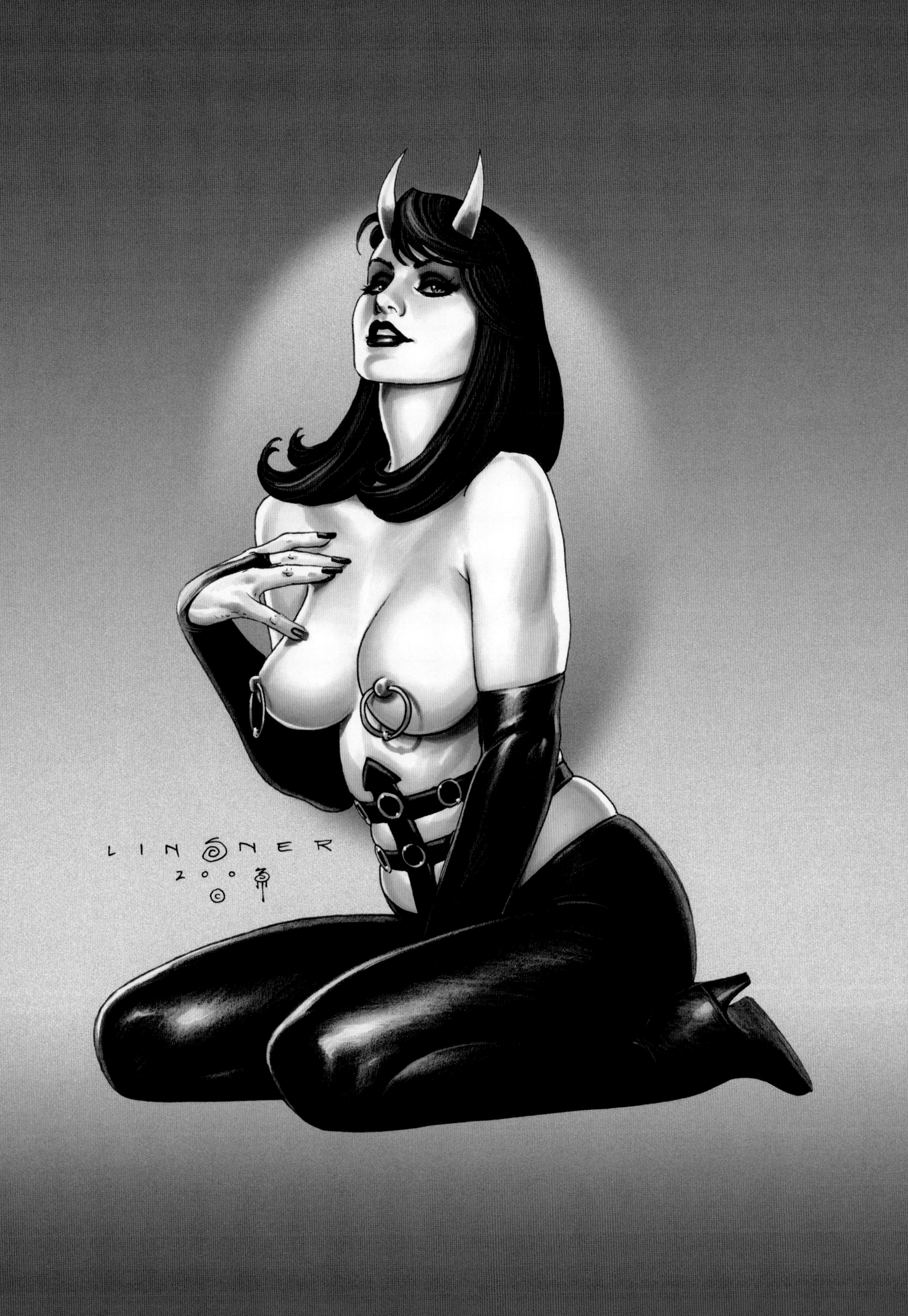
LINSNER
2003
©

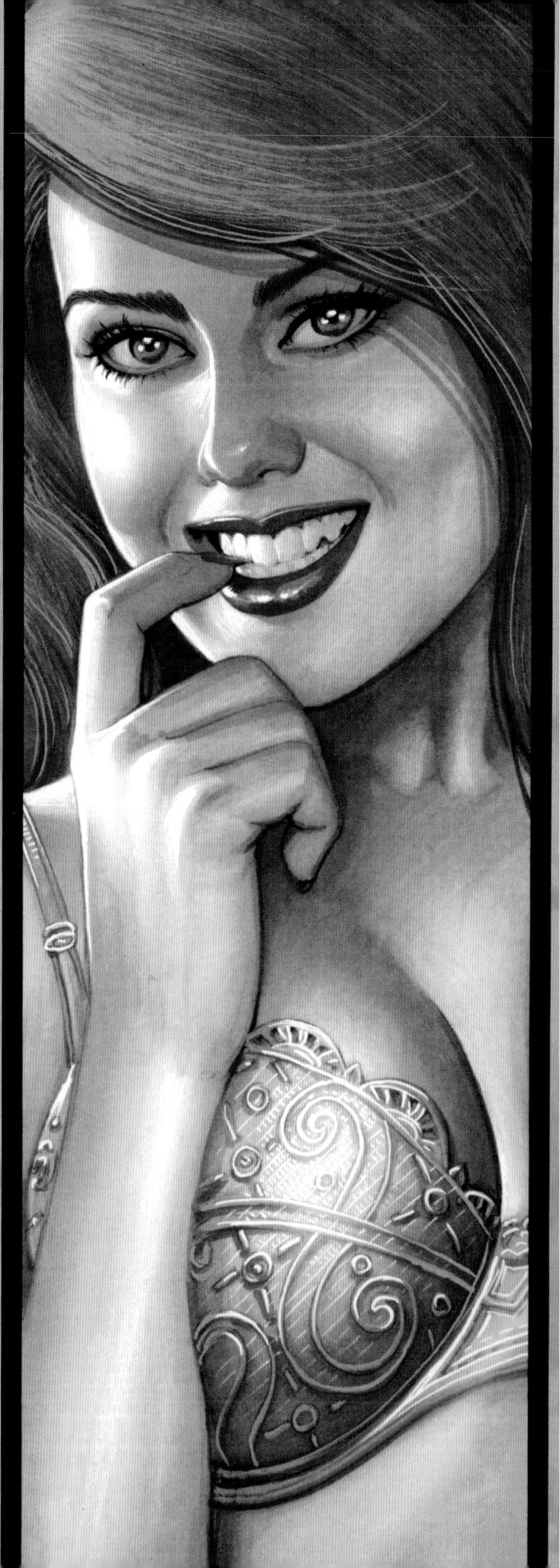

Linsner Girls

La Chica

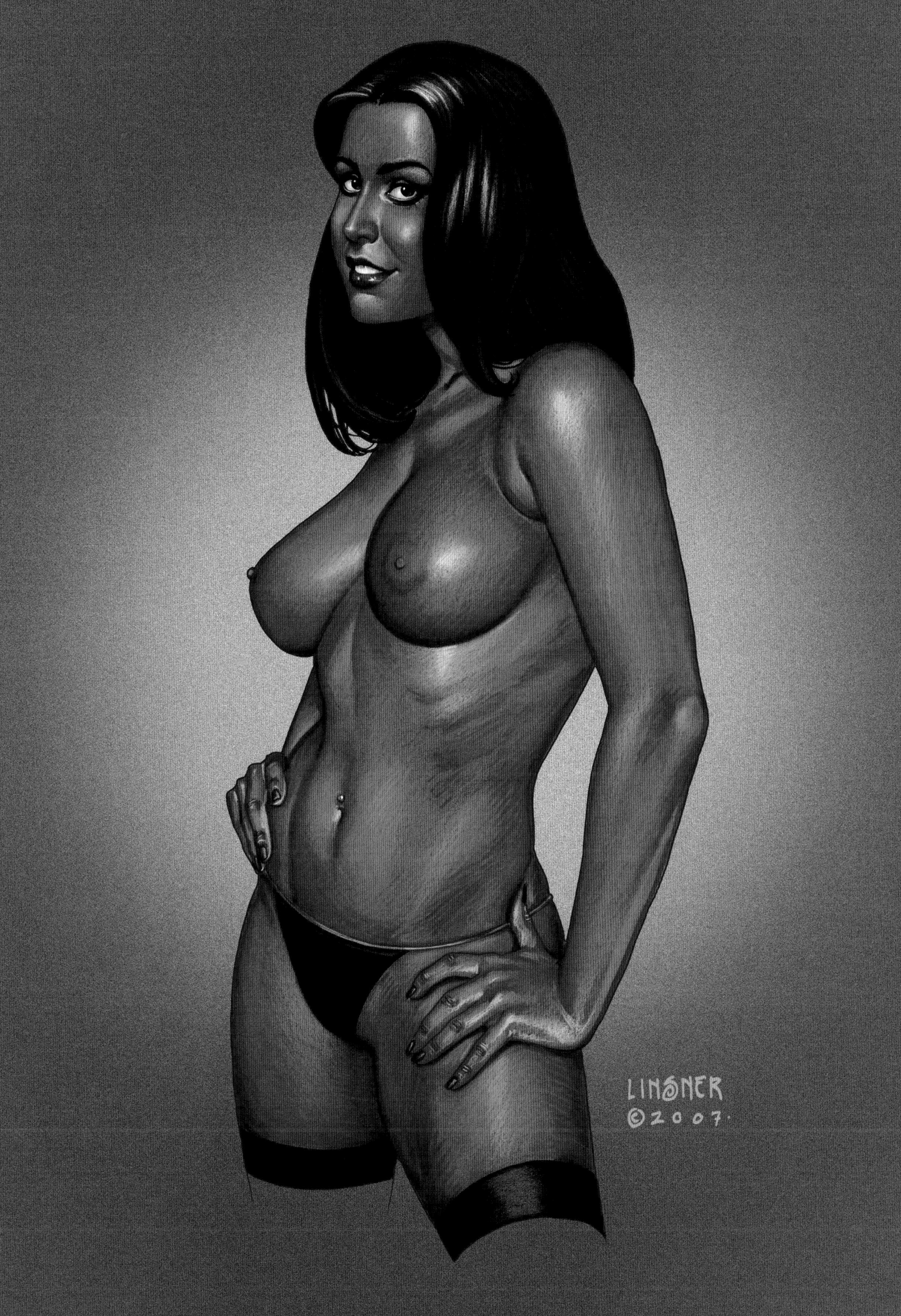
LINSNER
©2007.

DRAMA!

June

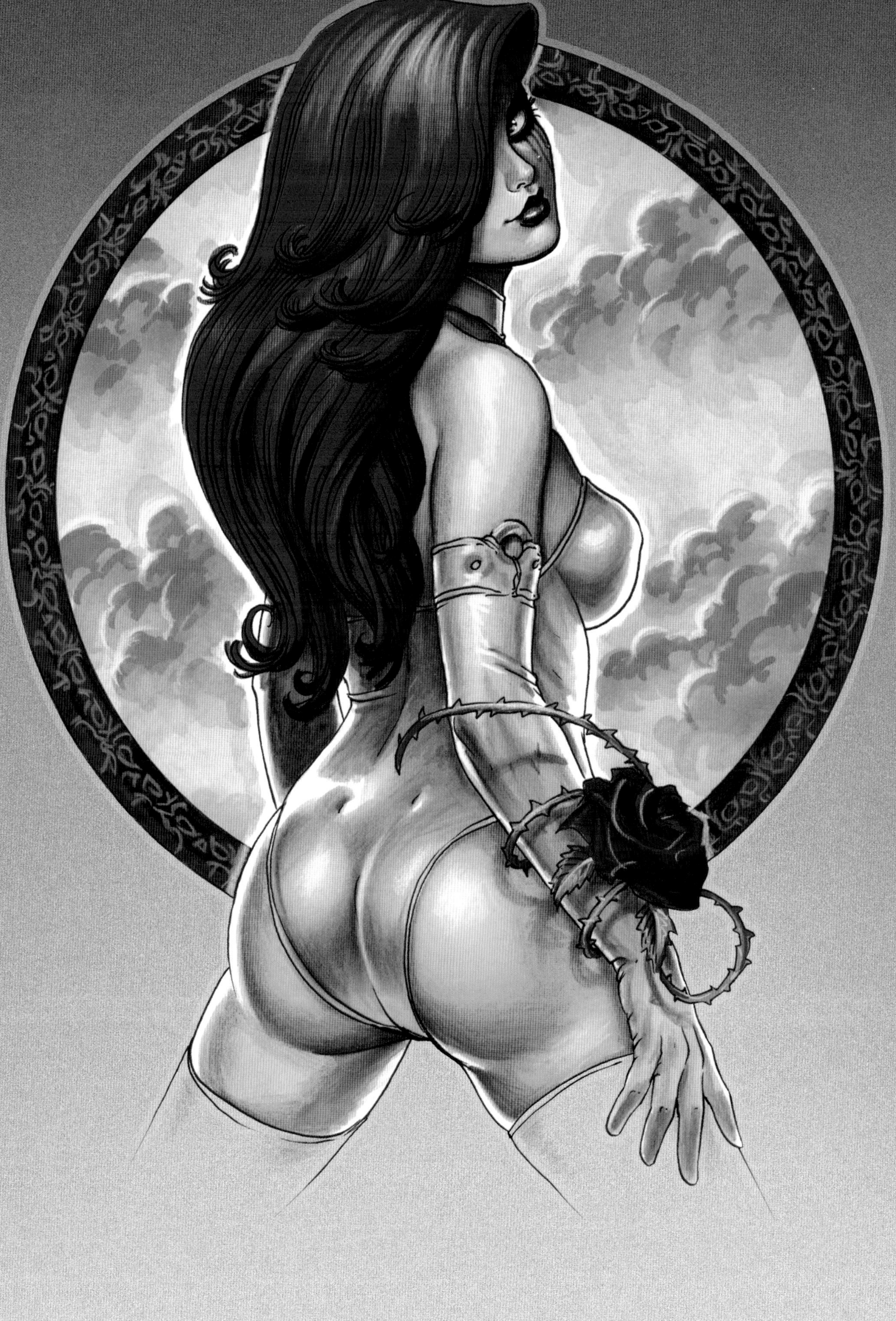

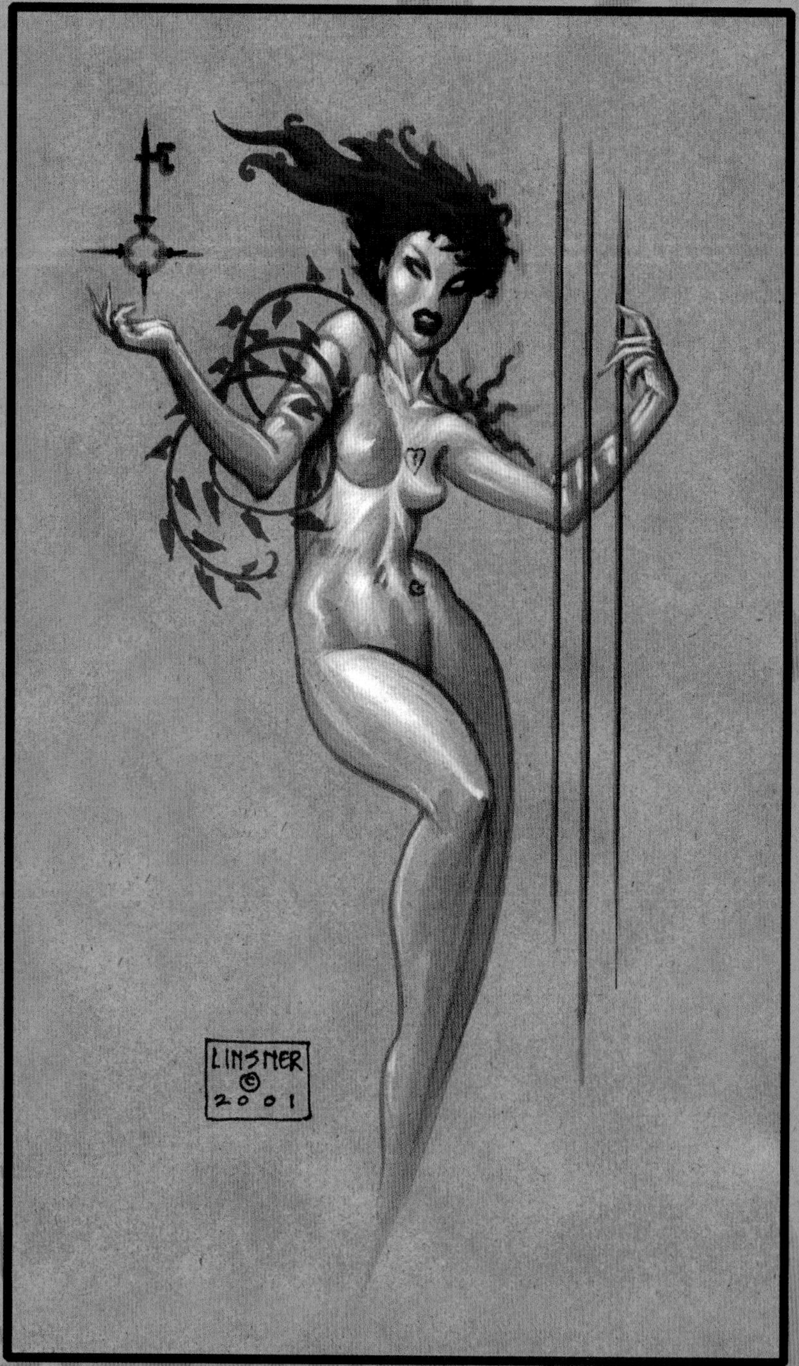
LINSNER © 2001

Red Sprite

Pink Stripes

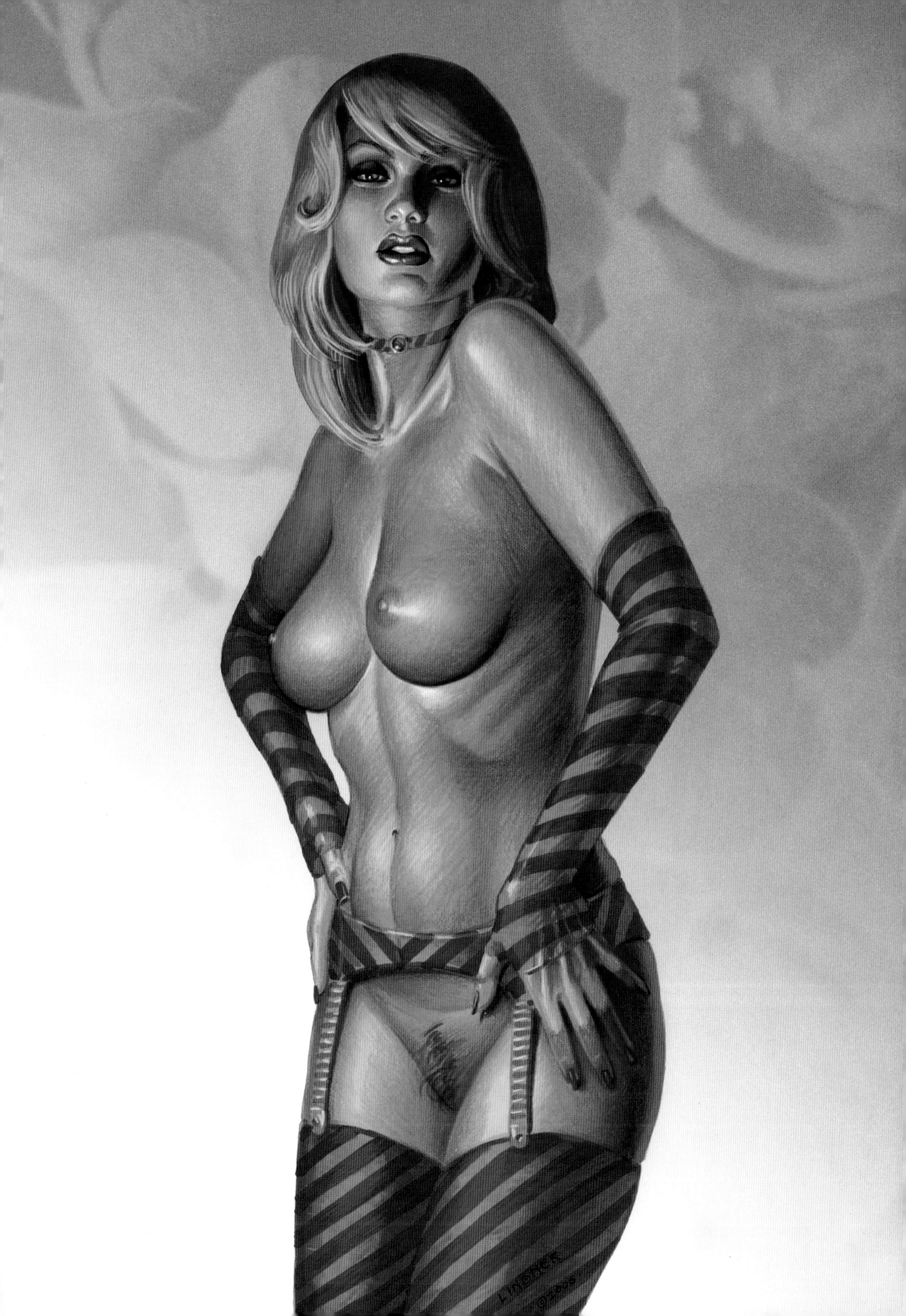

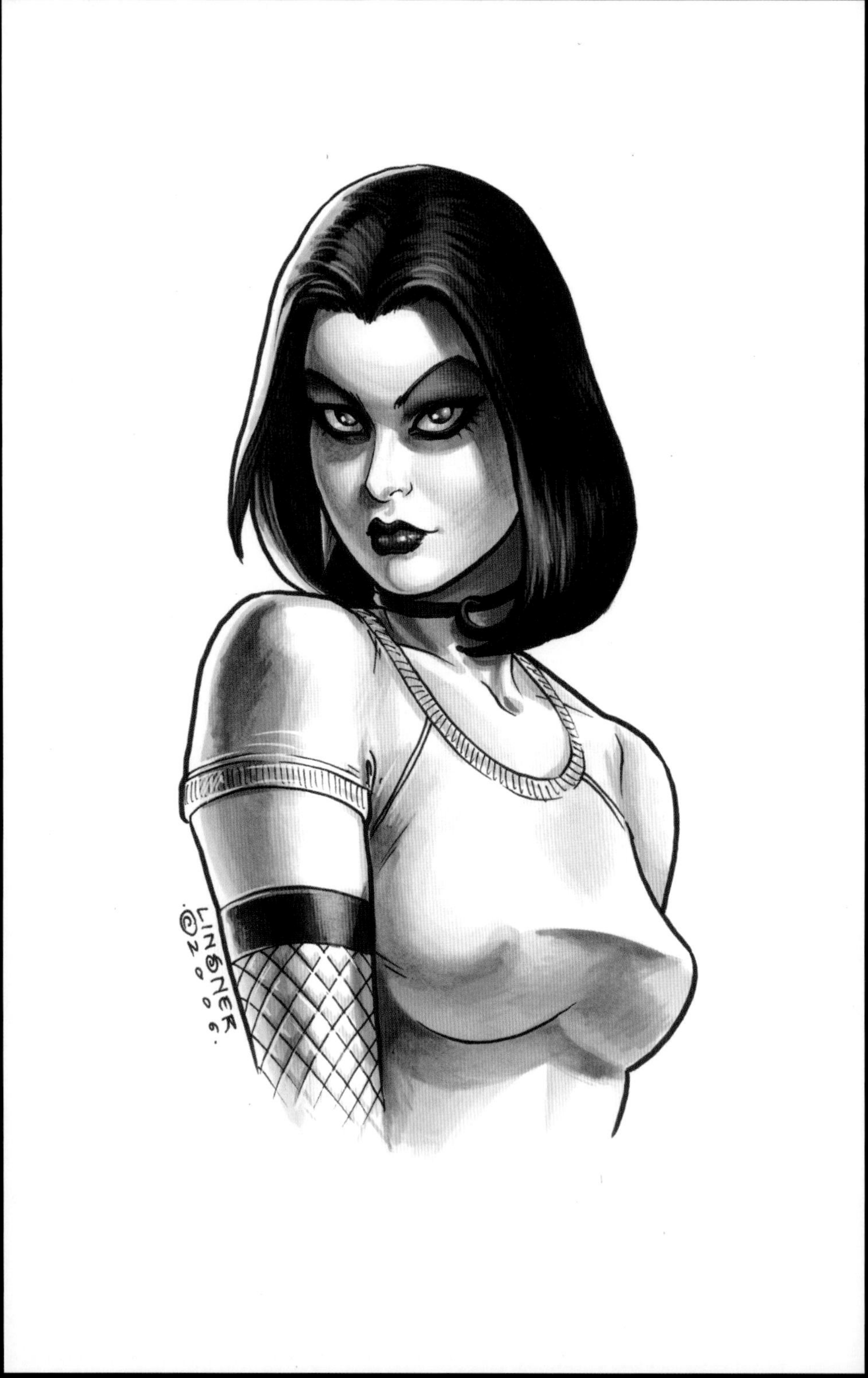
LINSNER ©2006.

Ivory

Ivory Lotus

DARK IVORY is a graphic novel I am currently working on with **Eva Hopkins** as my writing partner. It is about a cynical teenage girl who listens to all the goth music she can & dreams about leading the charmed life of a vampire, the eternal cool and the endless night. She discovers it's not nearly as much fun as it looks, once it actually happens to her. *Except for the wings...*

Dark Ivory is ultimately an unconventional vampire love story, one that explores the balance between giving and taking in all relationships. Dark Ivory debuts in late 2007 through Image Comics.

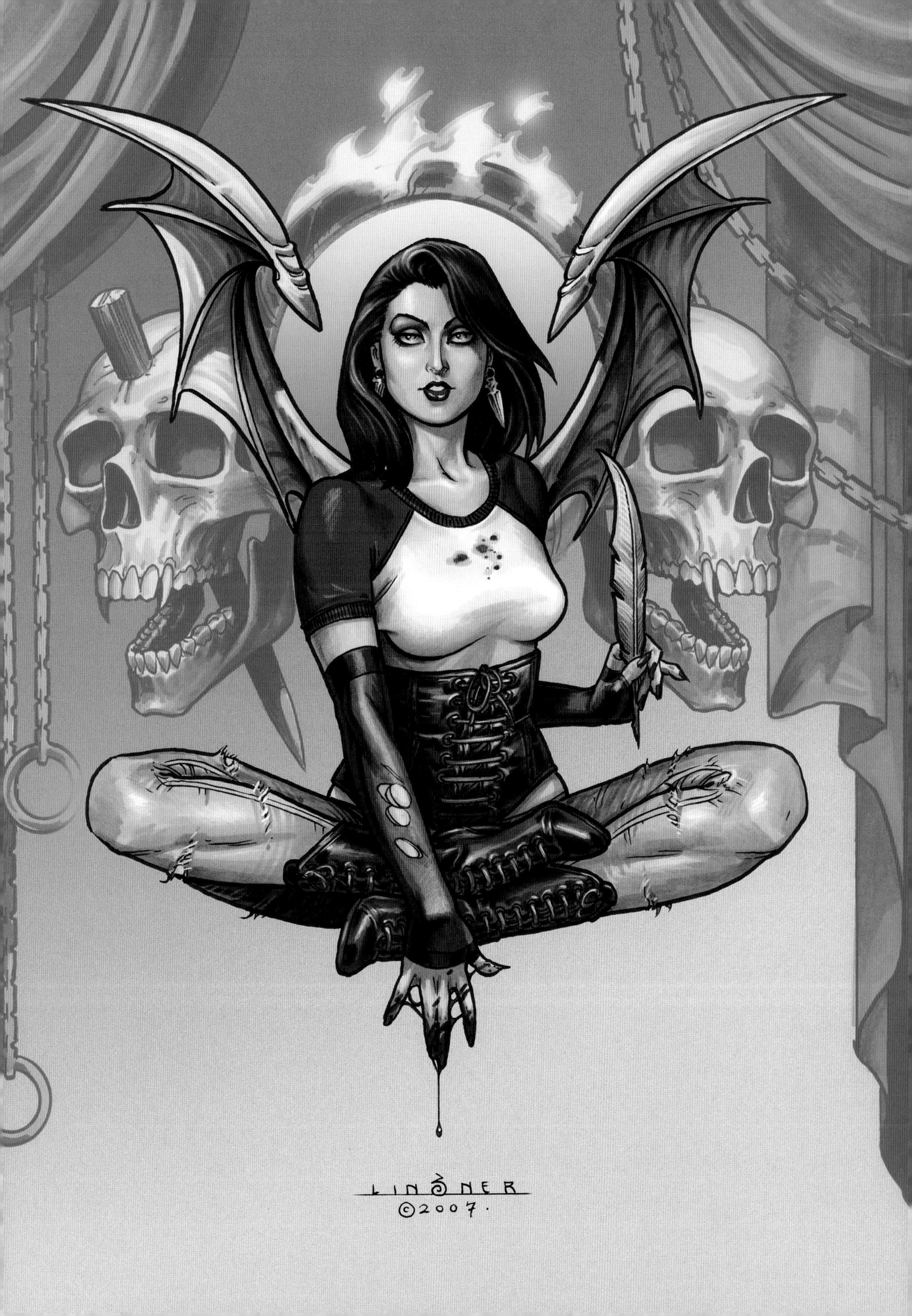

LINSNER
©2007.

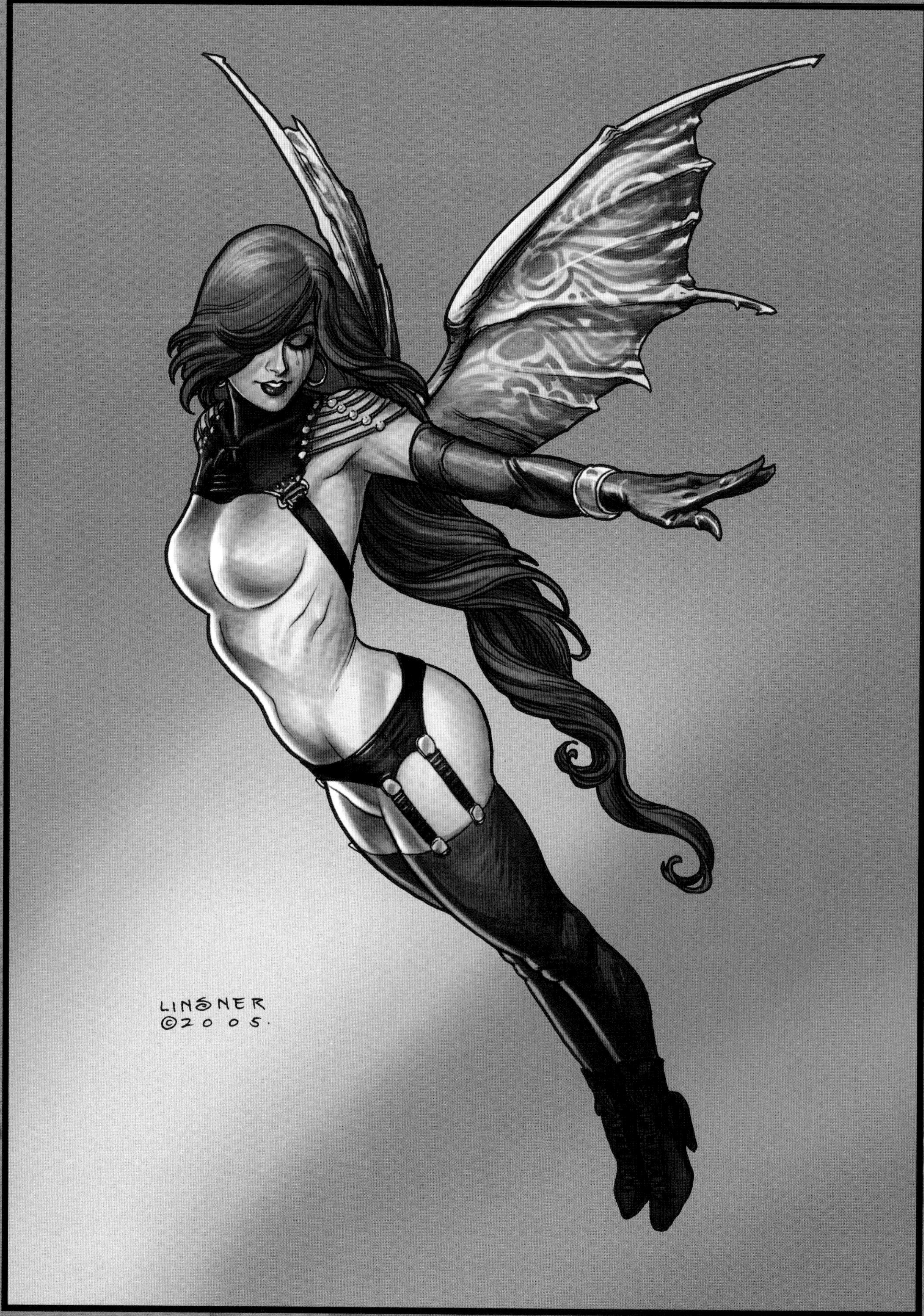
LINSNER
©2005.

Wings

Butterfly

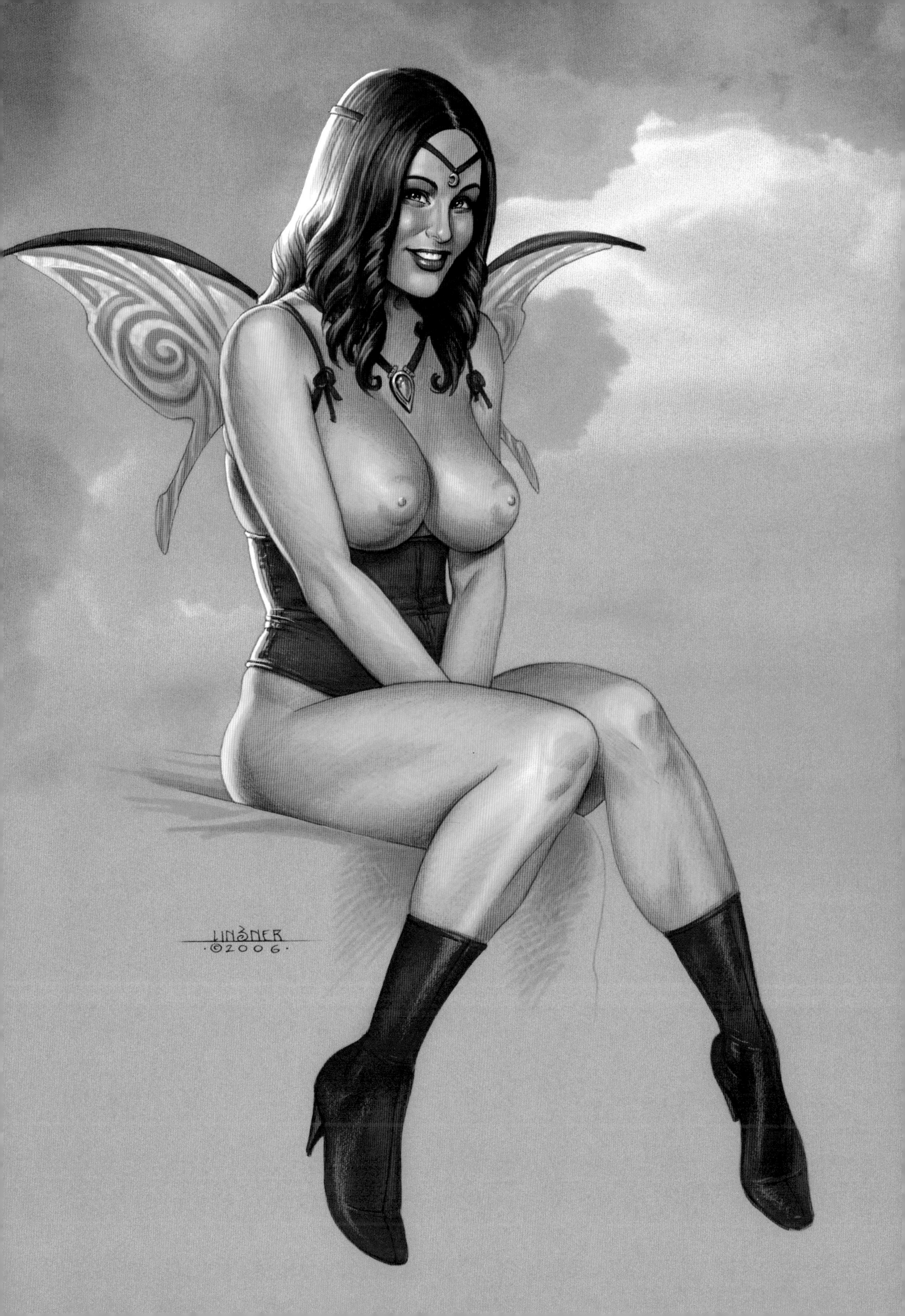
LINSNER
©2006

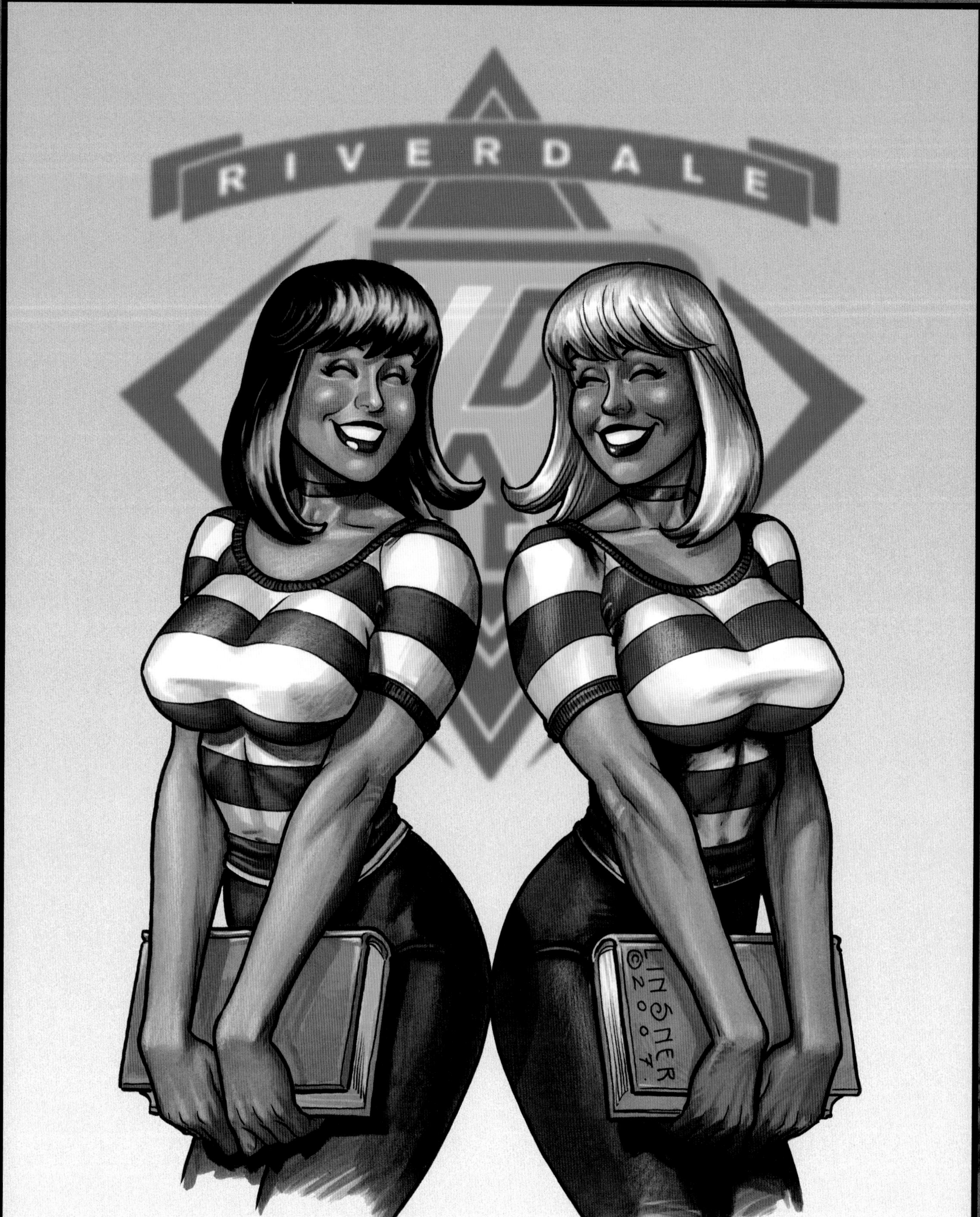
RIVERDALE
LINSNER ©2007

Riverdale Girls

Batty Betty

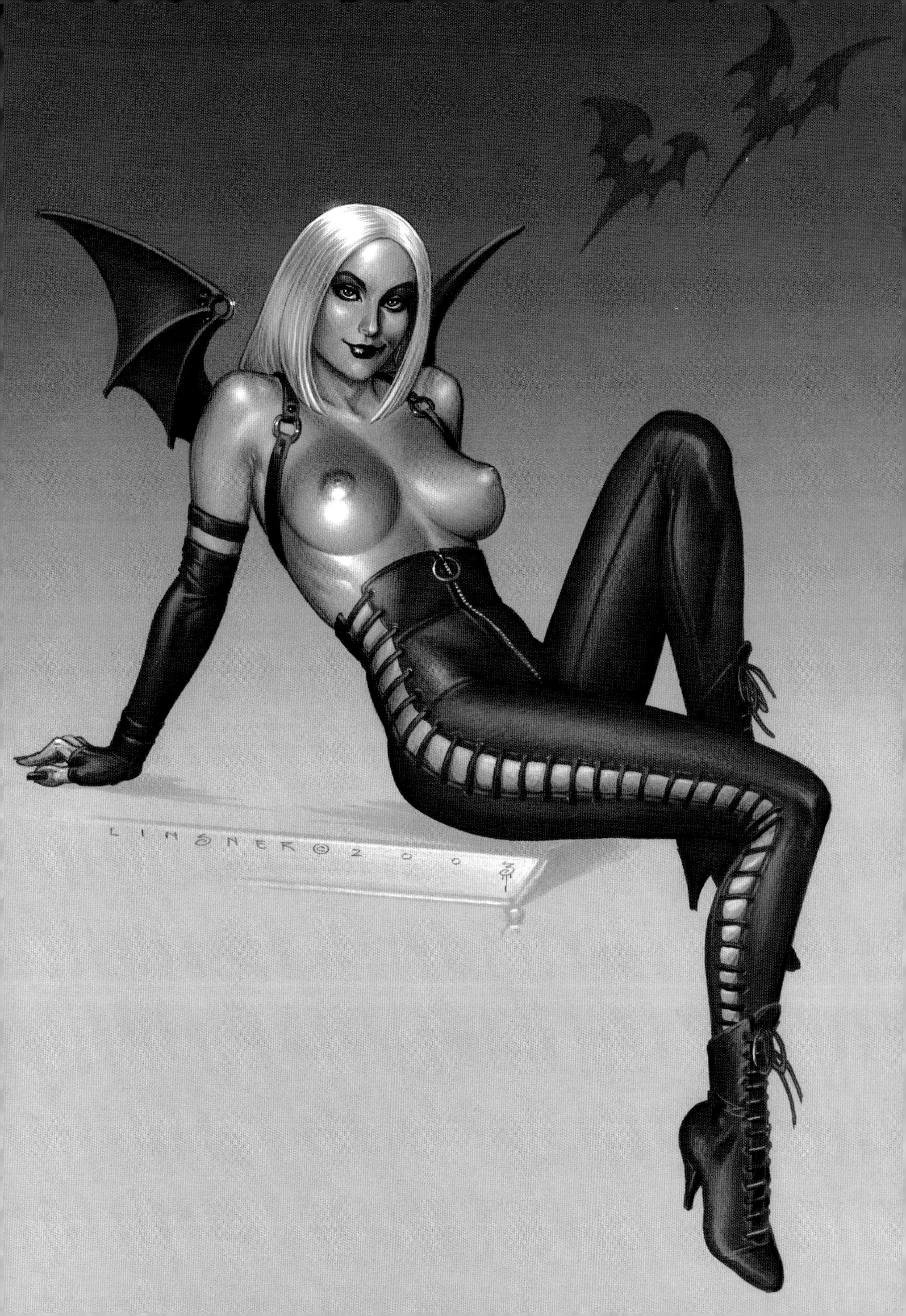
LINSNER©200

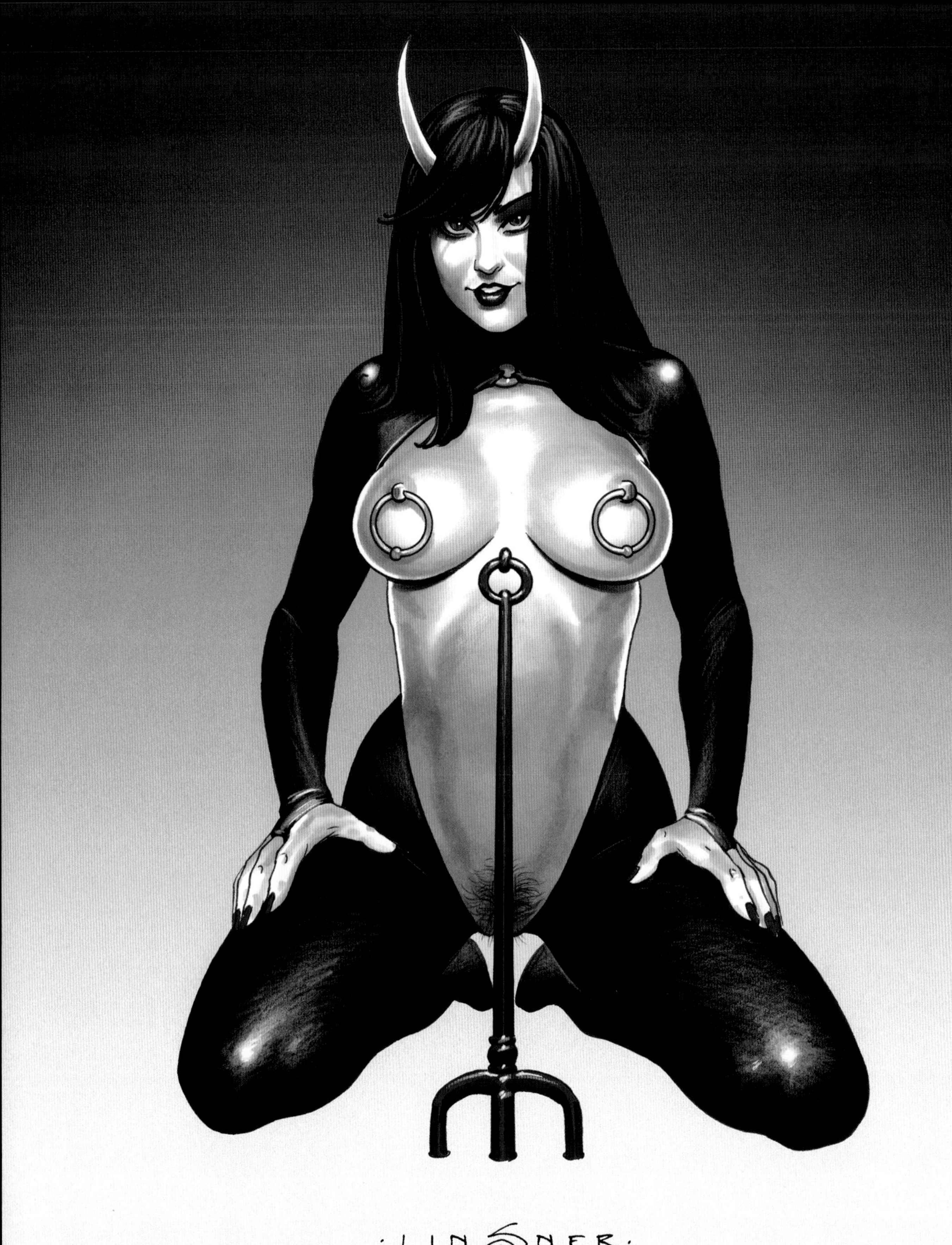
·LINSNER·
2003
©

Red Hot Ronnie

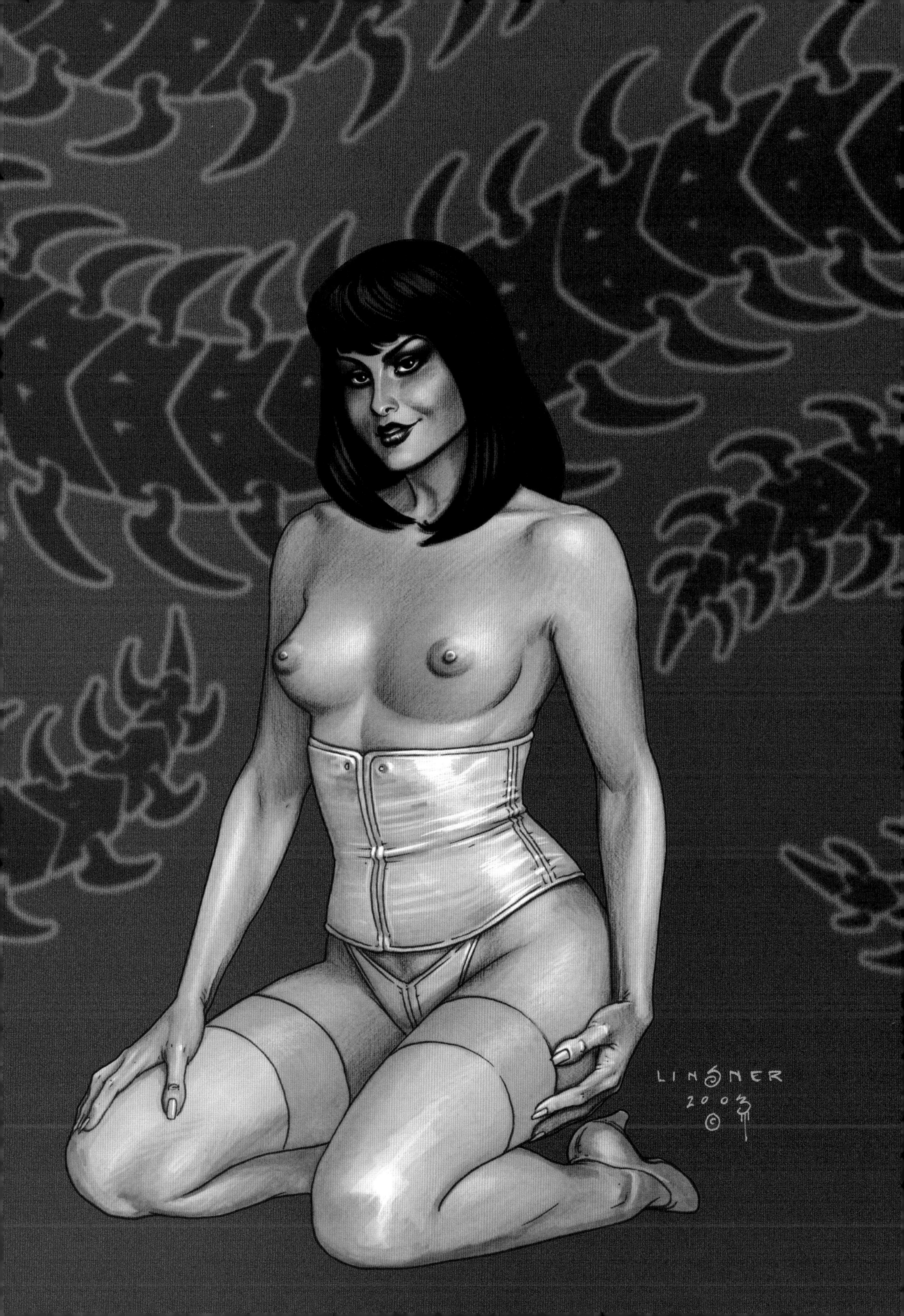
LINSNER
2003
©

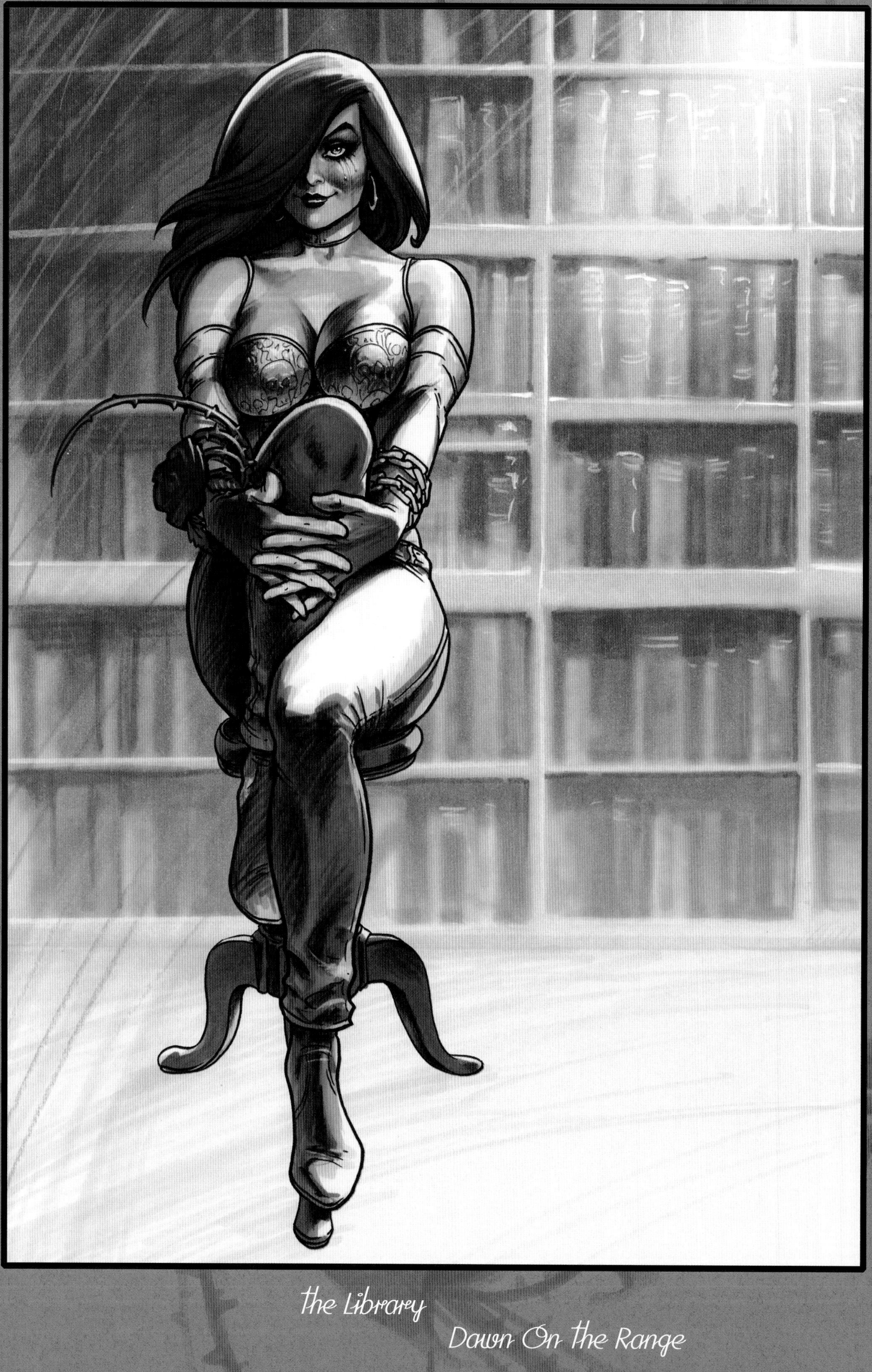

the Library

Dawn On the Range

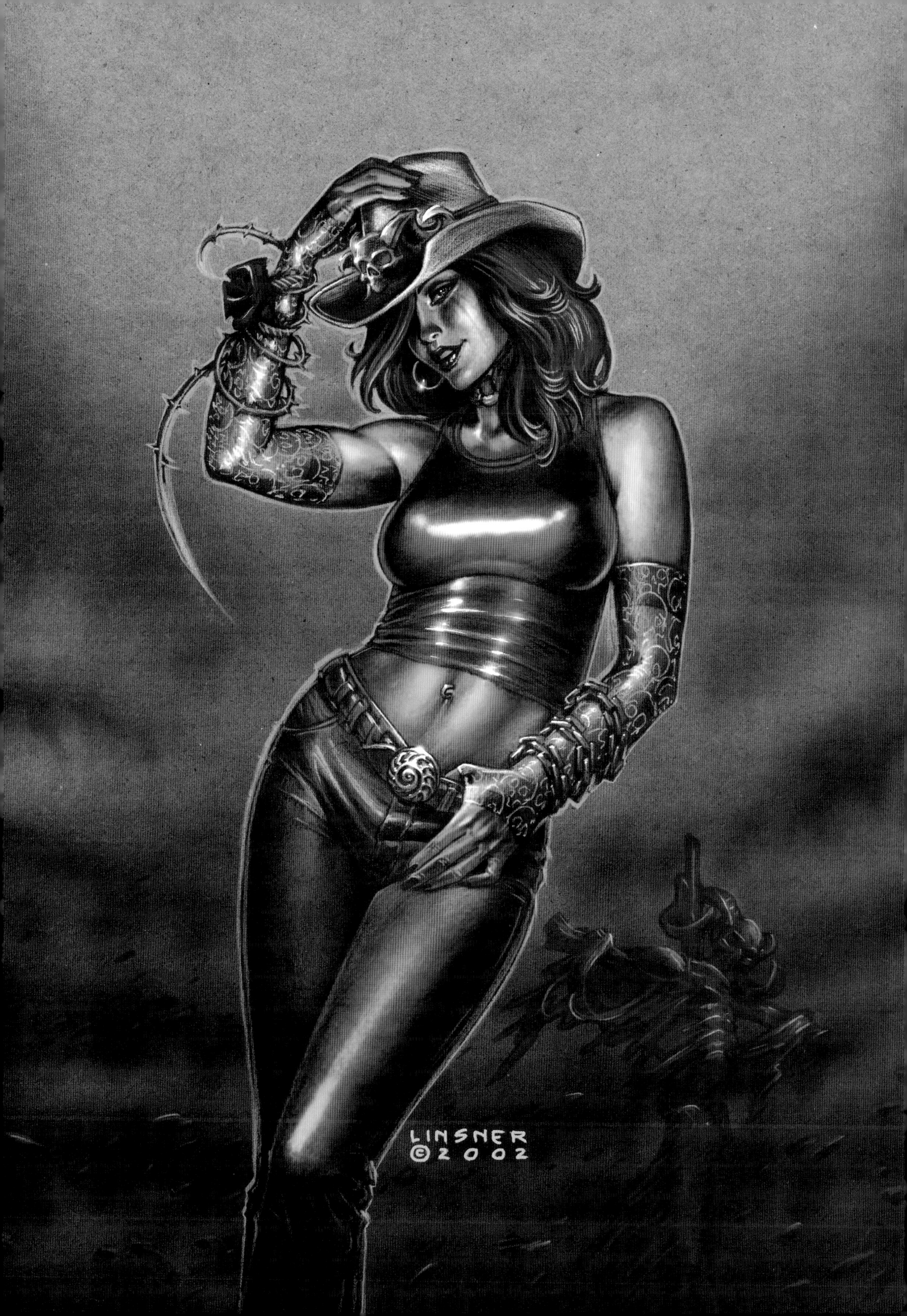
LINSNER
©2002

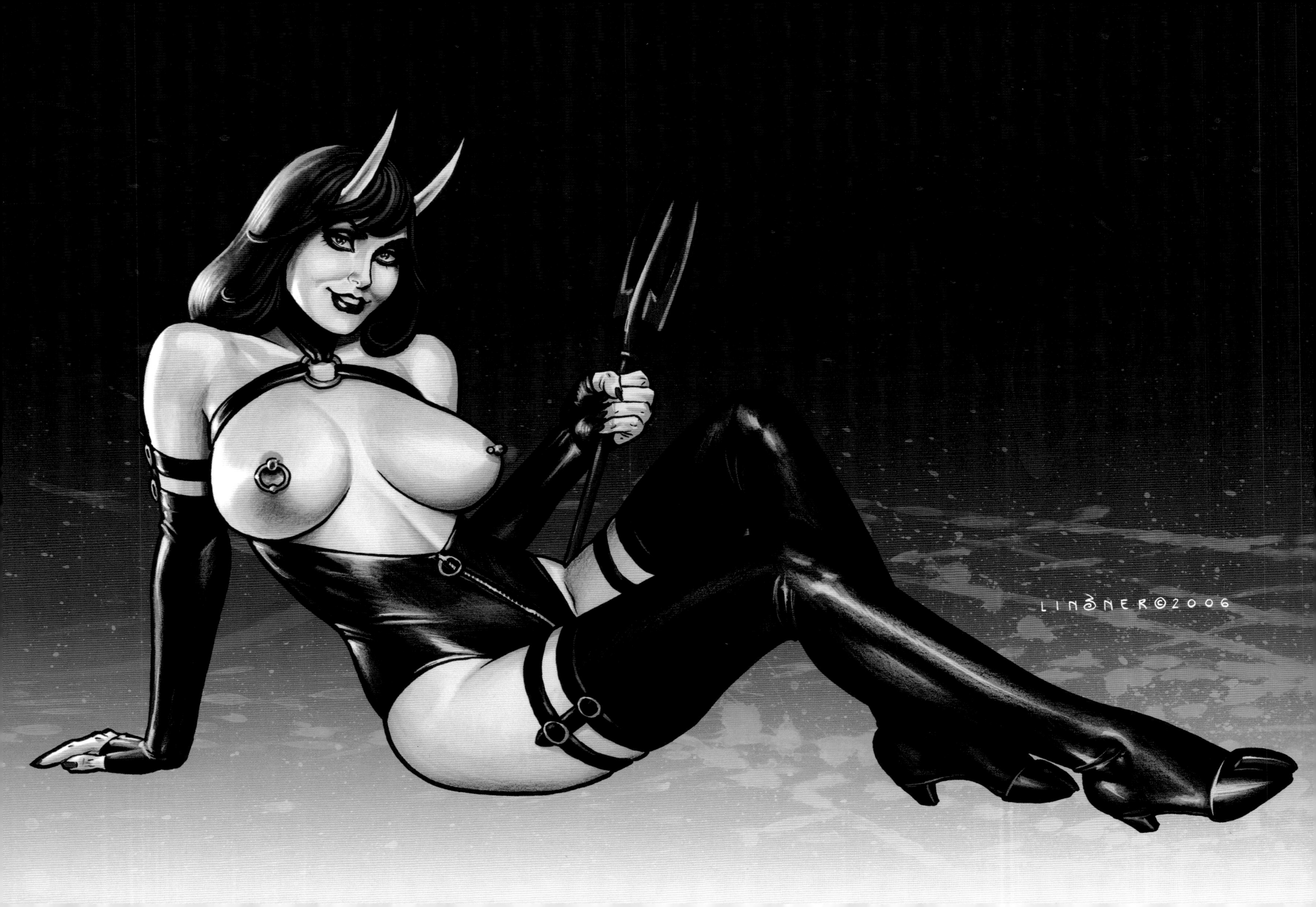
LINDNER©2006

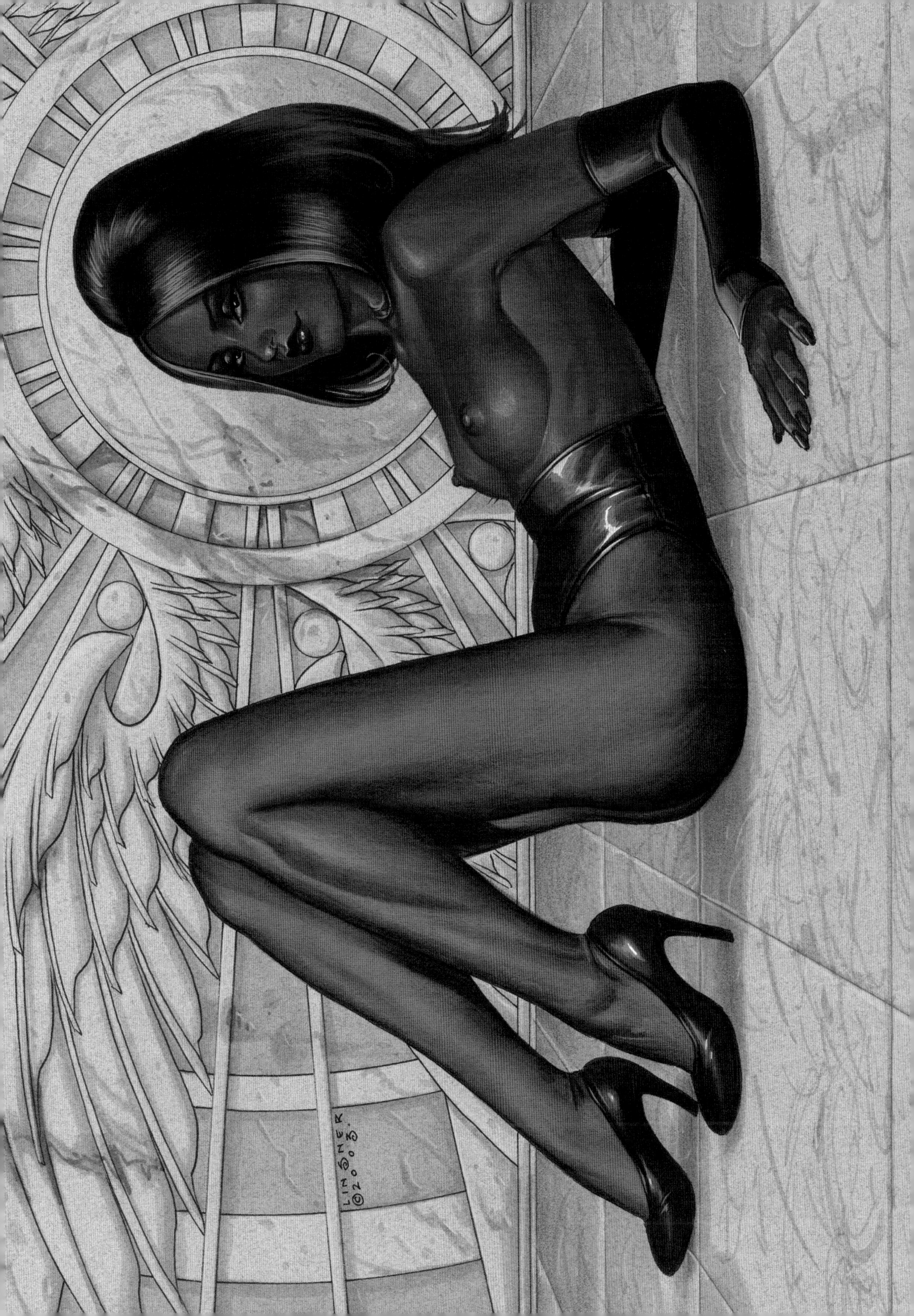
LINSNER
©2003.

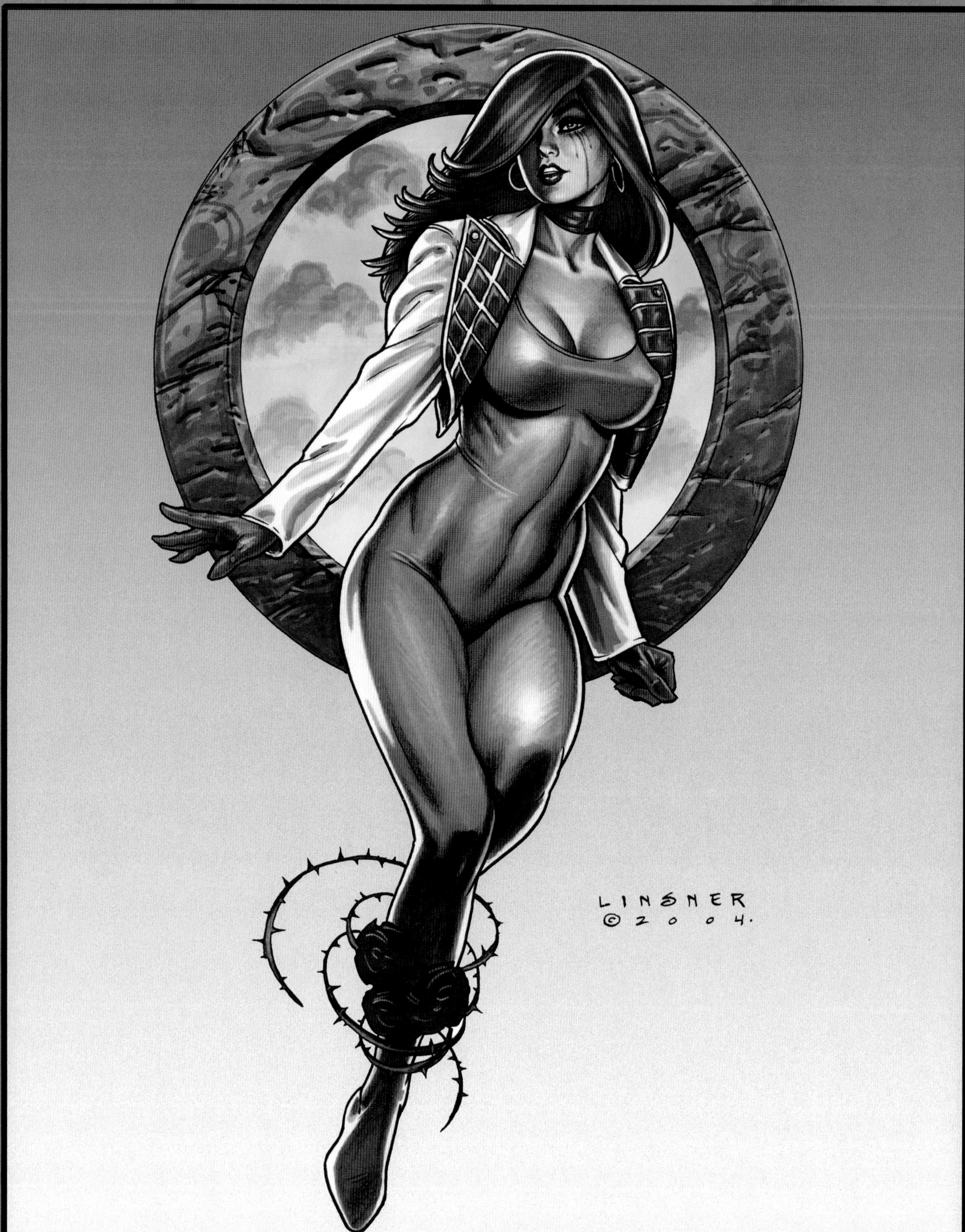
LINSNER
©2004.

Green Sky

Screaming Skull & Violaceous
(Pages 46 & 47)

Garters

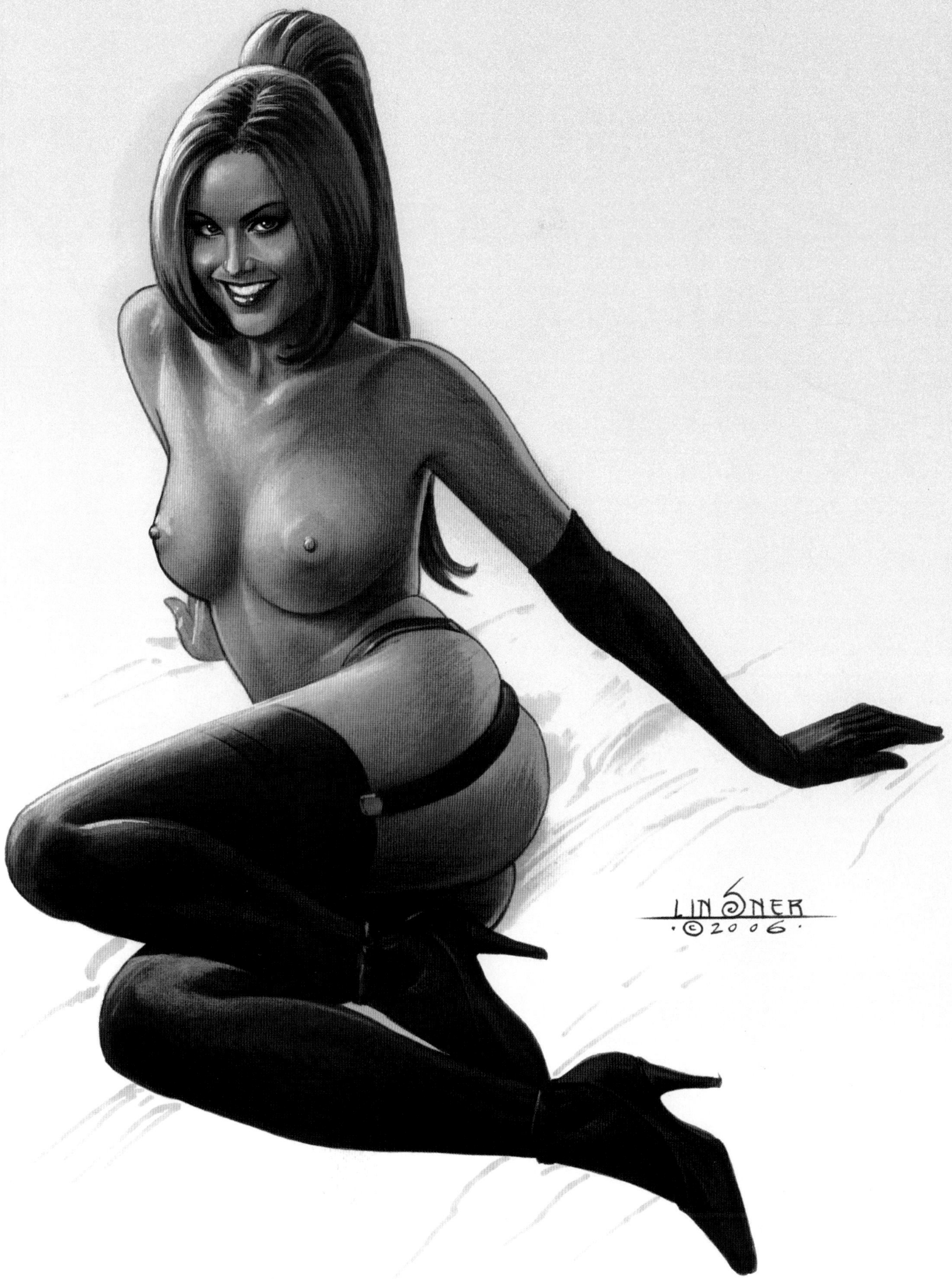
LINSNER
©2006

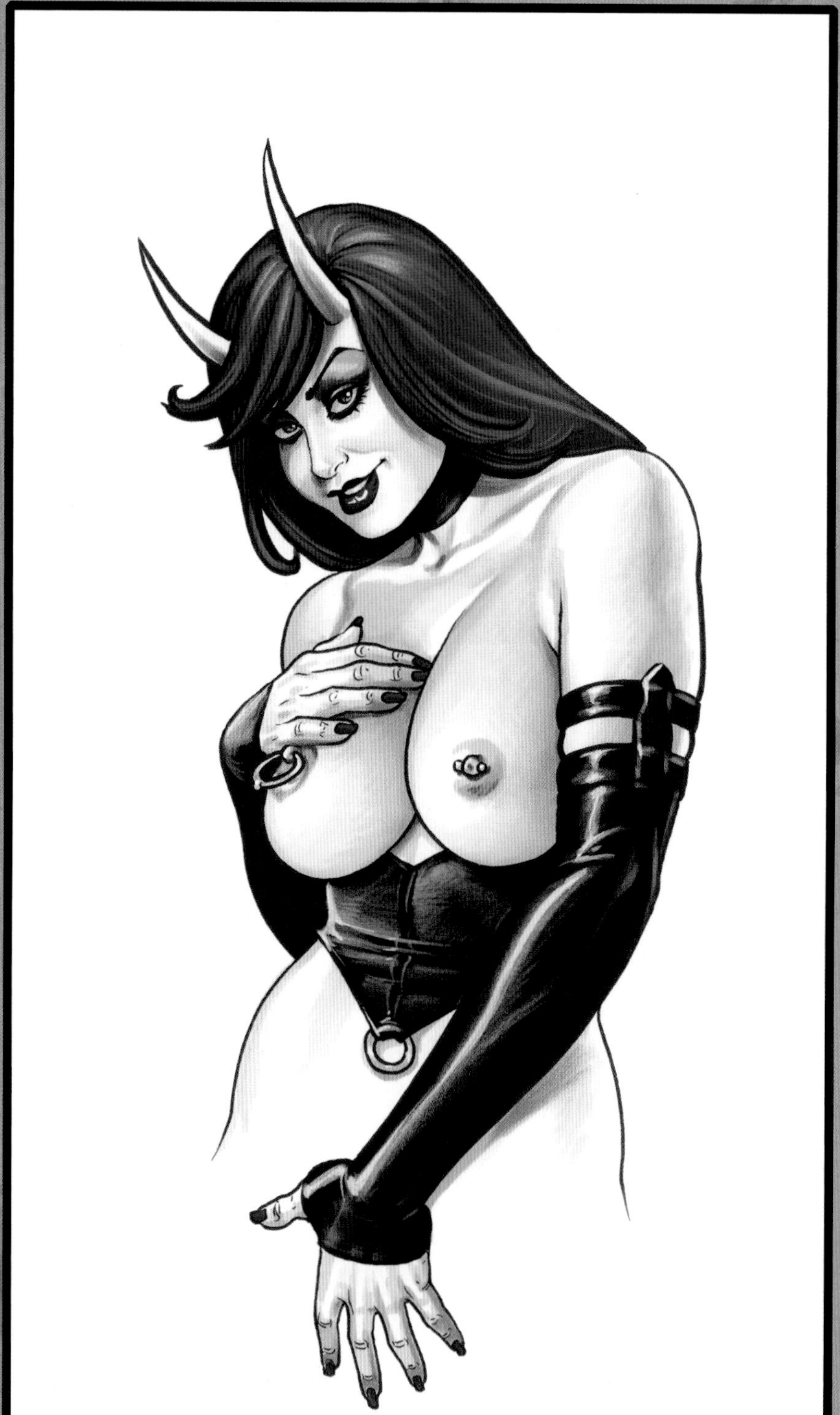
LINSNER
·©2006·

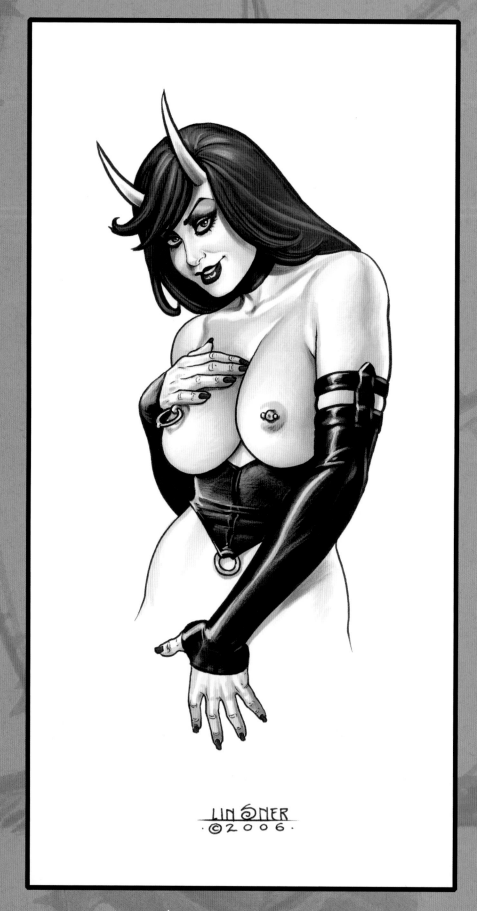

Squeeze Me, Please Me

Freckles

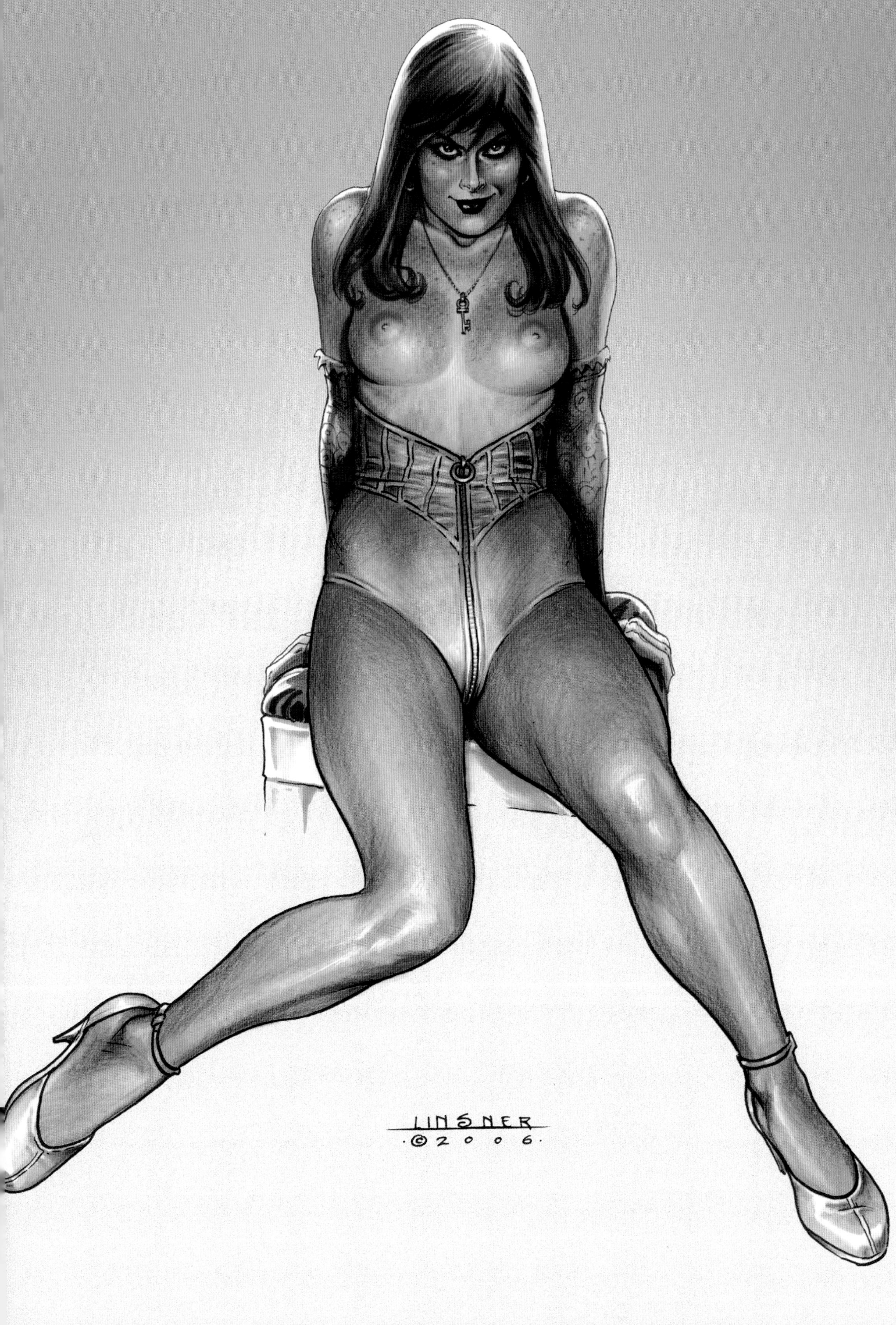
LINSNER
©2006

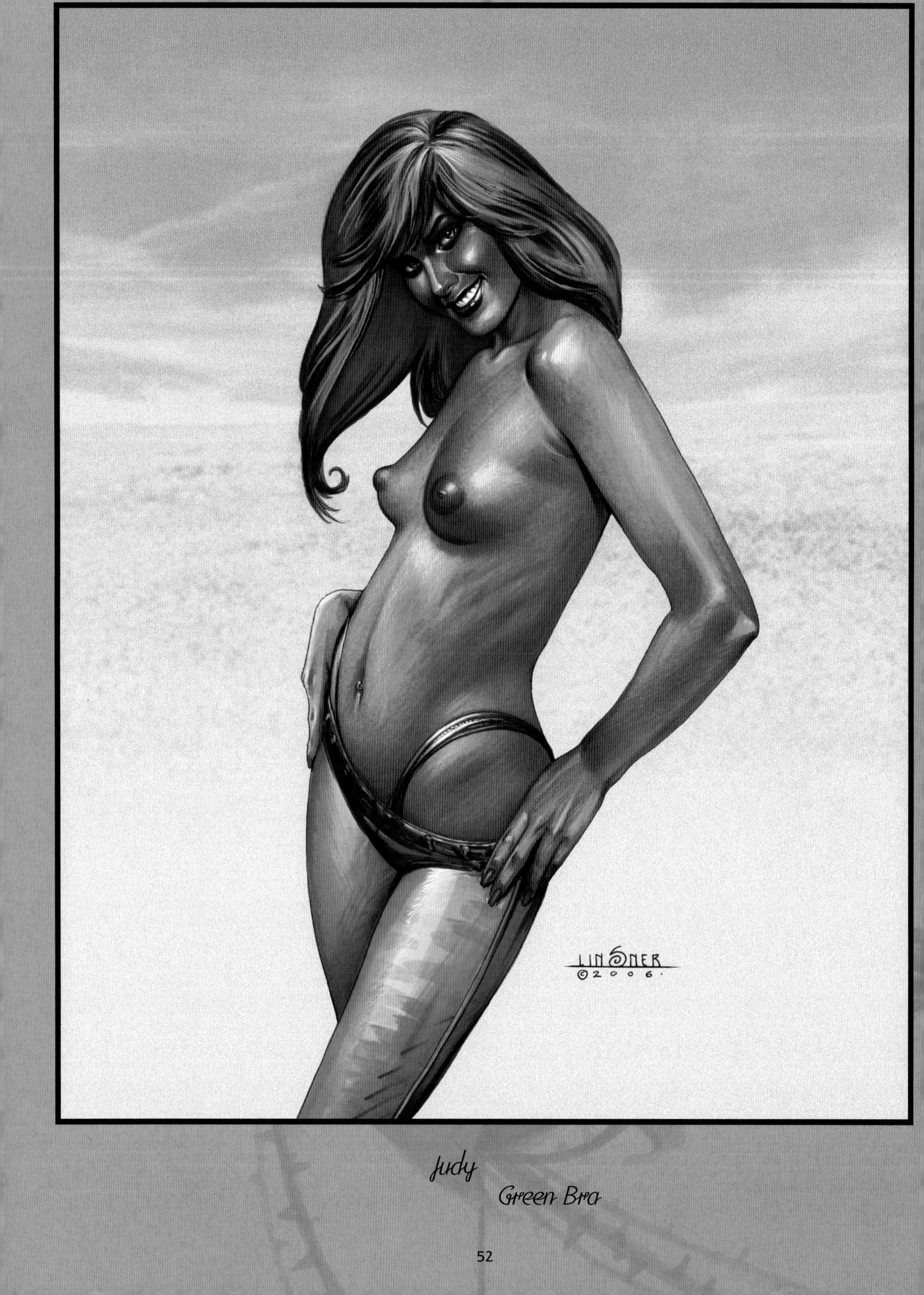
LINSNER
©2006.

Judy

Green Bra

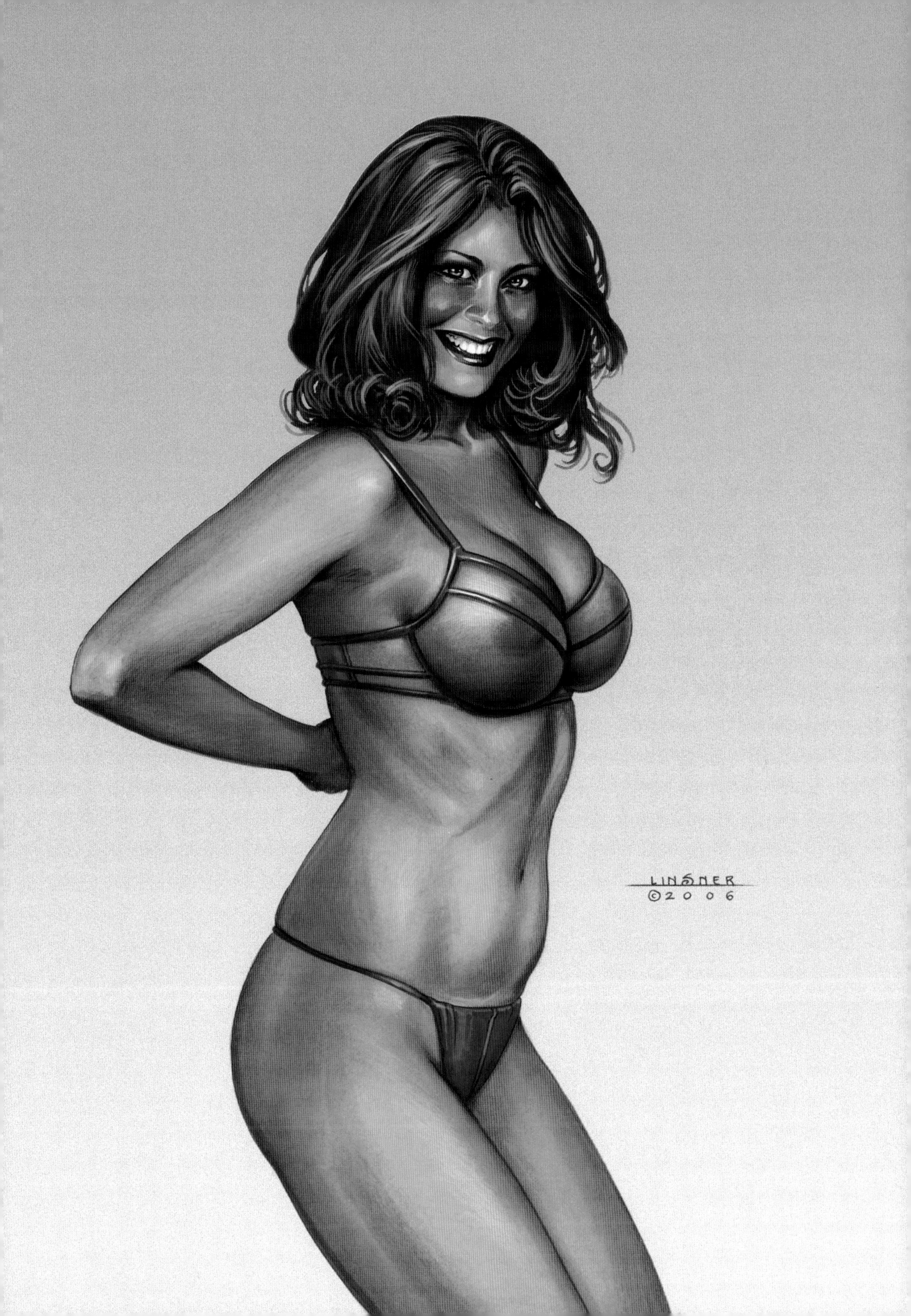
LINSNER
©2006

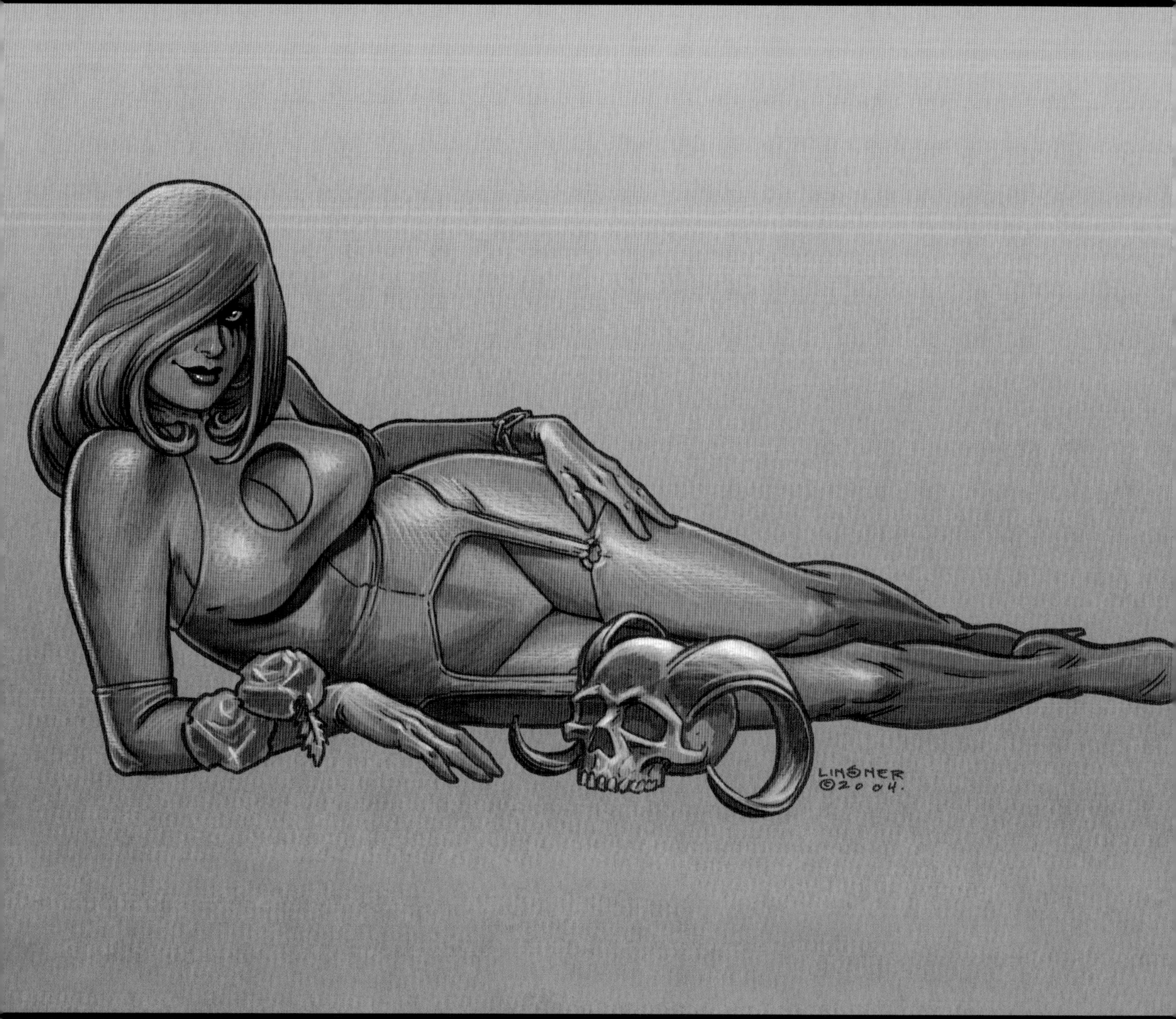
LIMSNER
©2004.

Reclining Dawn

Show Me the Money

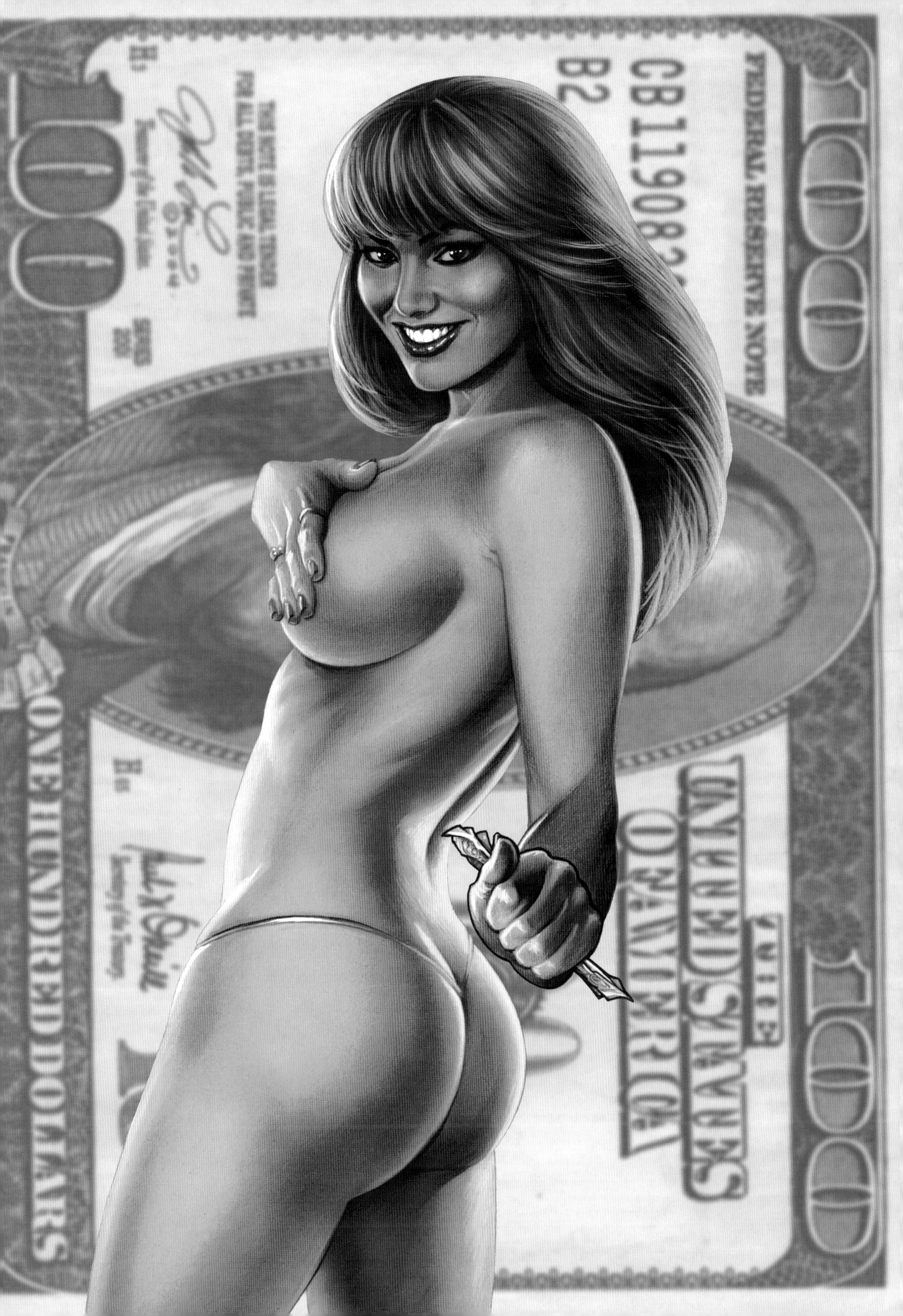
FEDERAL RESERVE NOTE
ONE HUNDRED DOLLARS

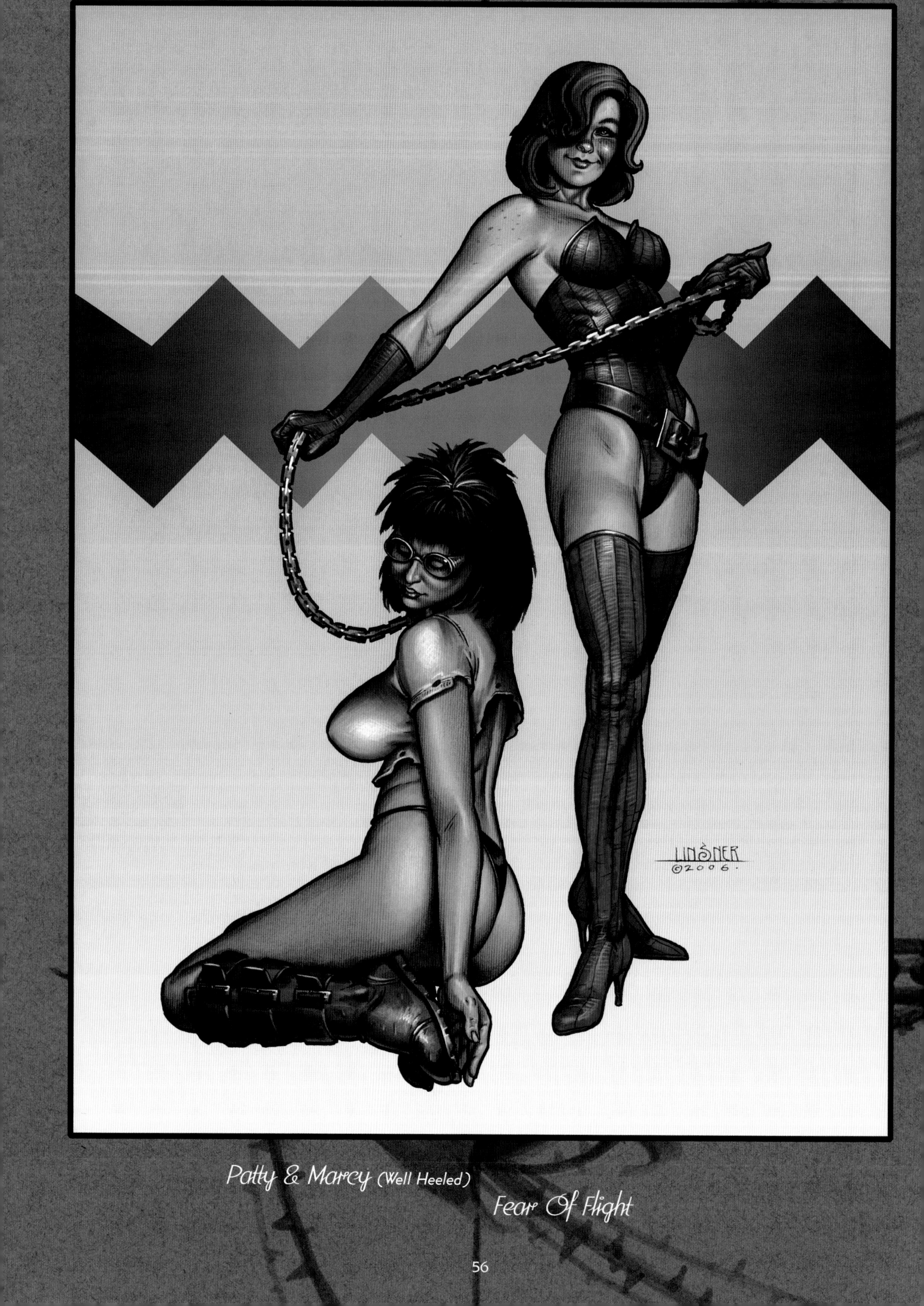
LINSNER
©2006.

Patty & Marcy (Well Heeled)

Fear Of Flight

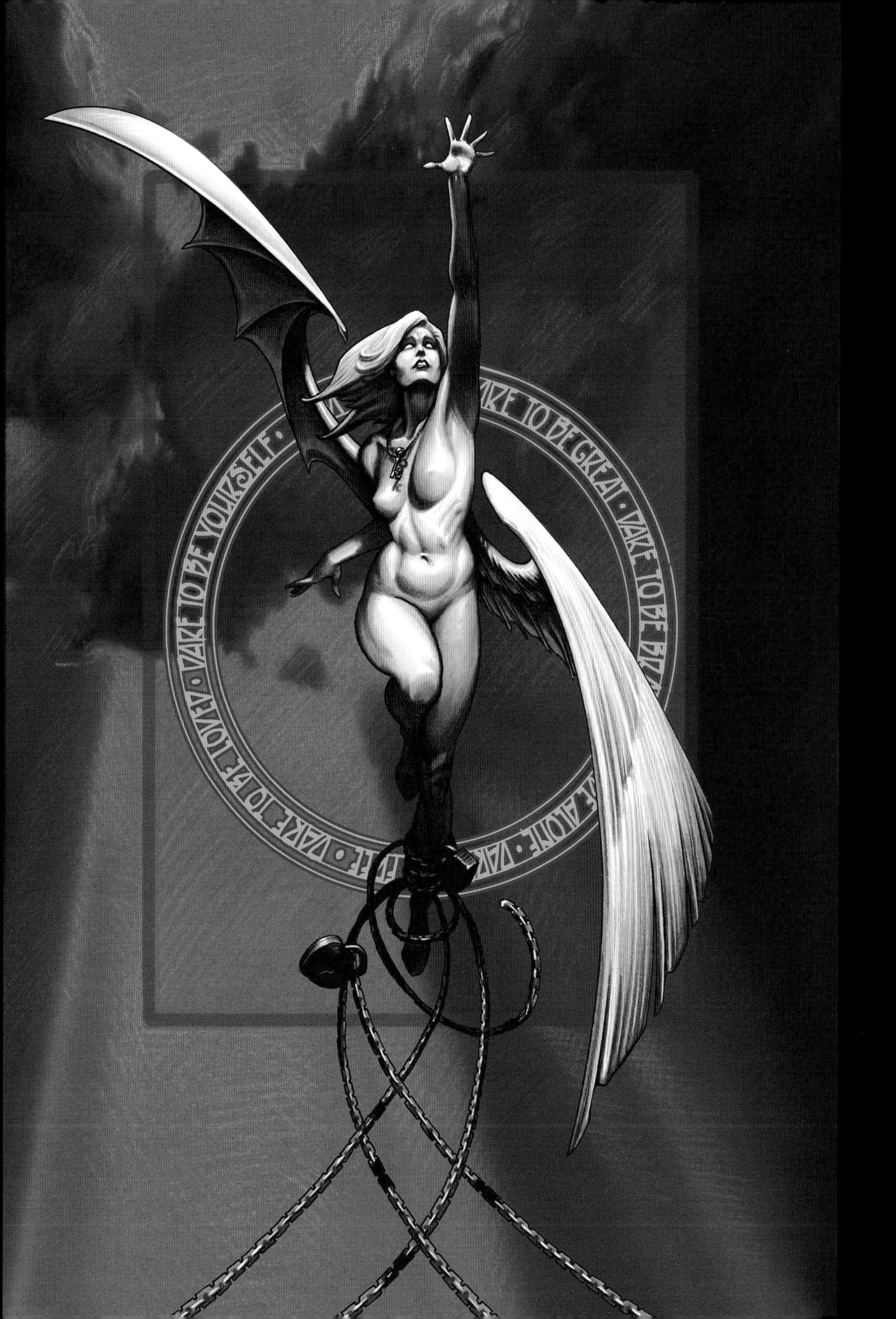

DARE TO BE YOURSELF
DARE TO BE GREAT
DARE TO BE LOVED

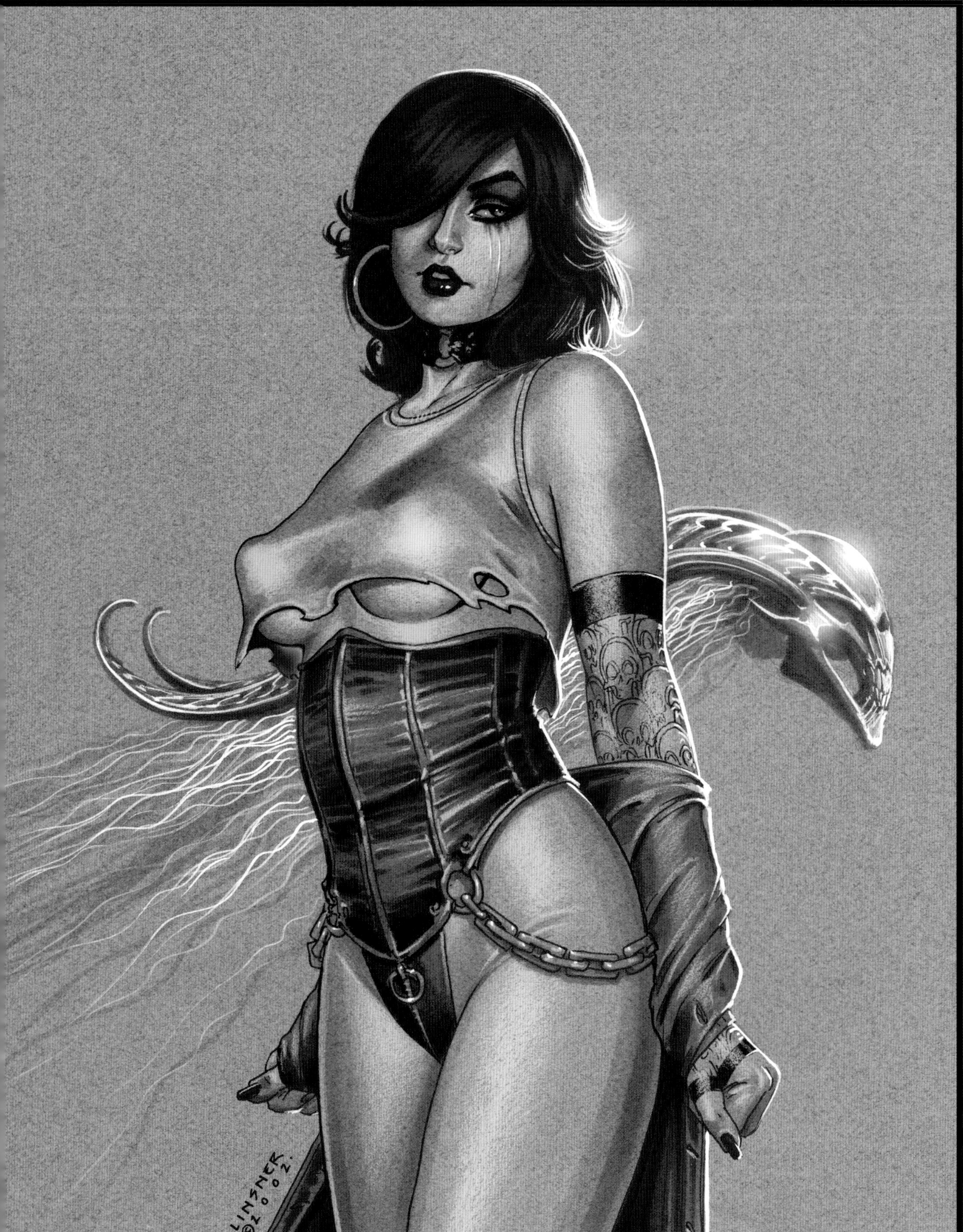
LINSNER
©2002.

Red & Gray

Fairy Dawn

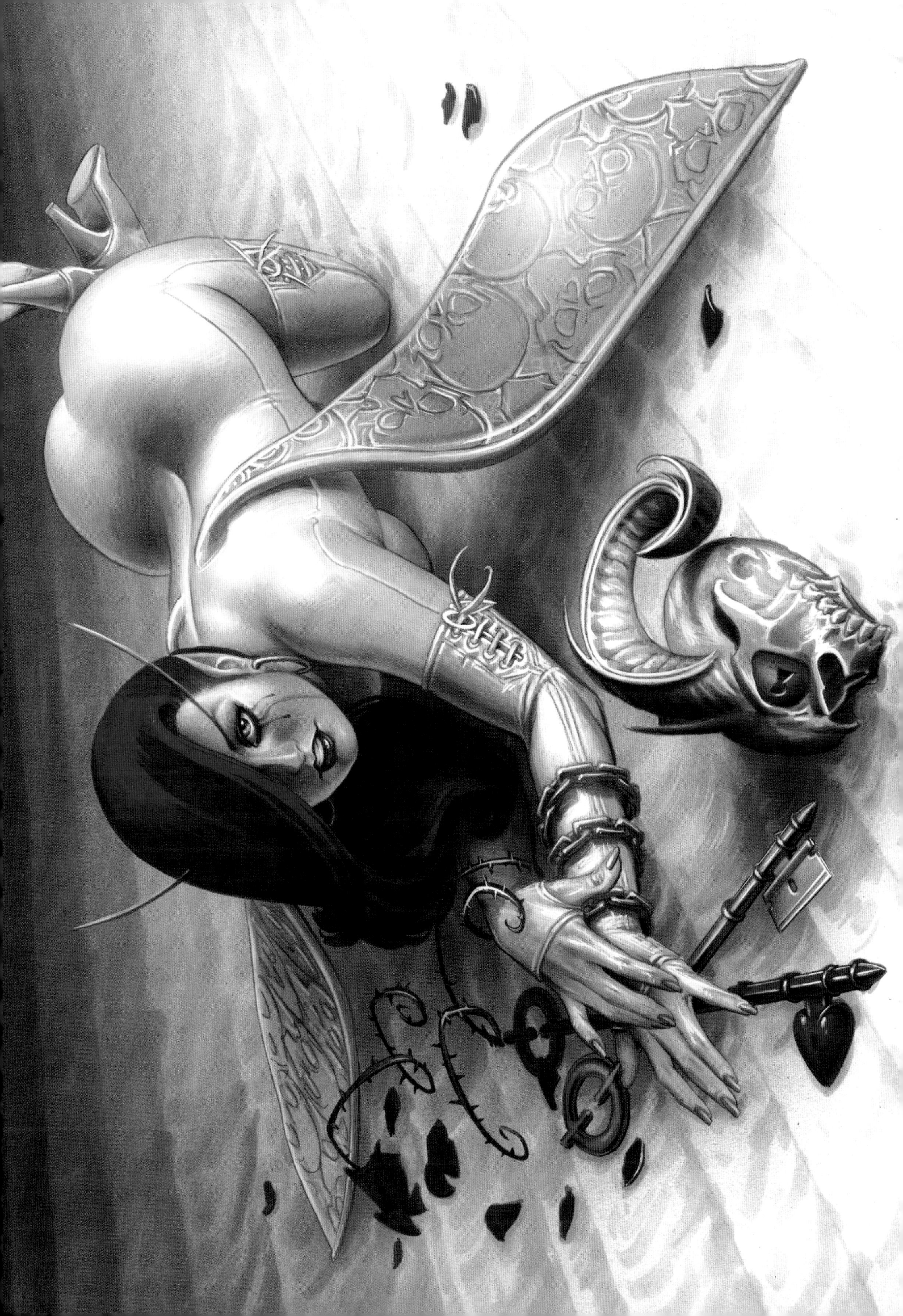

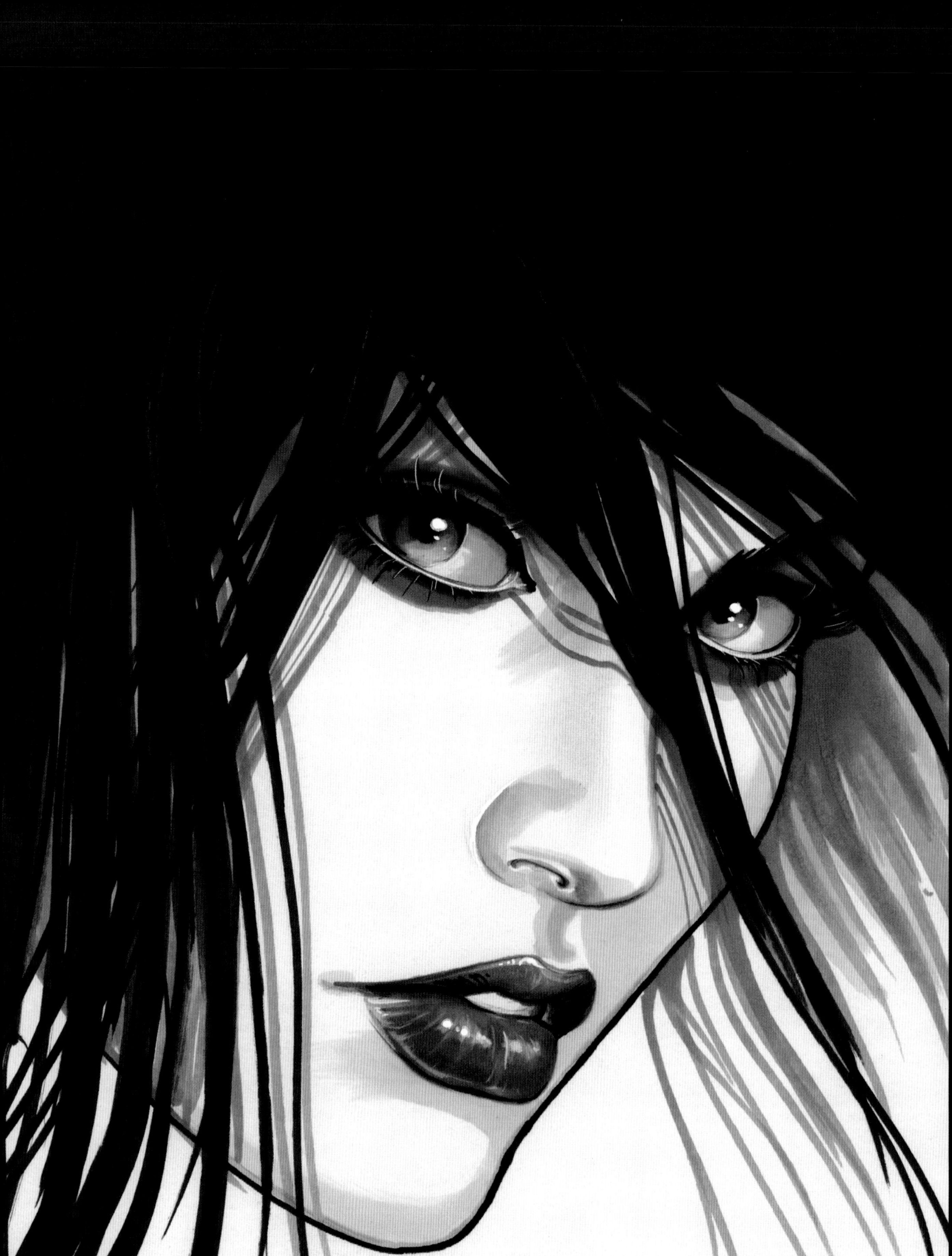

Ivory Eyes

My Confession

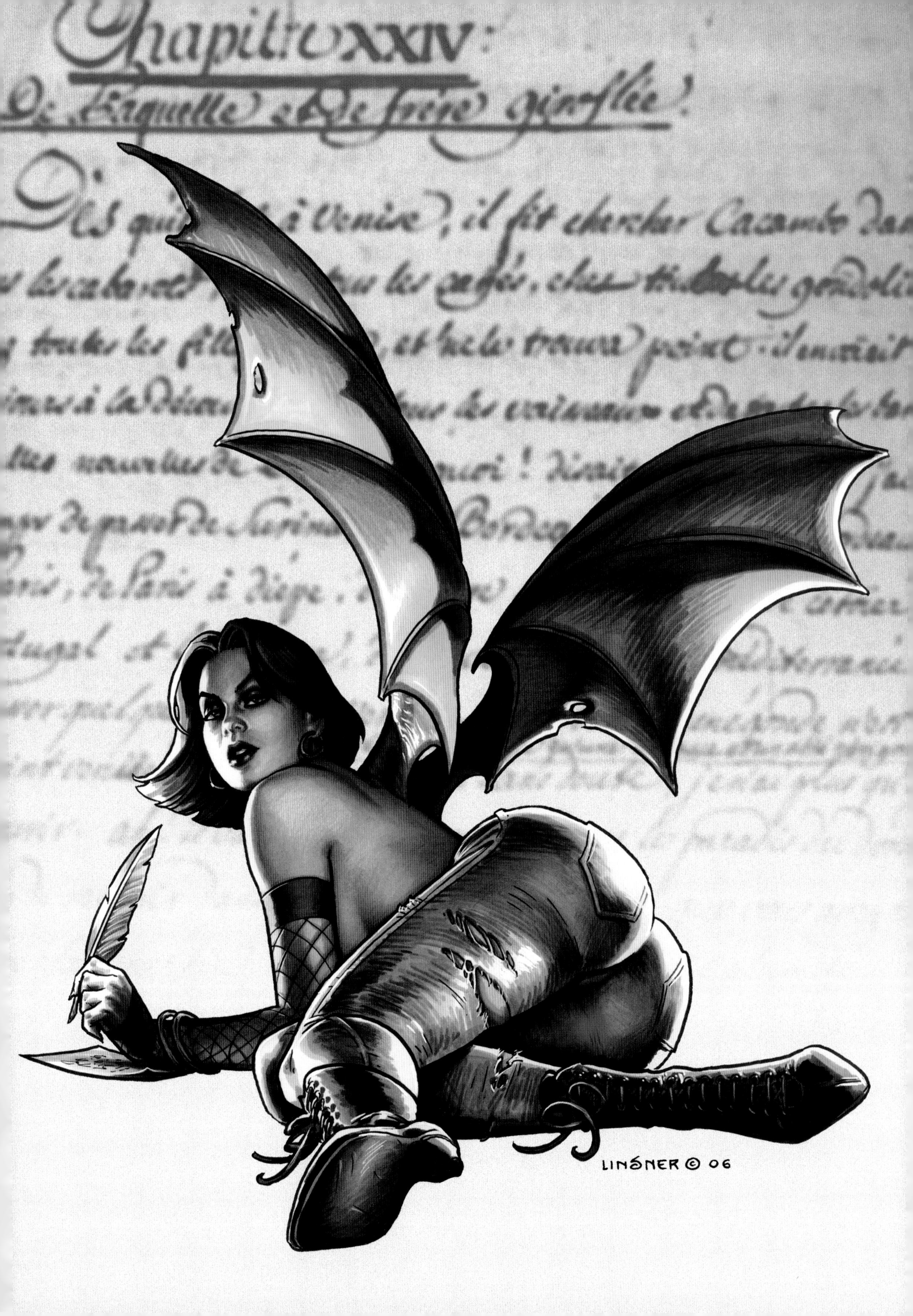
Chapitre XXIV:
LINSNER © 06

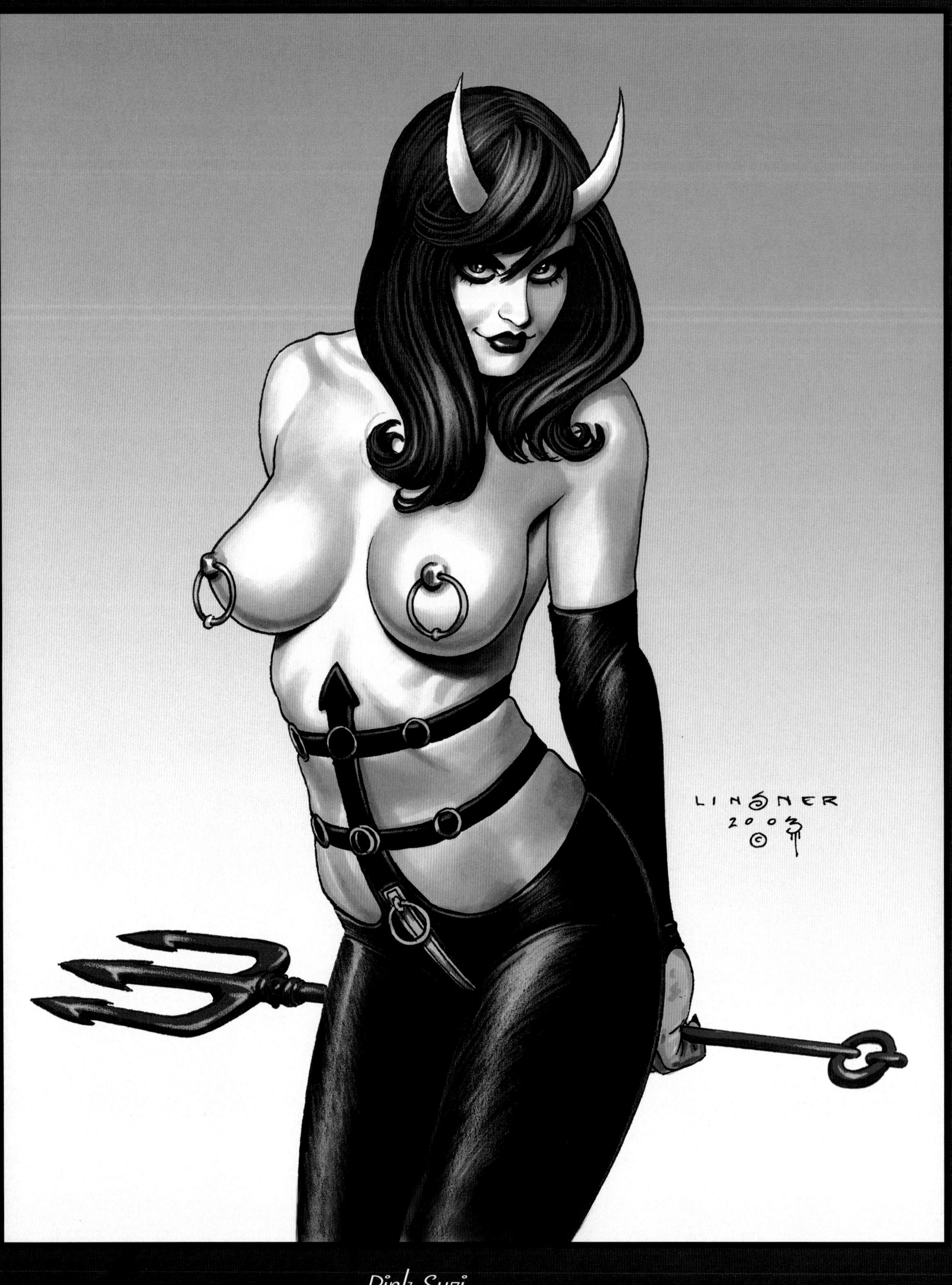
LINSNER
2003
©

Pink Suzi

Purple Skin

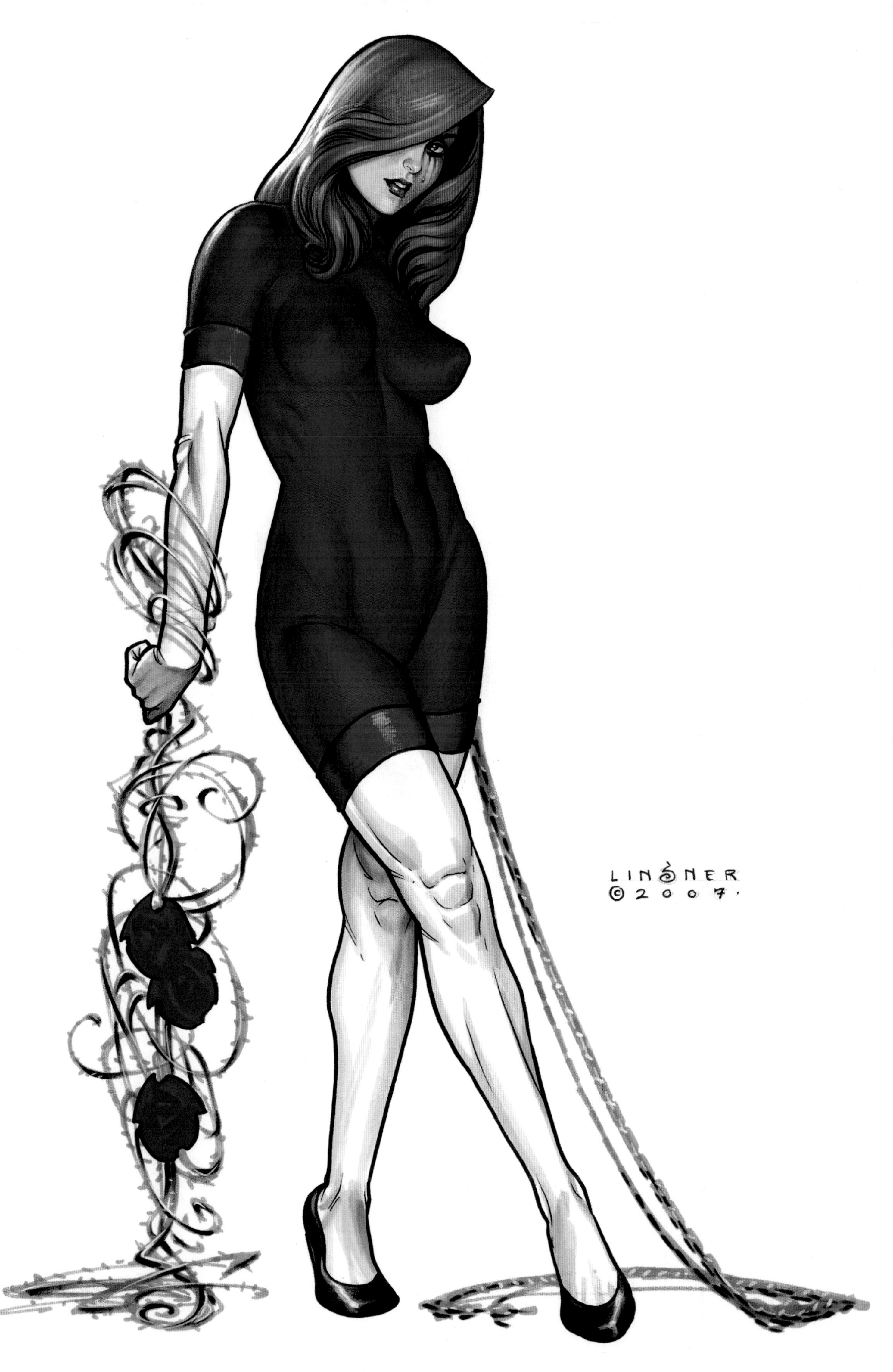
LINSNER
©2007.

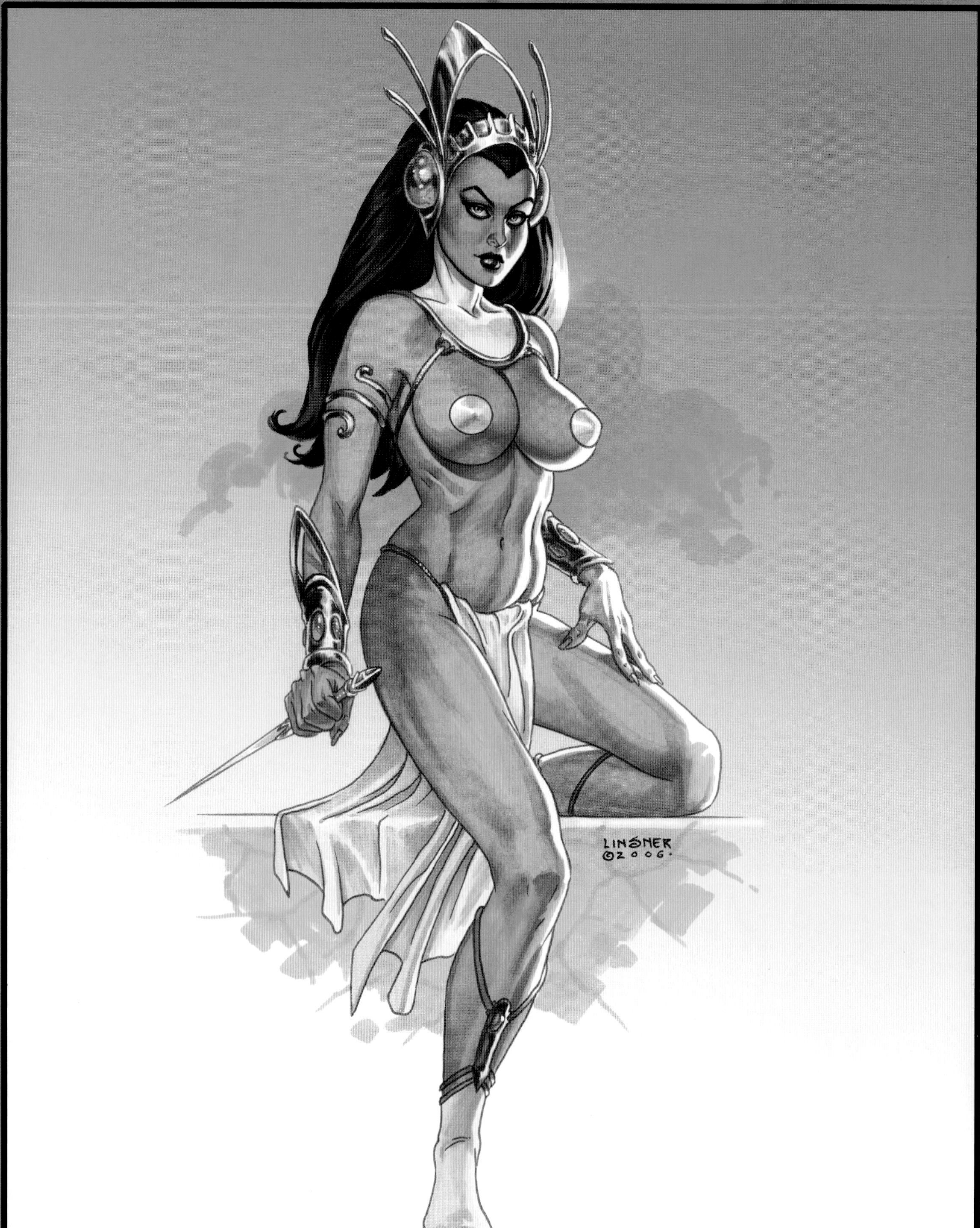
LINSNER
©2006.

Martian Maiden

Burgundy Corset

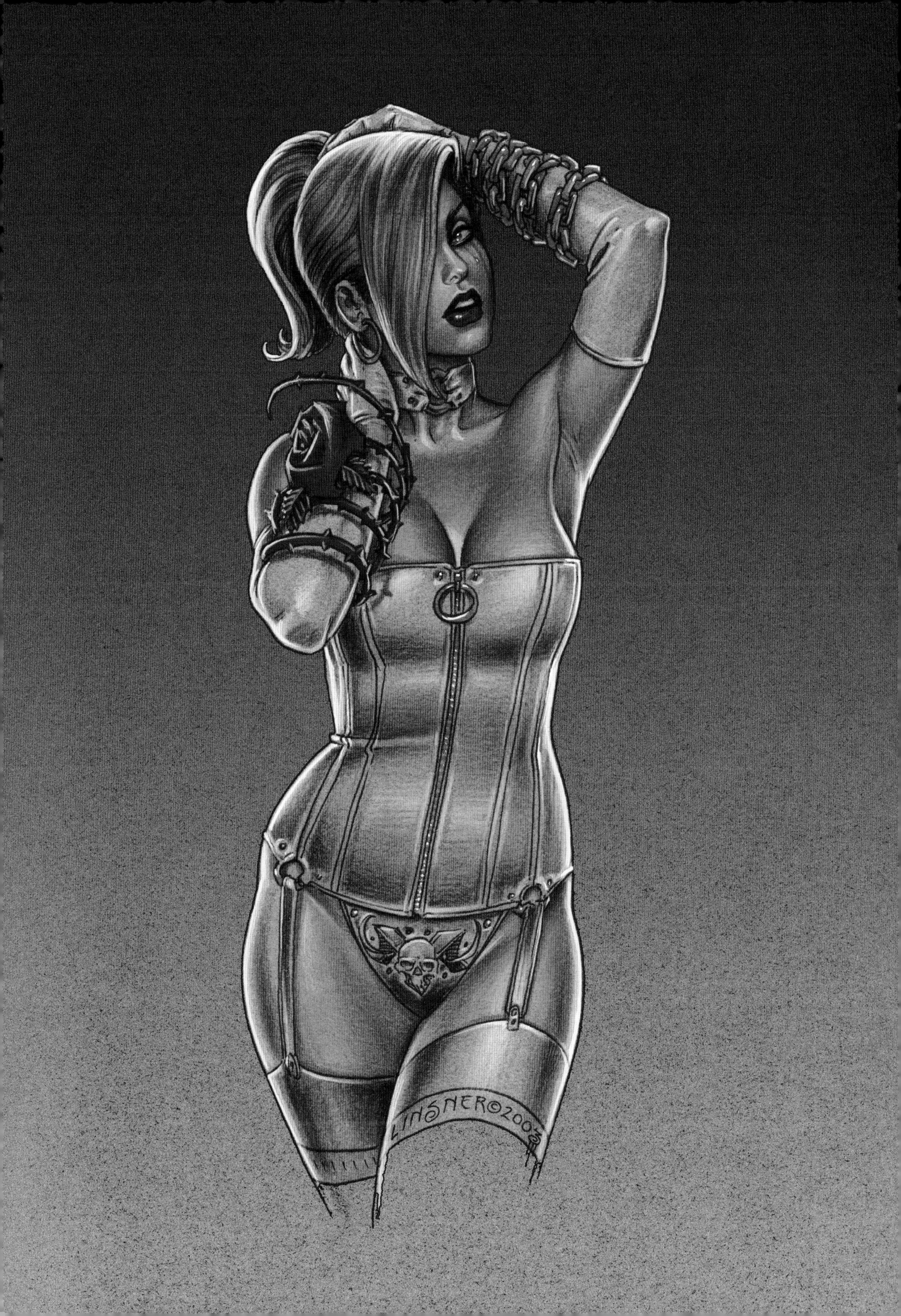
LINSNER

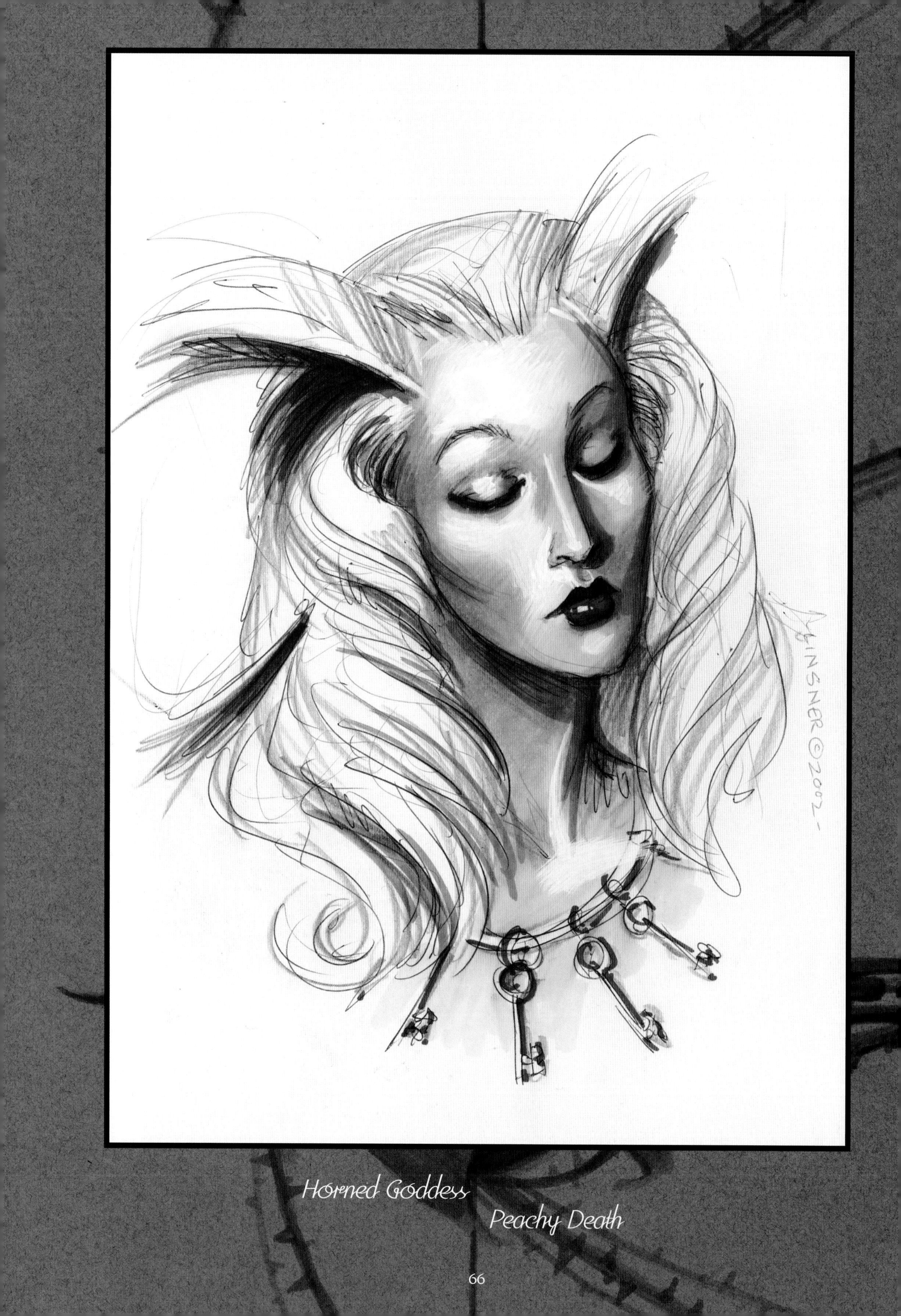

Horned Goddess

Peachy Death

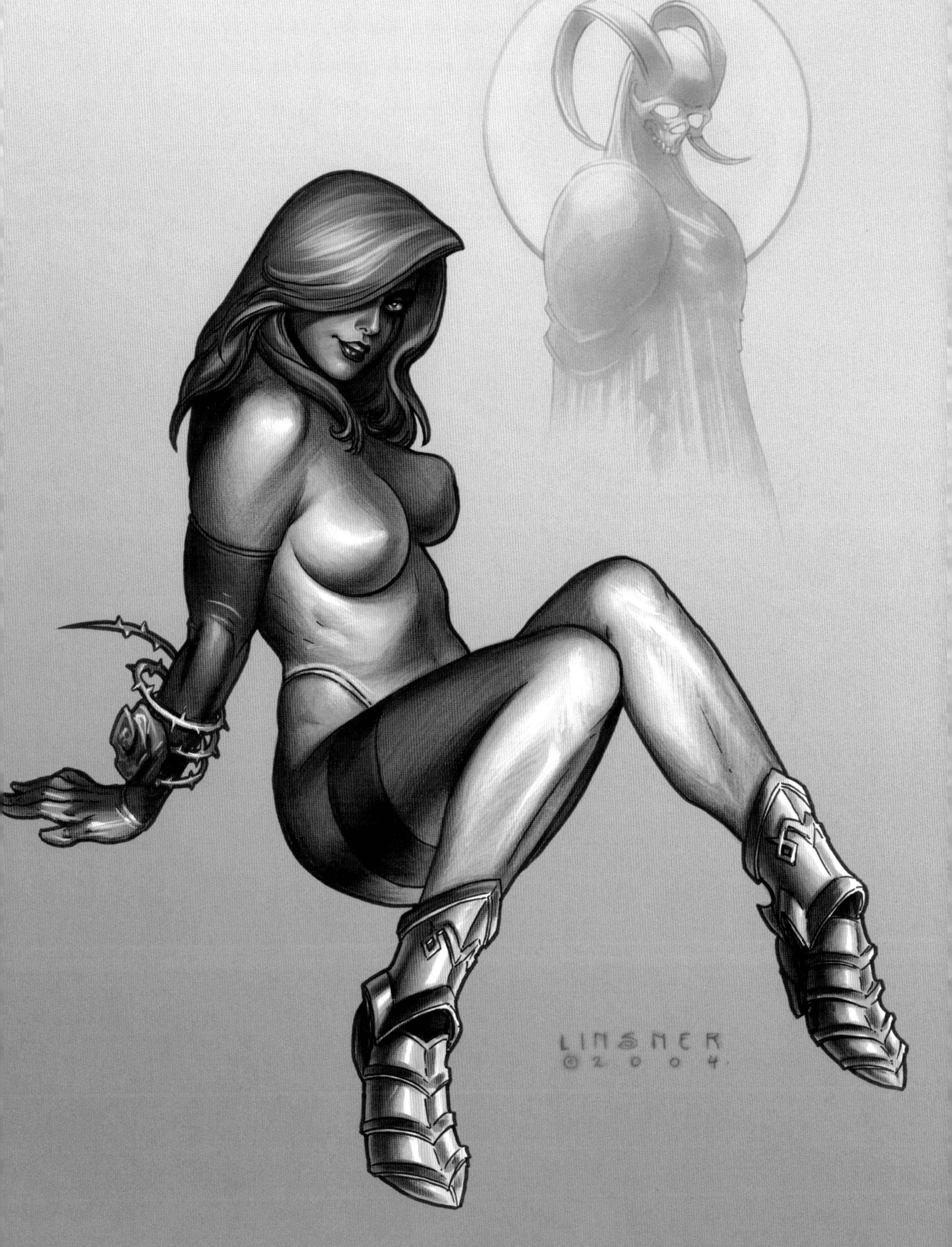
LINSNER
©2004.

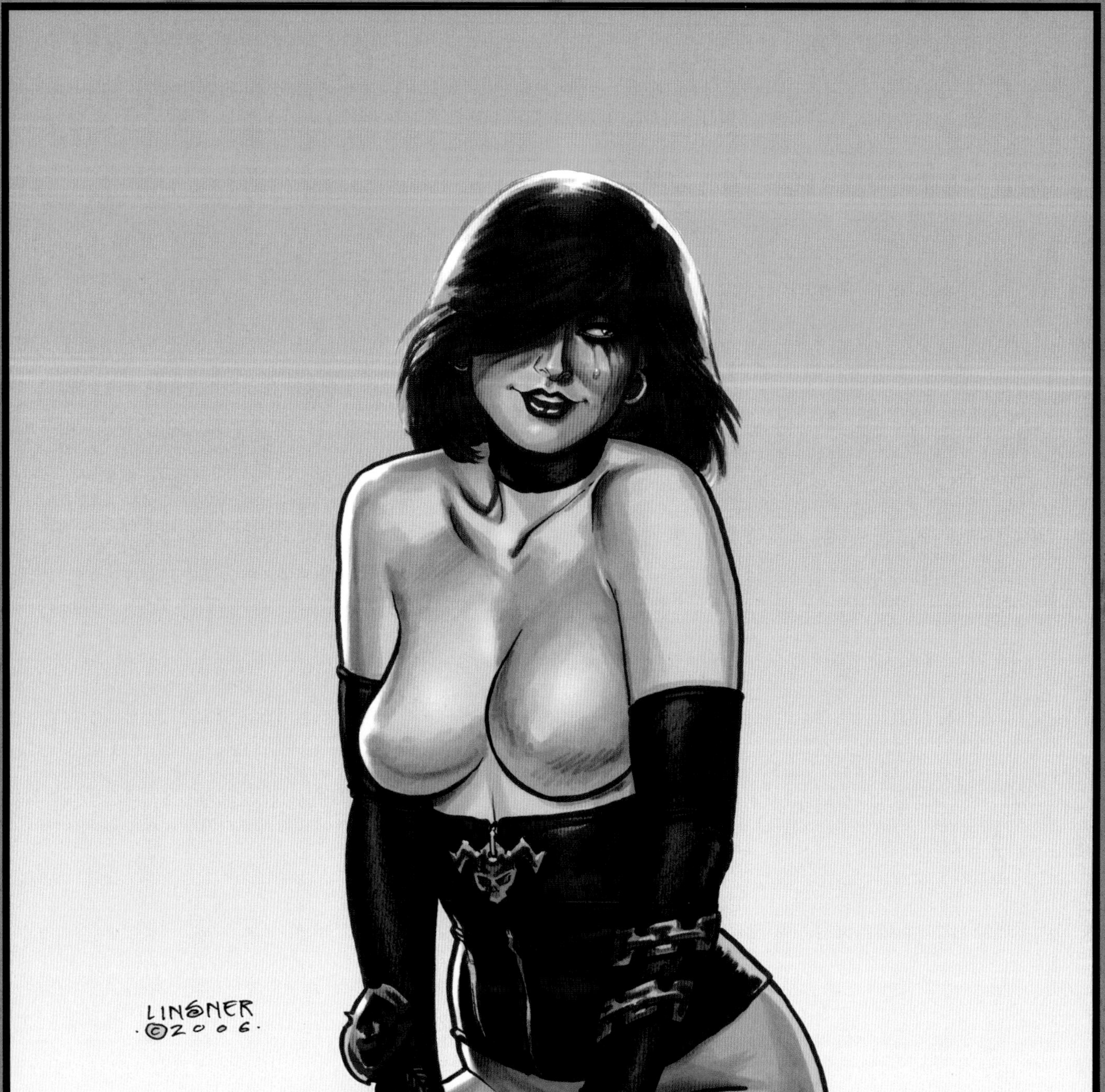
LINSNER
©2006

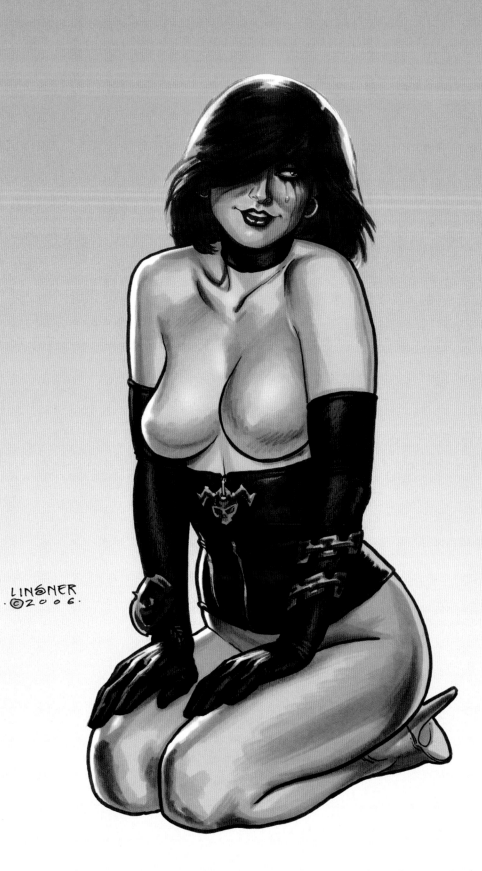

Sunshine

Sinful Suzi

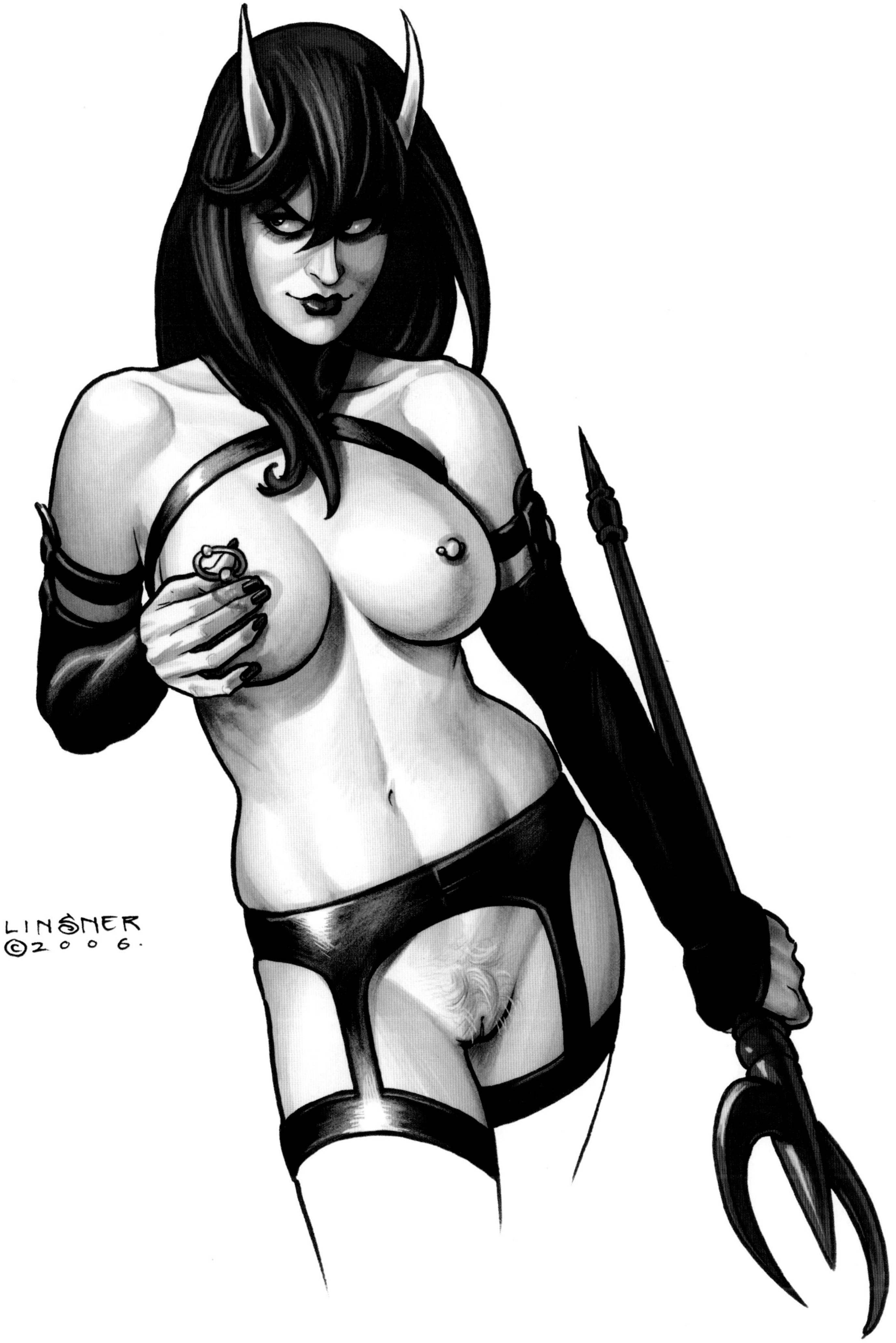
LINSNER
©2006.

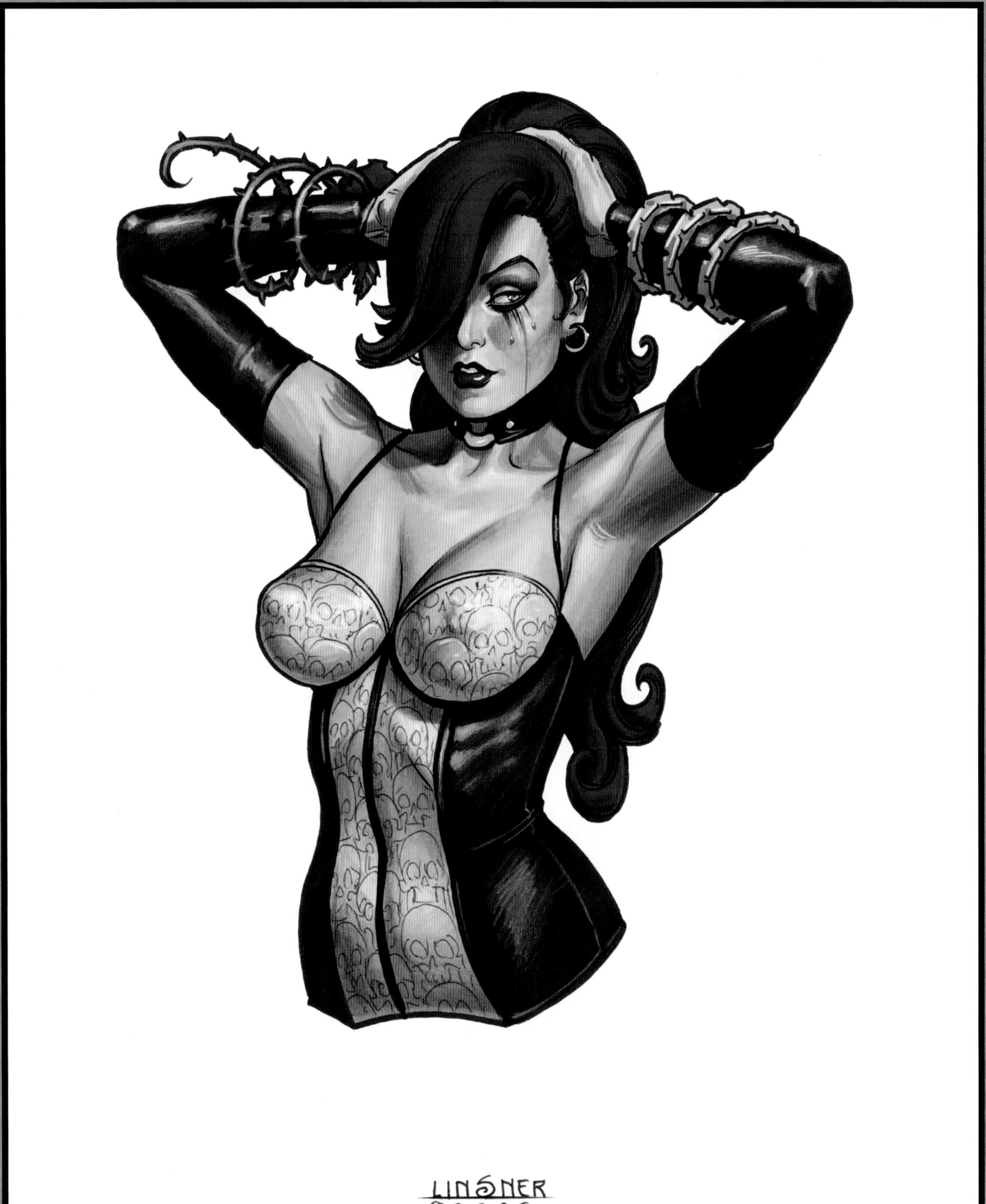
LINSNER
©2006

Stretch

Kiss Me

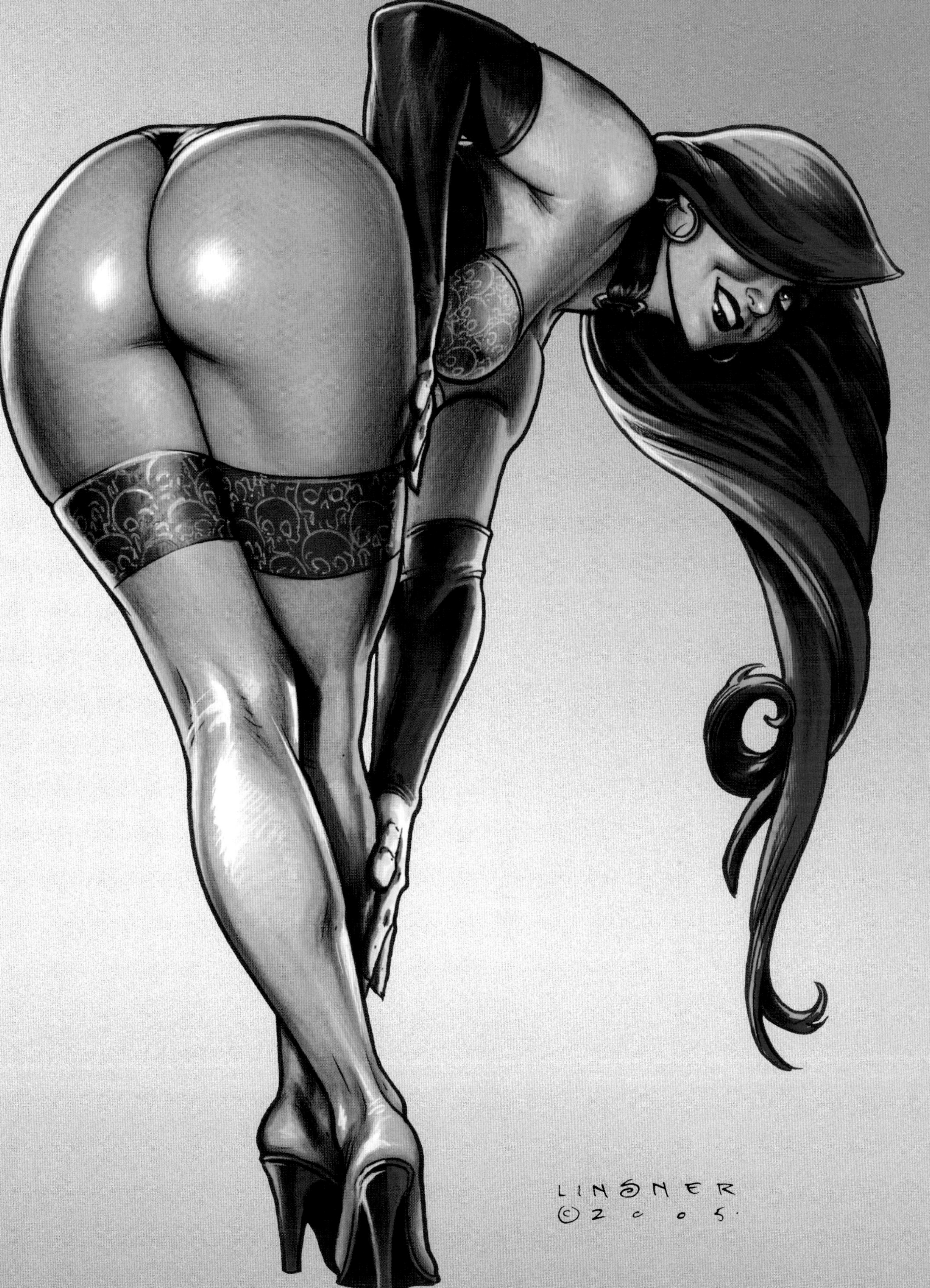
LINSNER
©2005.

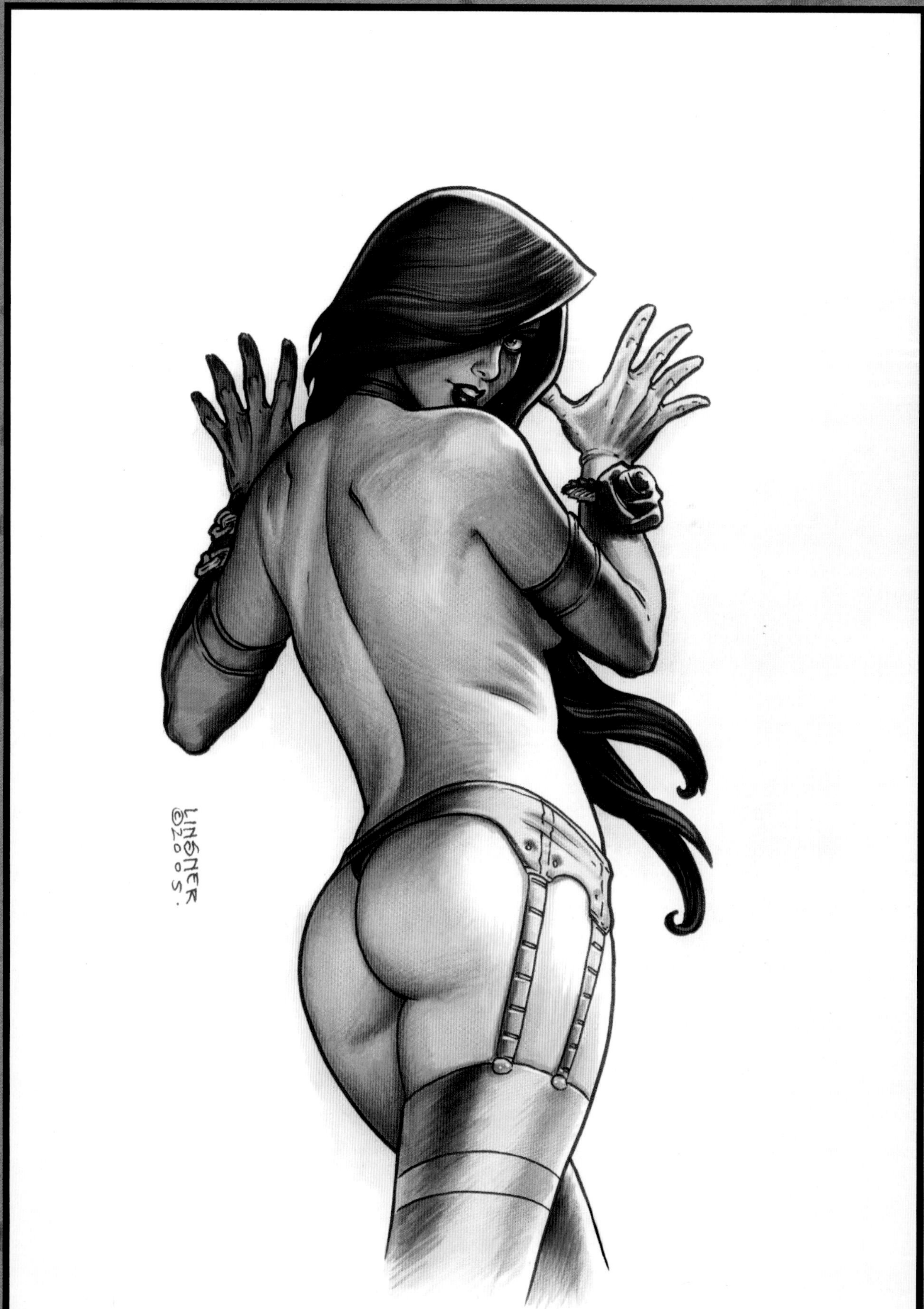
LINSNER ©2005.

Garterbelt
Suzi two

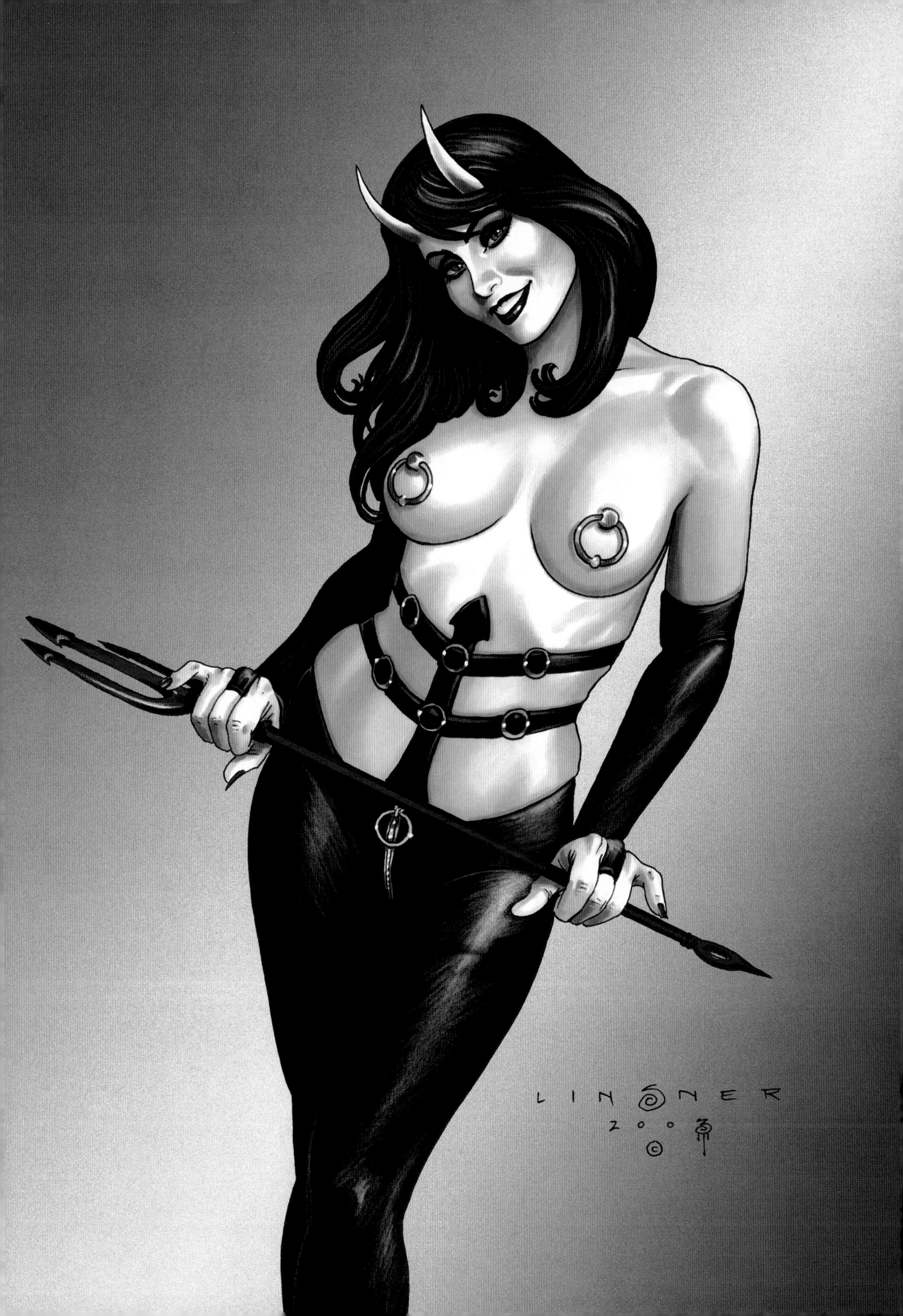

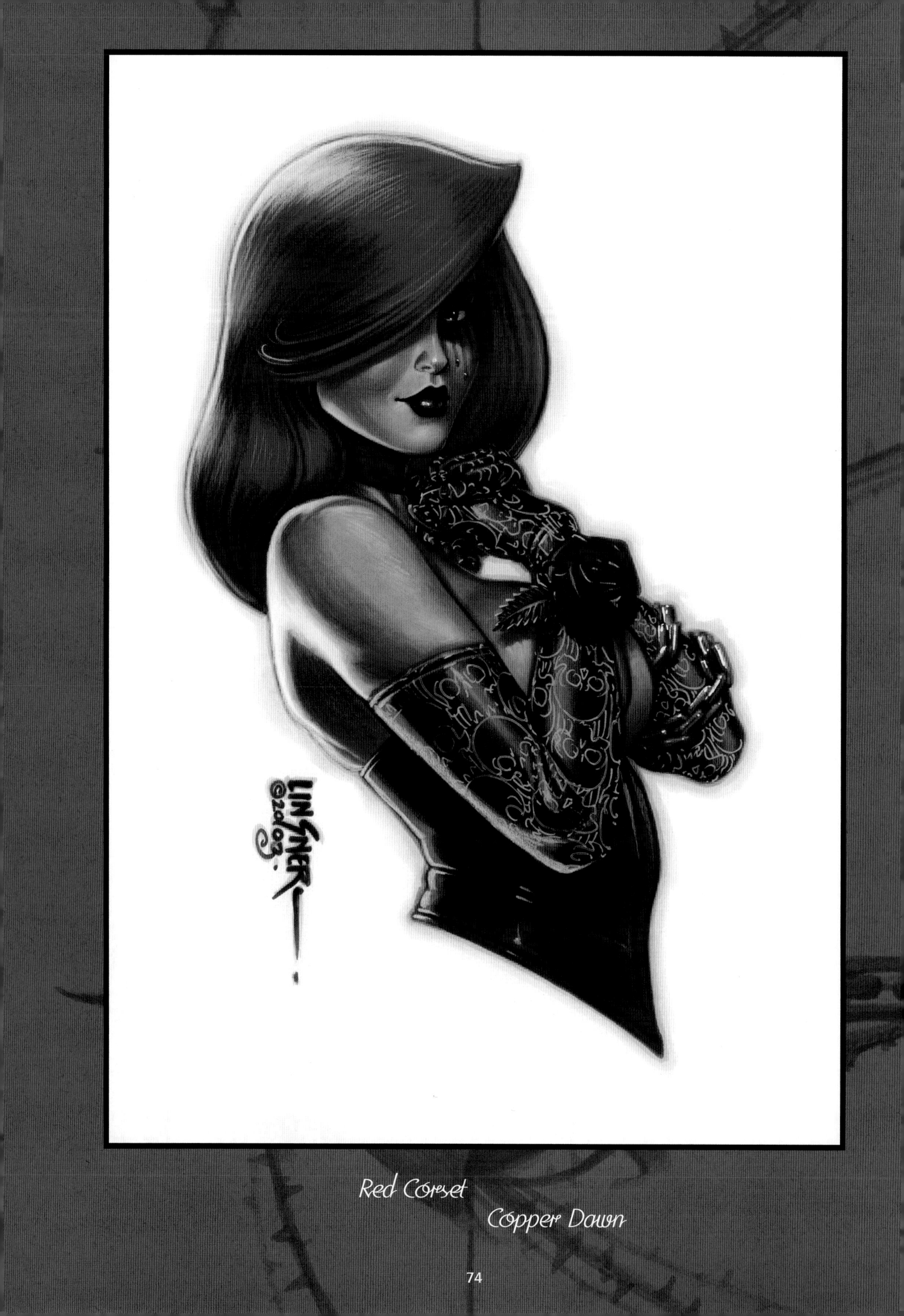
LINSNER
©2003

Red Corset

Copper Dawn

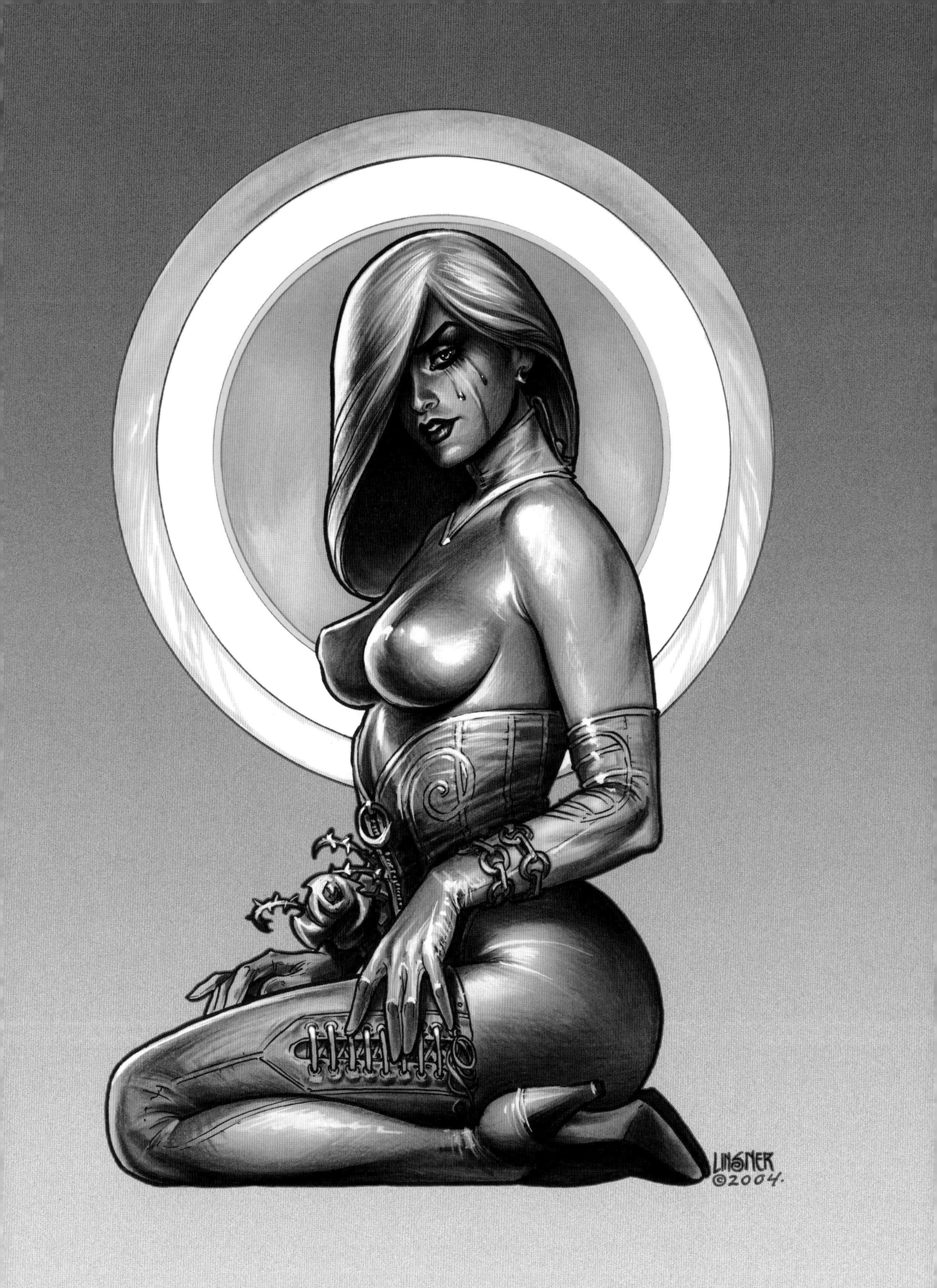
LINSNER
©2004.

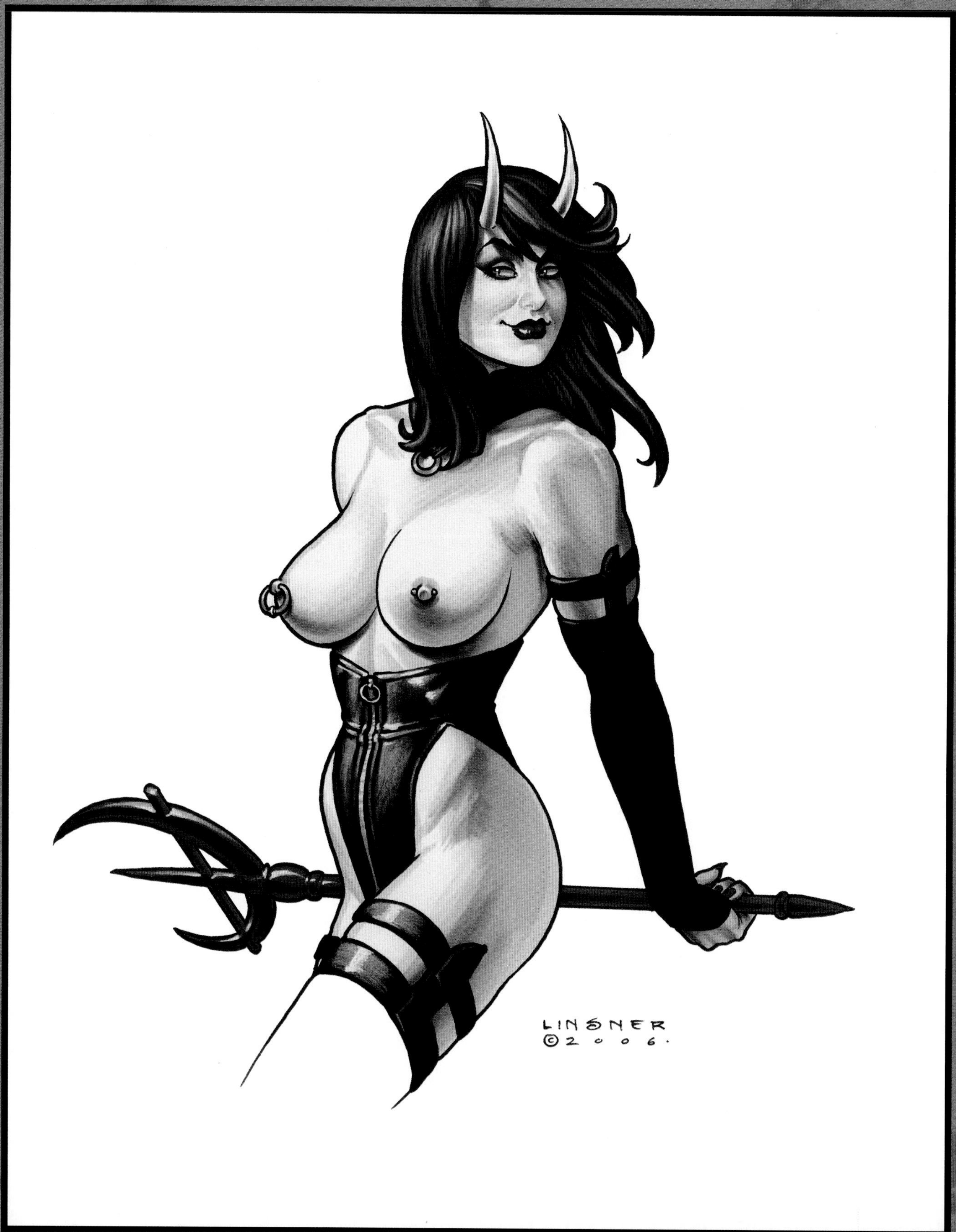
LINSNER
©2006.

Suzi Smiles

Brazen Raven

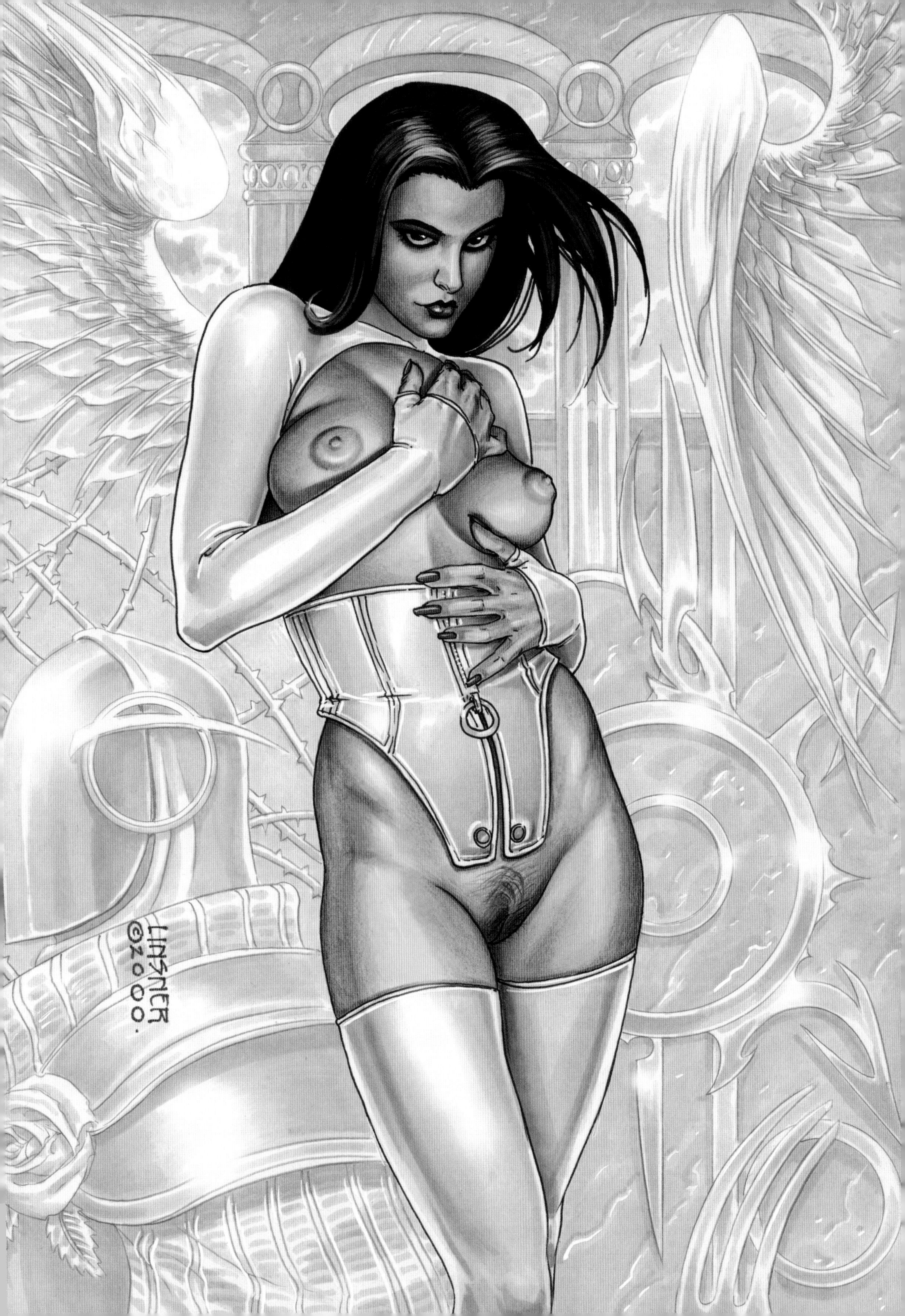
LINSNER
©2000.

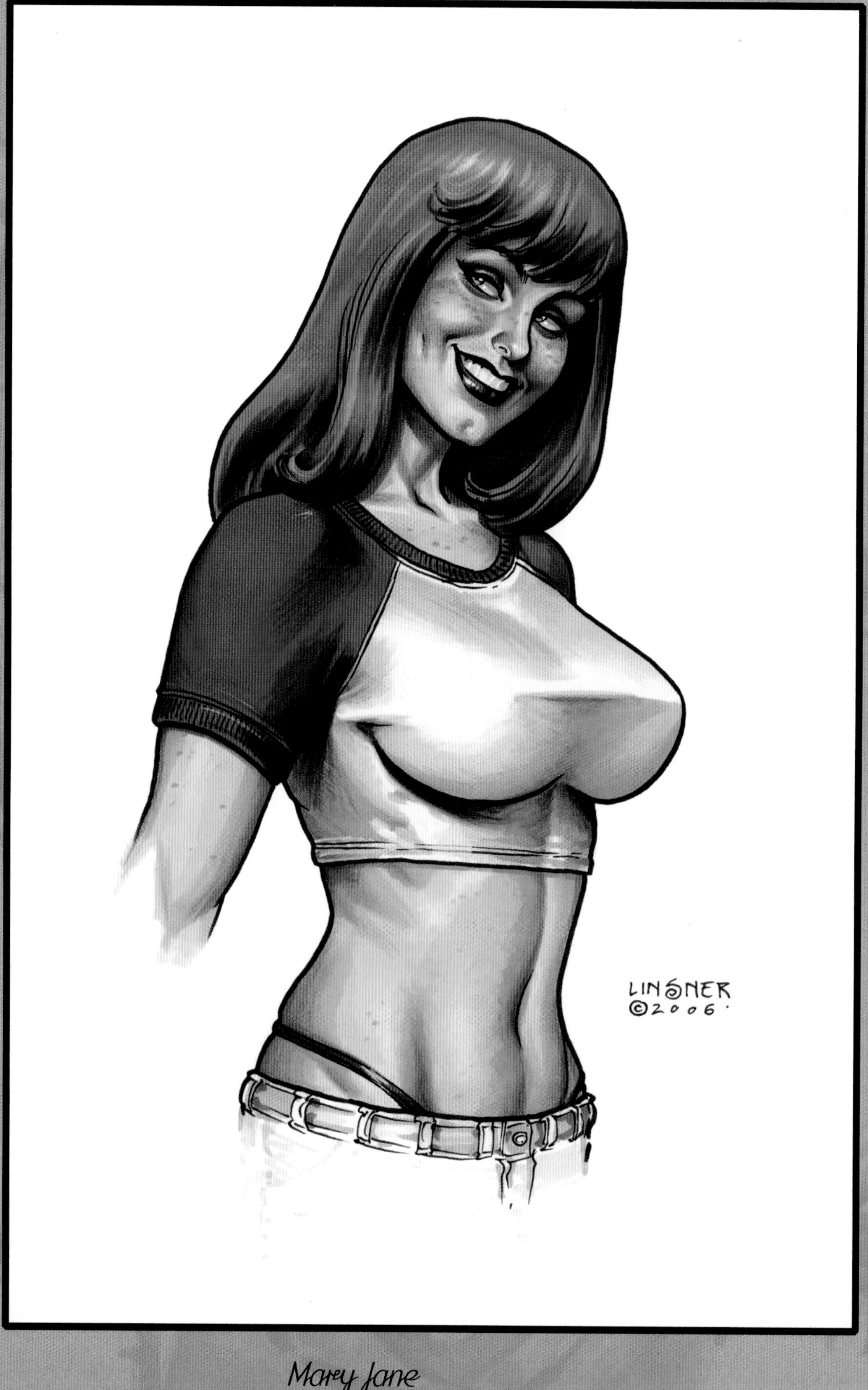
LINSNER
©2006

Mary Jane

After School Special

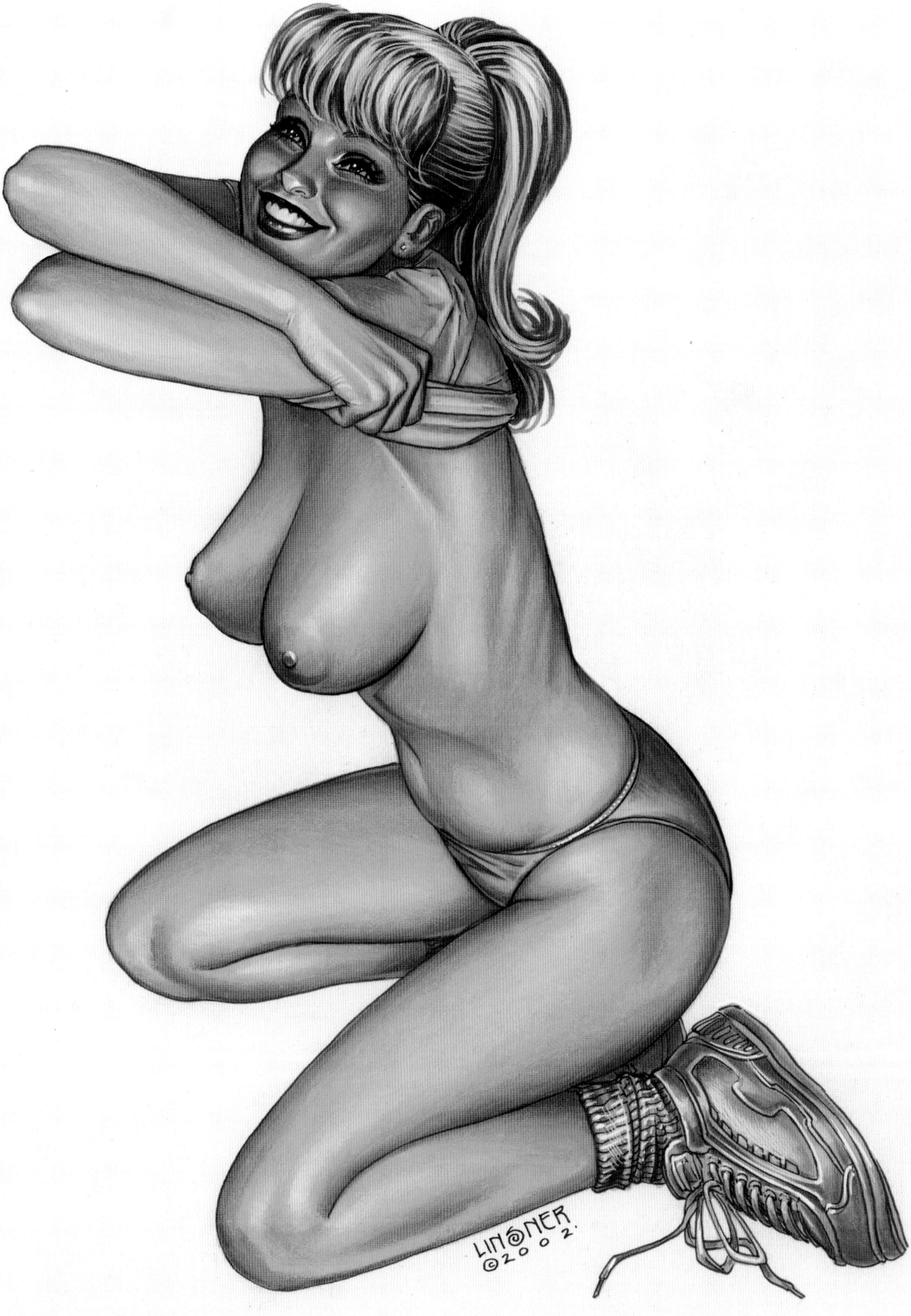
LINSNER
©2002.

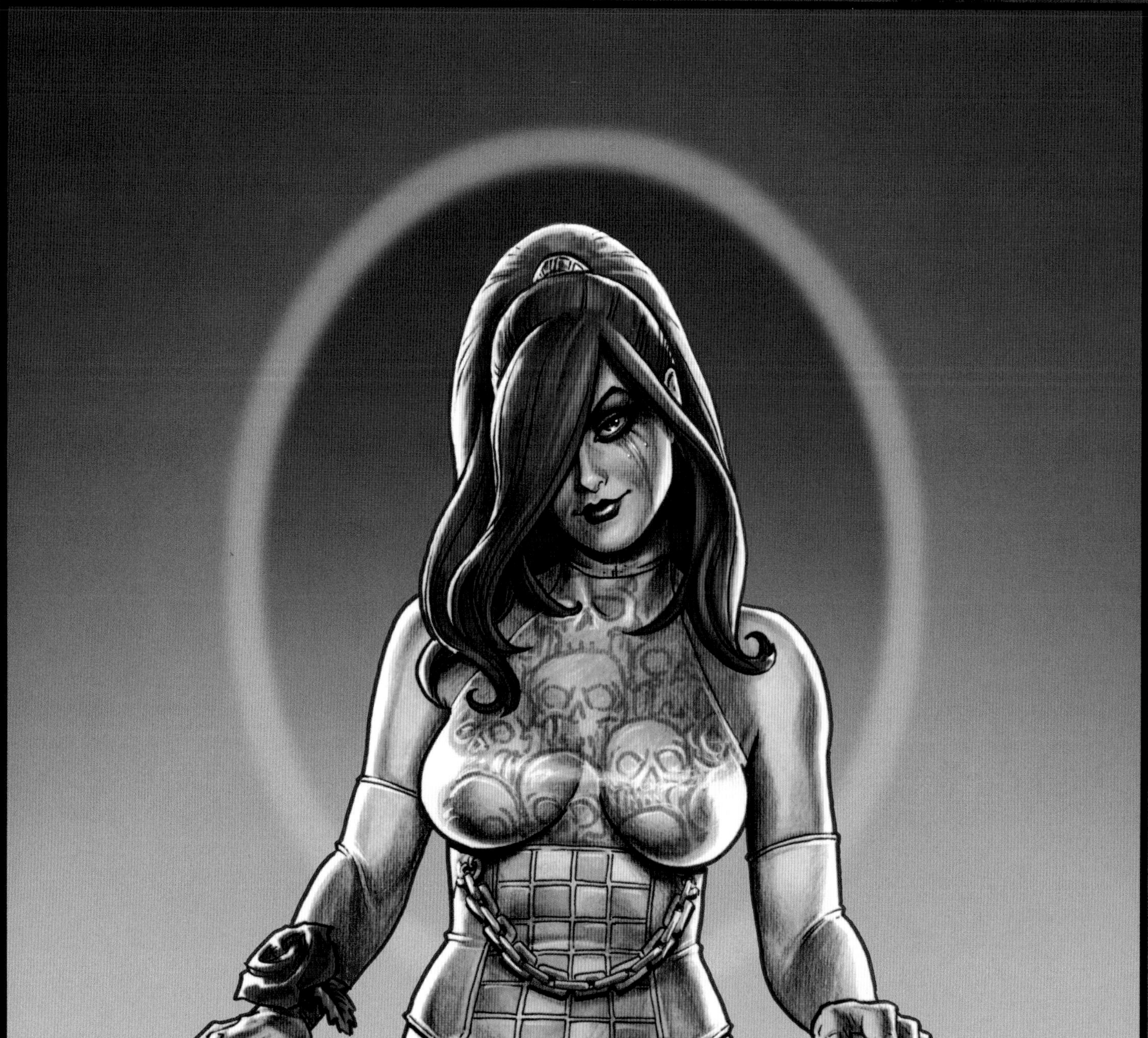
LINSNER
©2004.

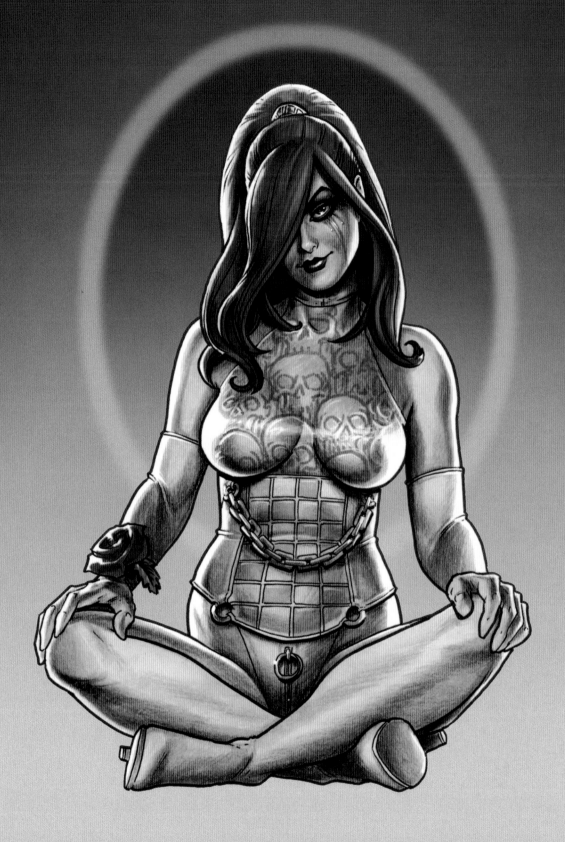

Sitting Pretty

transit

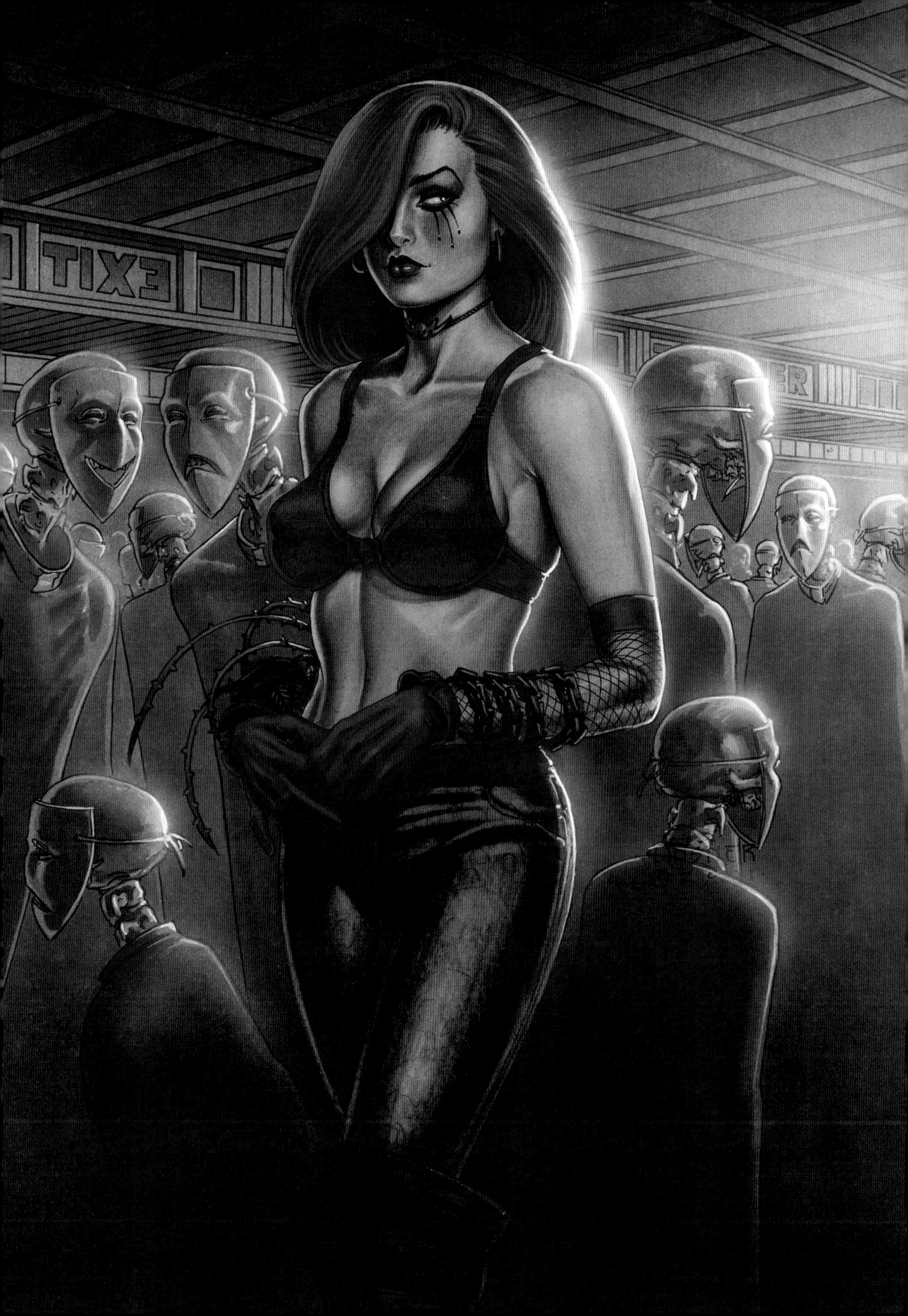

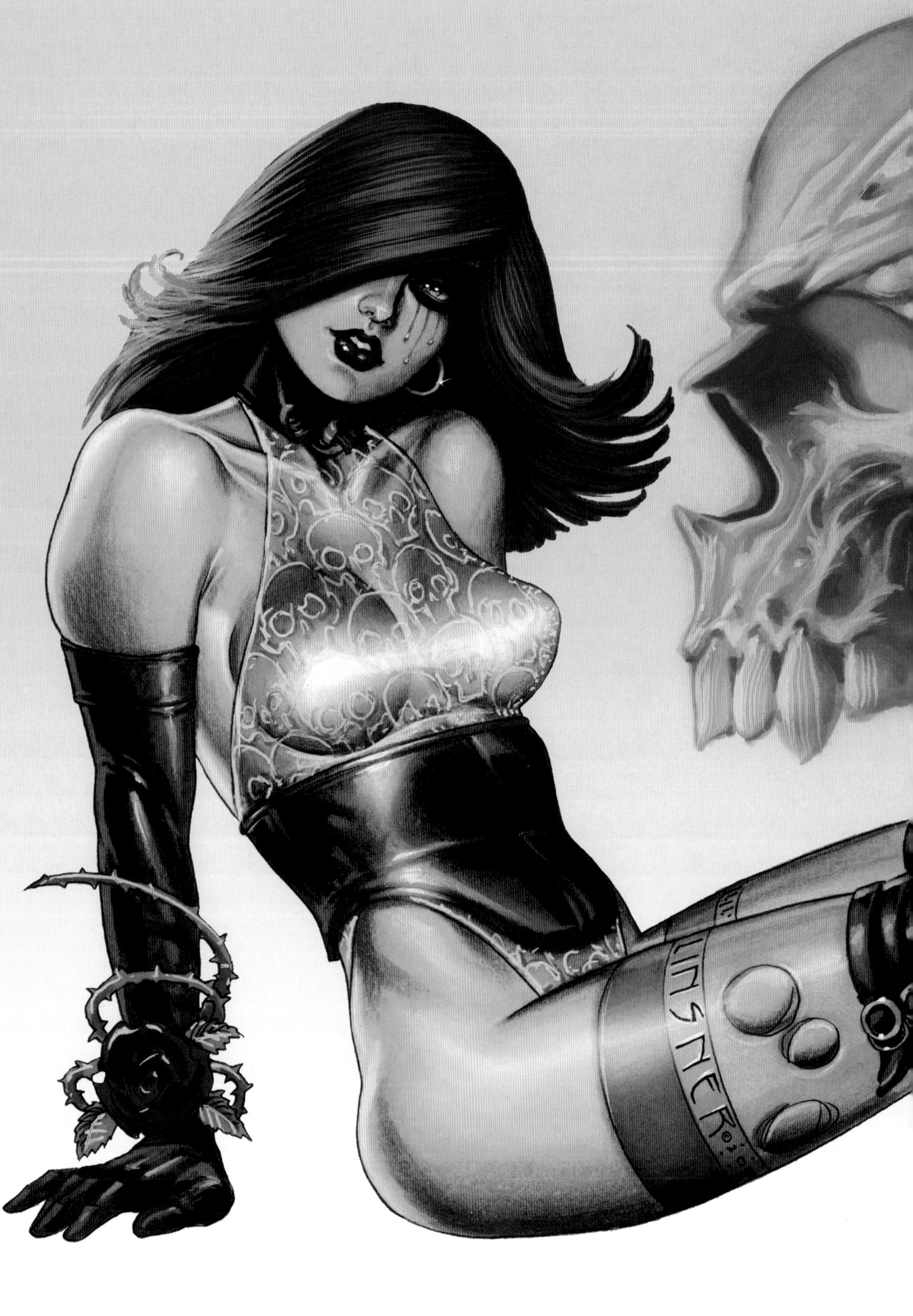
LINSNER

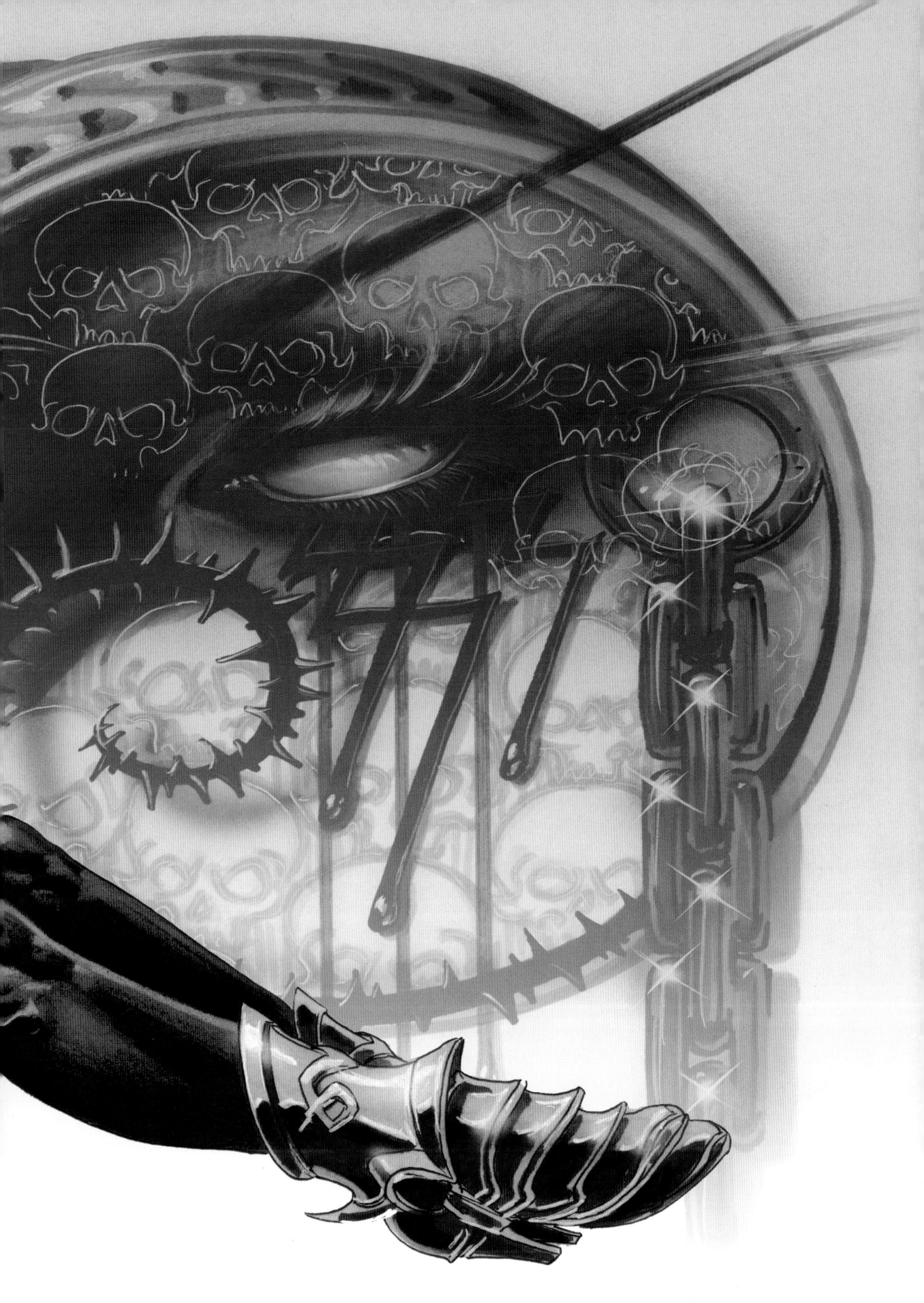

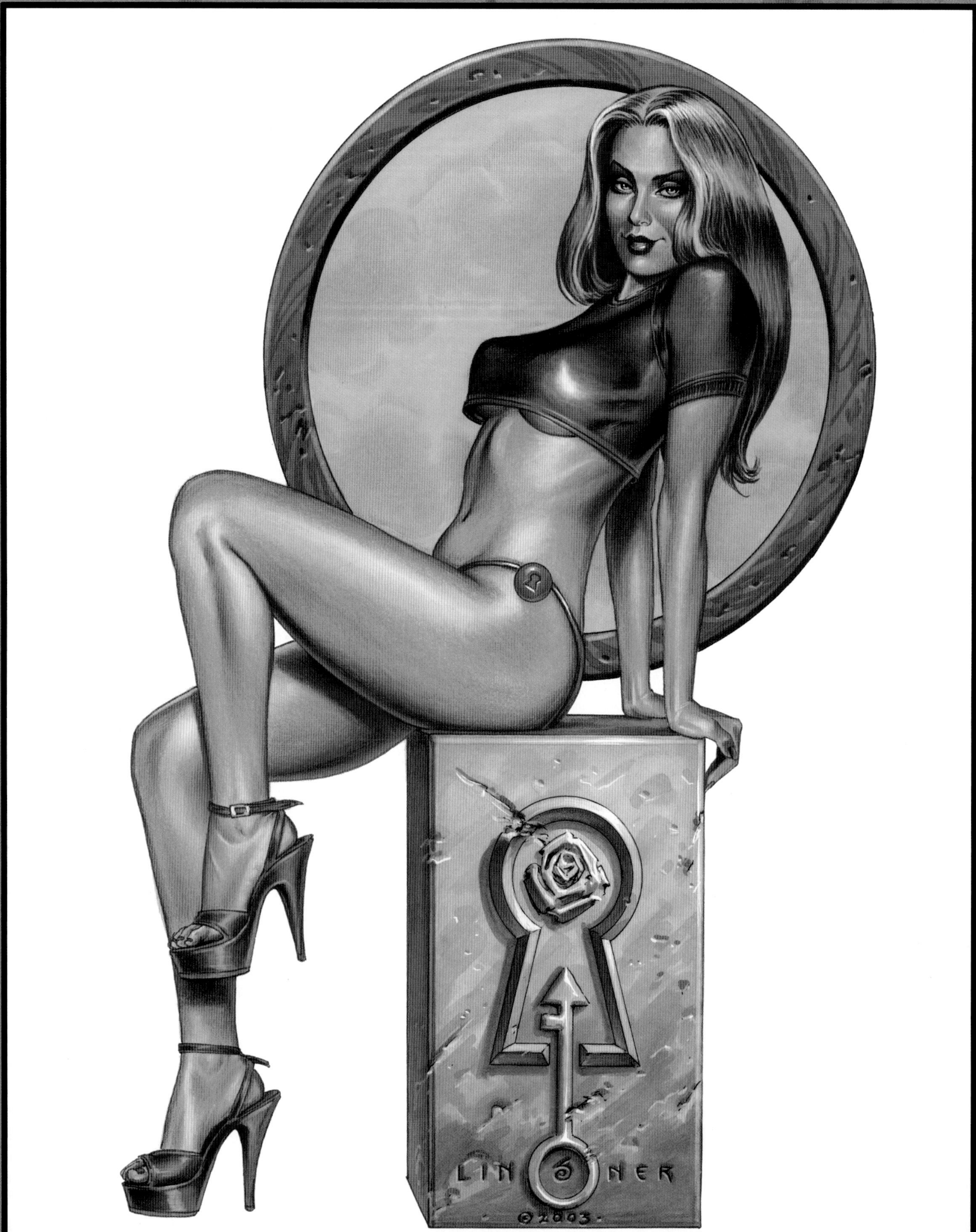
LIN NER
©2003

Got Key?

Death's Head
(Pages 82-83)

Rosebud

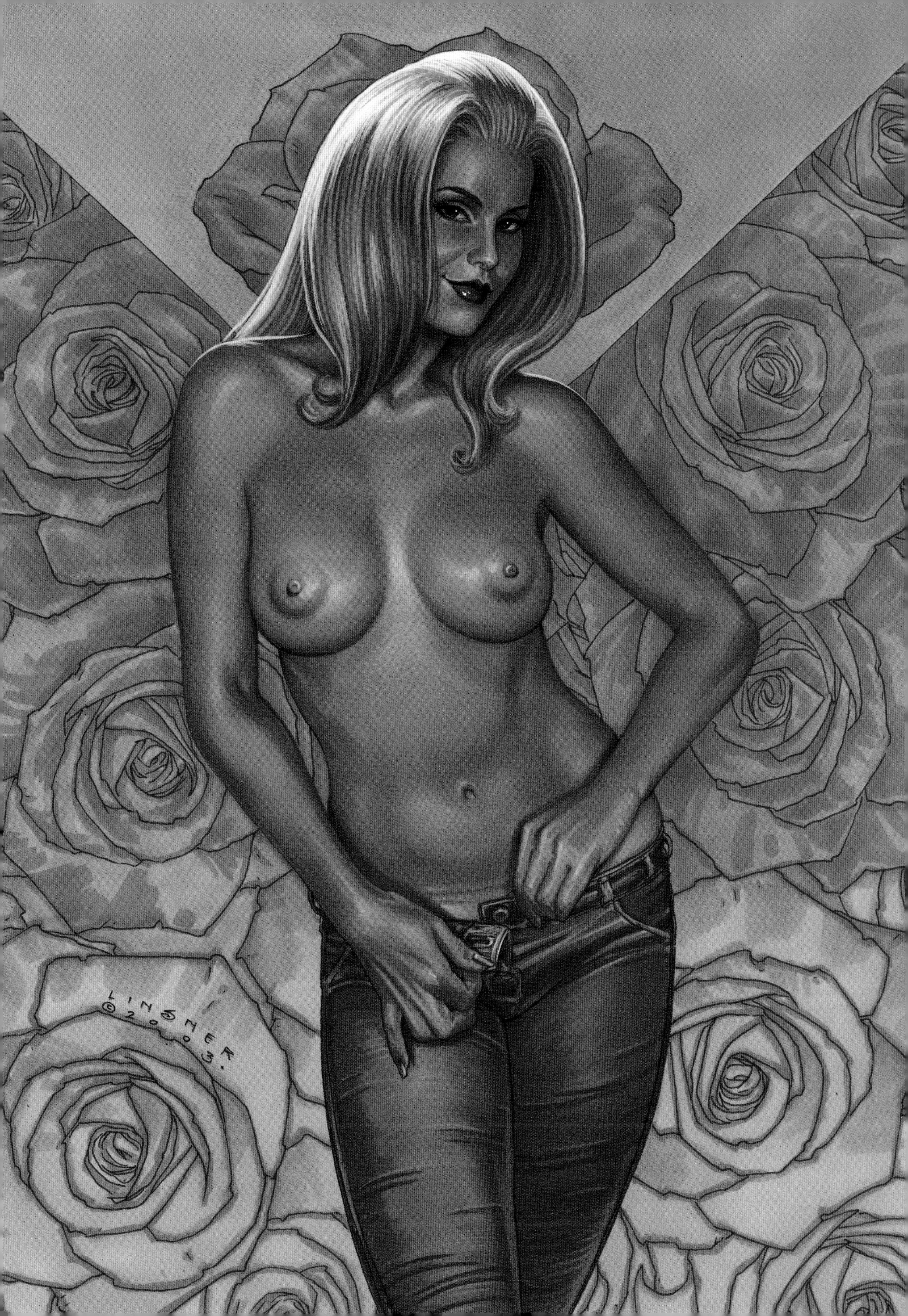
LINSNER
©2003.

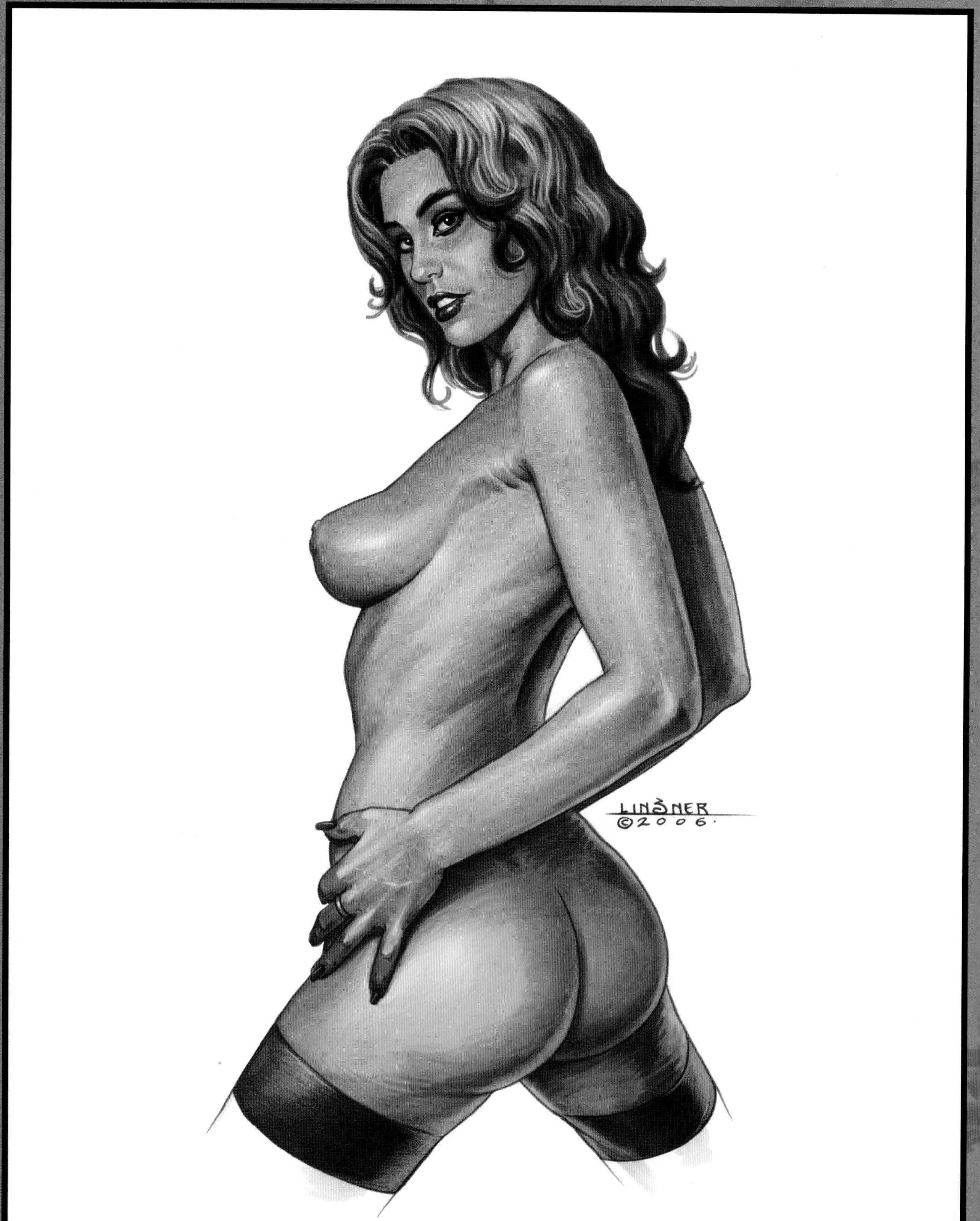
LINŠNER
©2006.

J C
Suzi Pearl

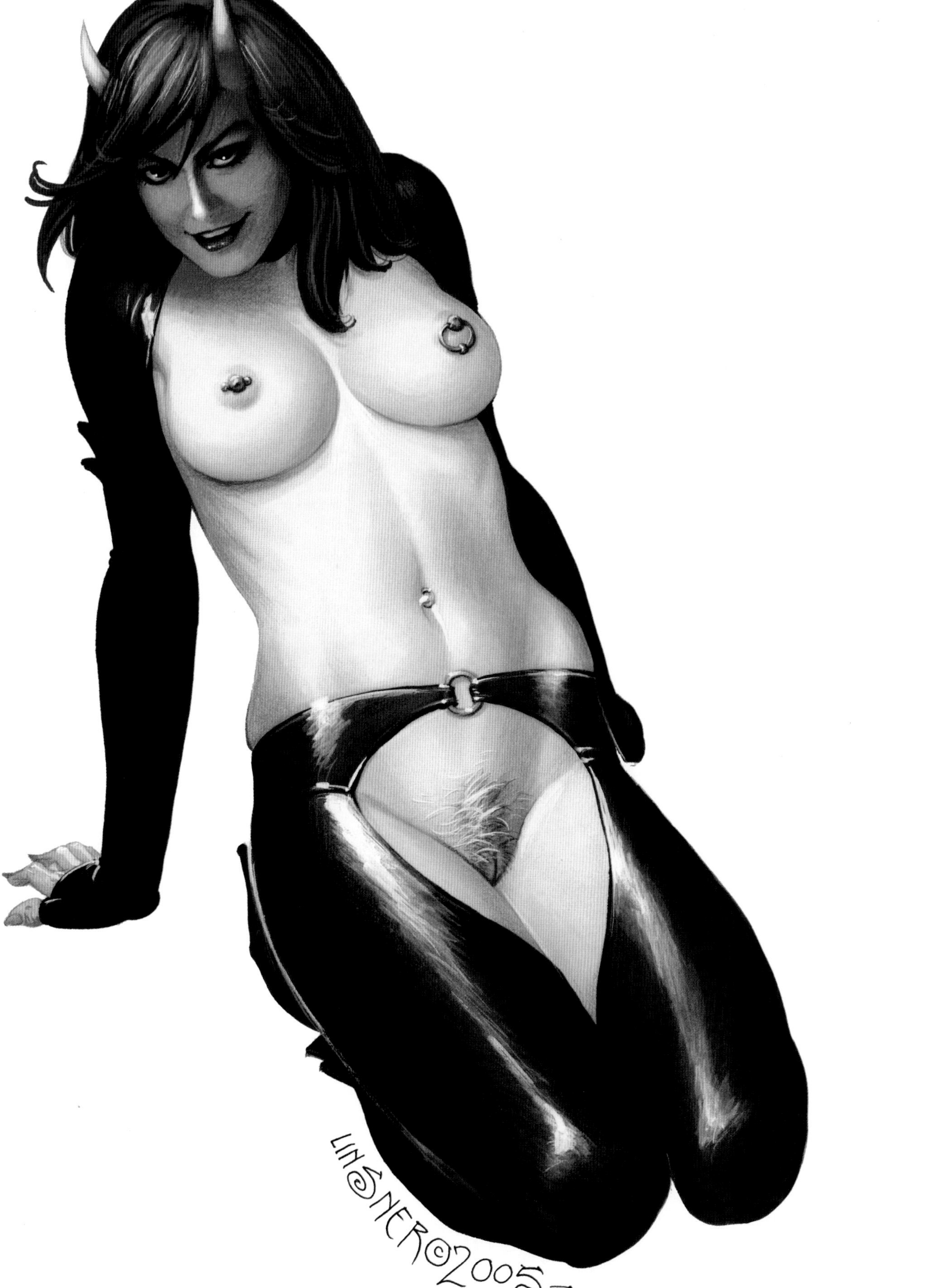
LINSNER©2005

Mucha Dawn
Guillotine

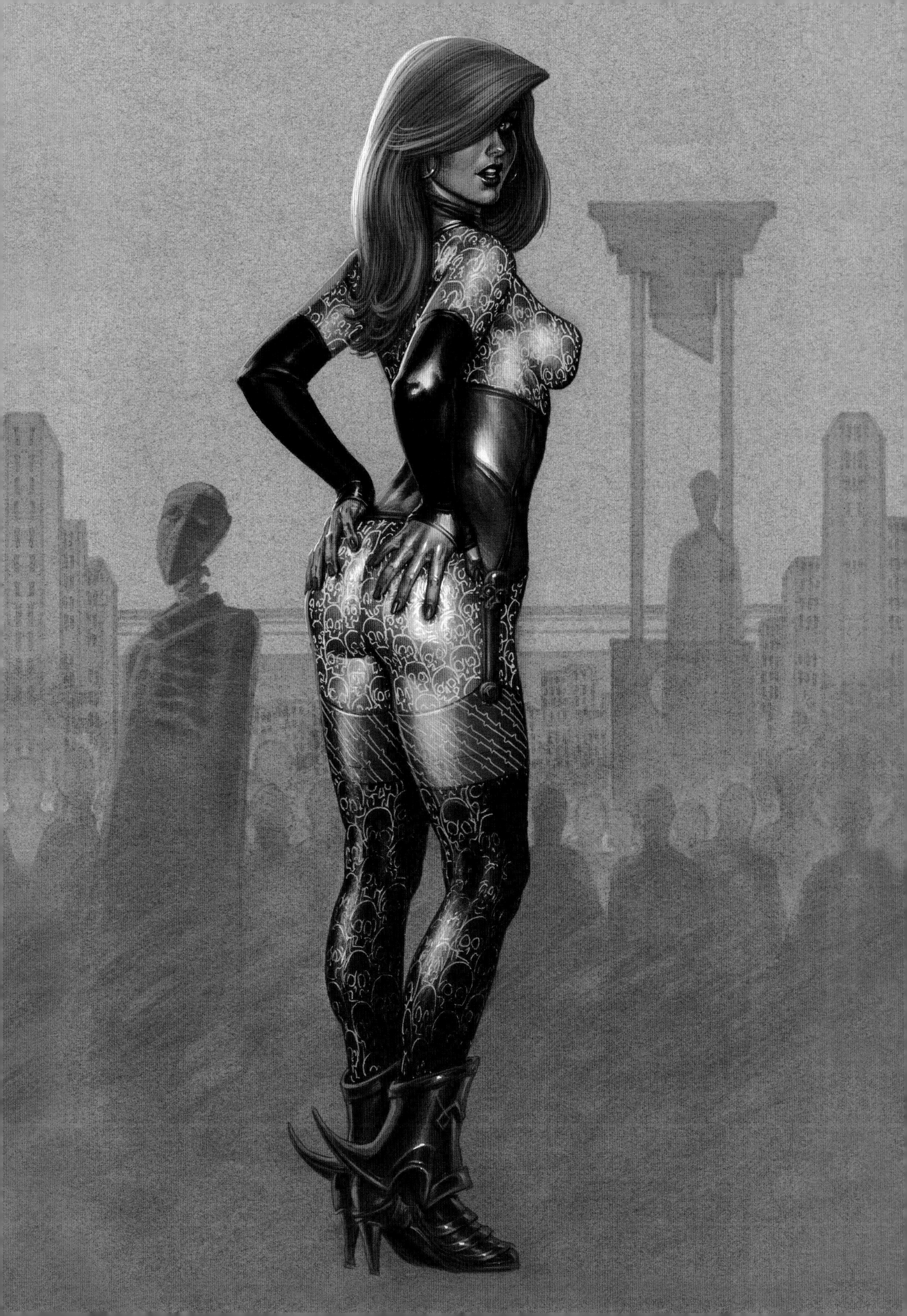

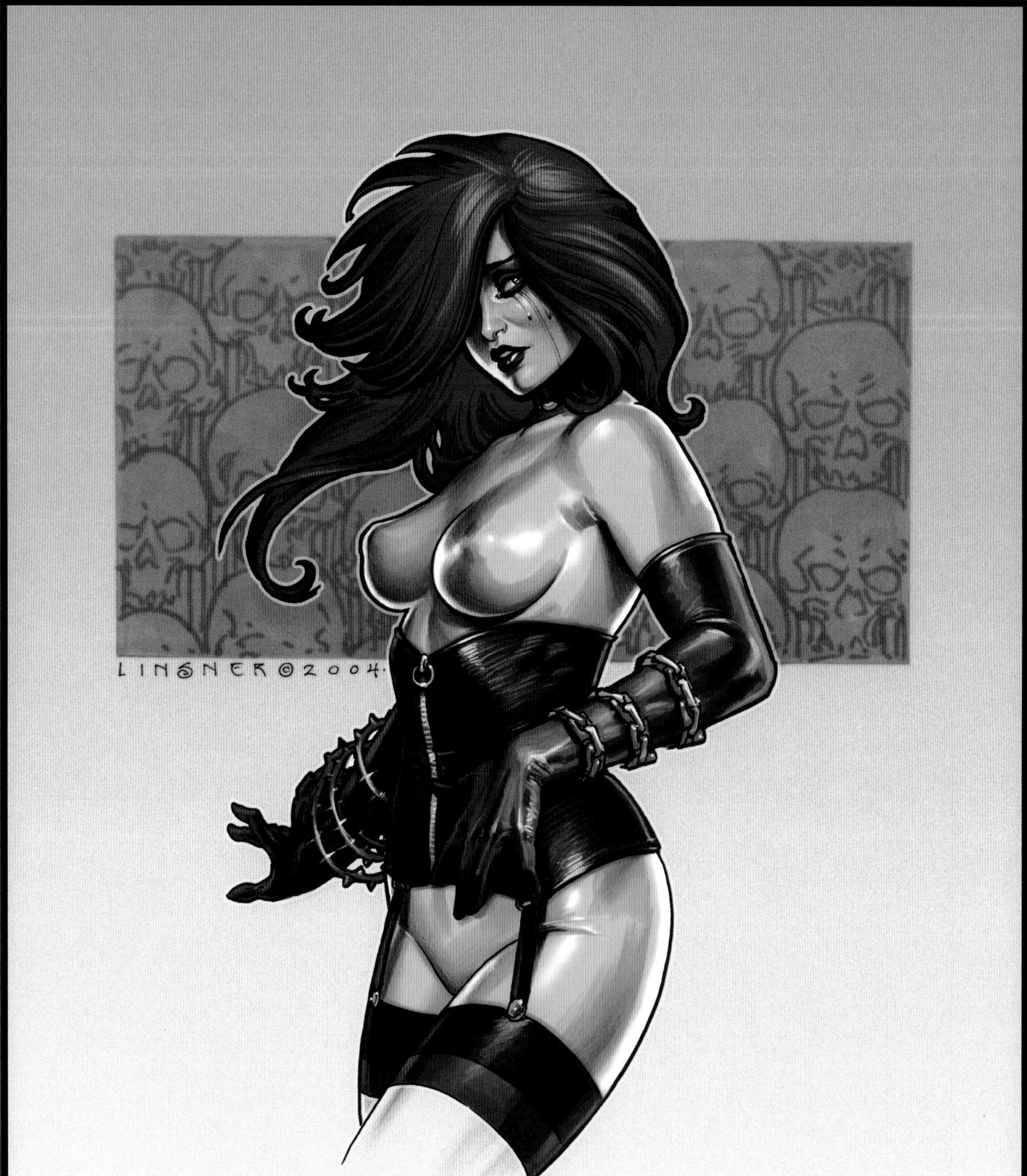
LINSNER©2004

Indigo
Starry Love

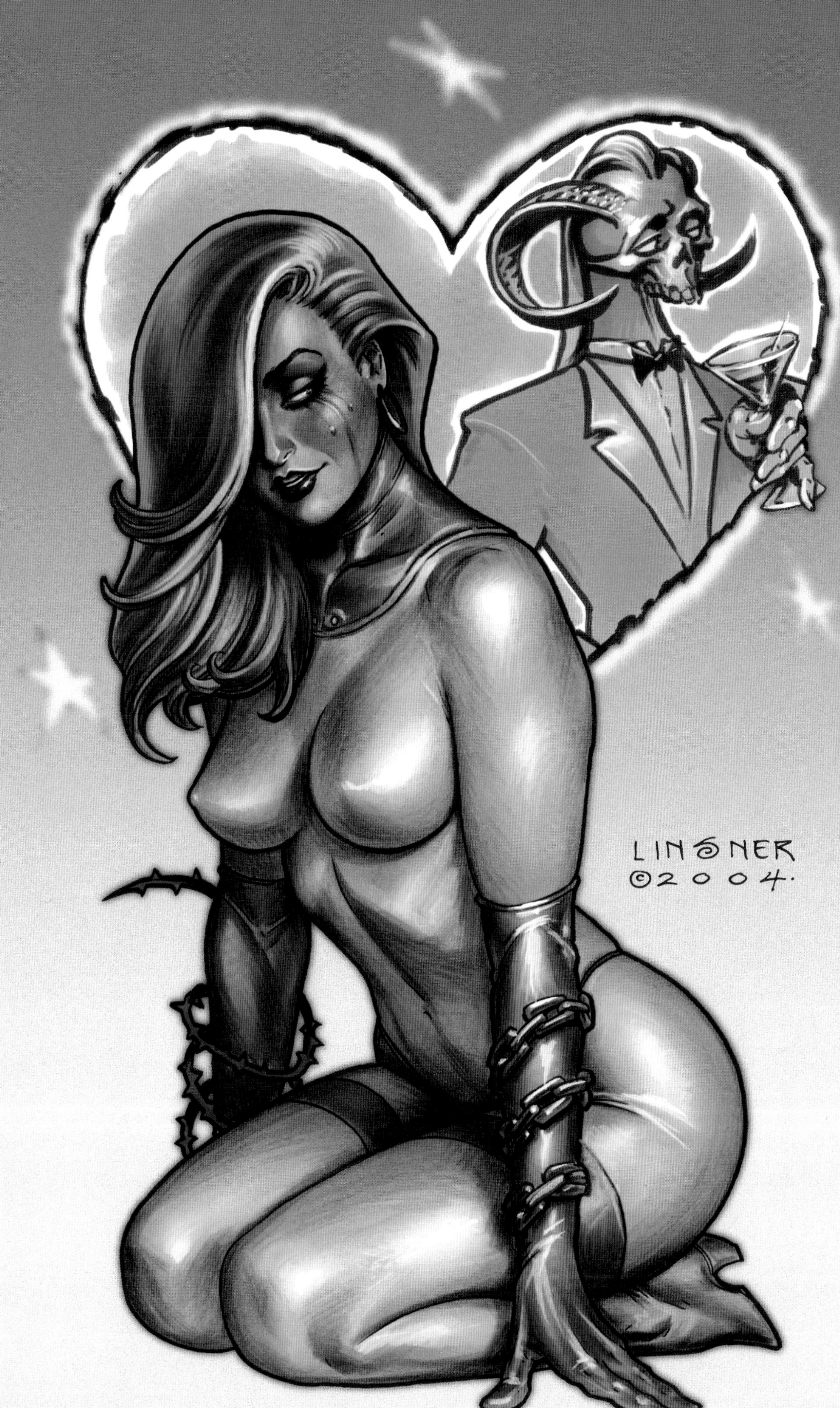
LINSNER
©2004.

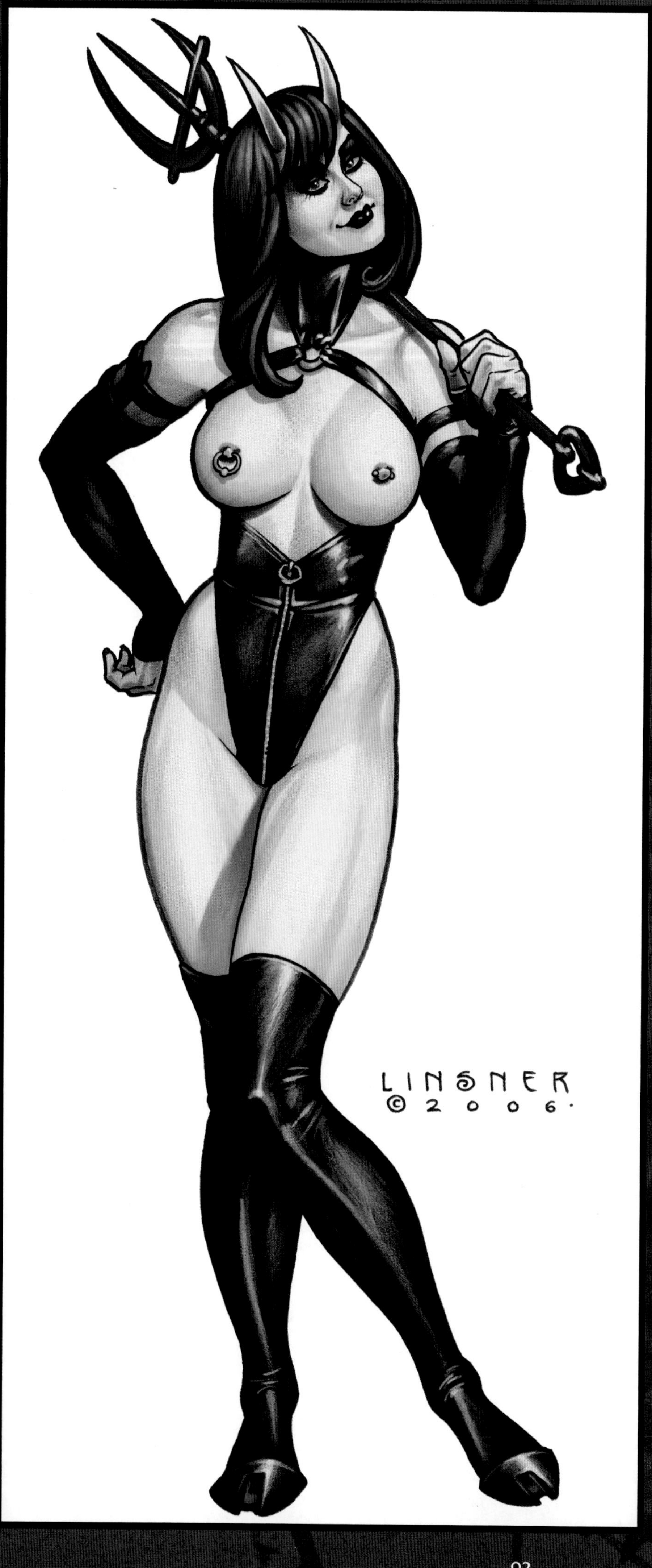
LINSNER
©2006.

Suzi Q

Pinch Me, I Must Be Dreamin

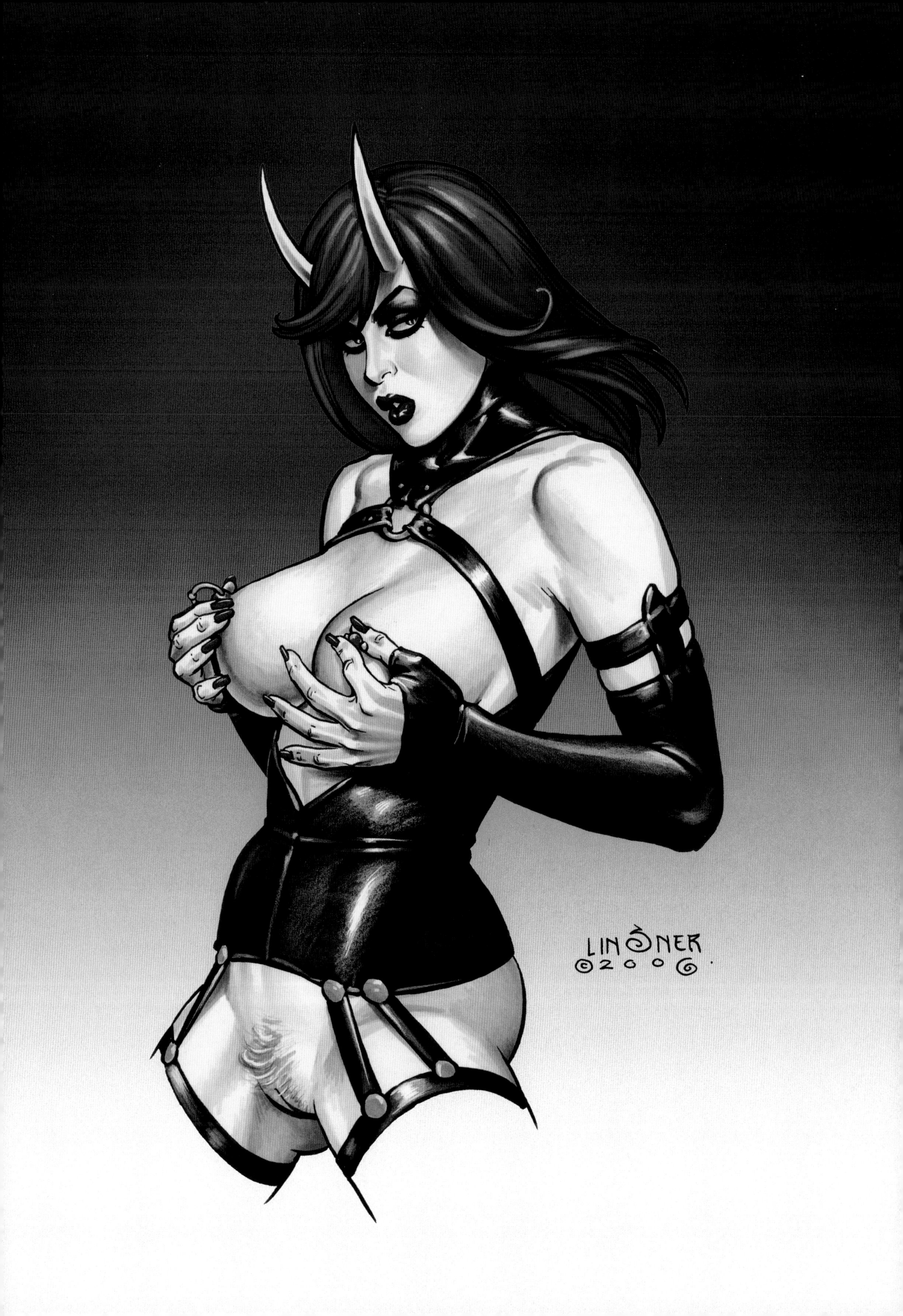
LINSNER
©2006.

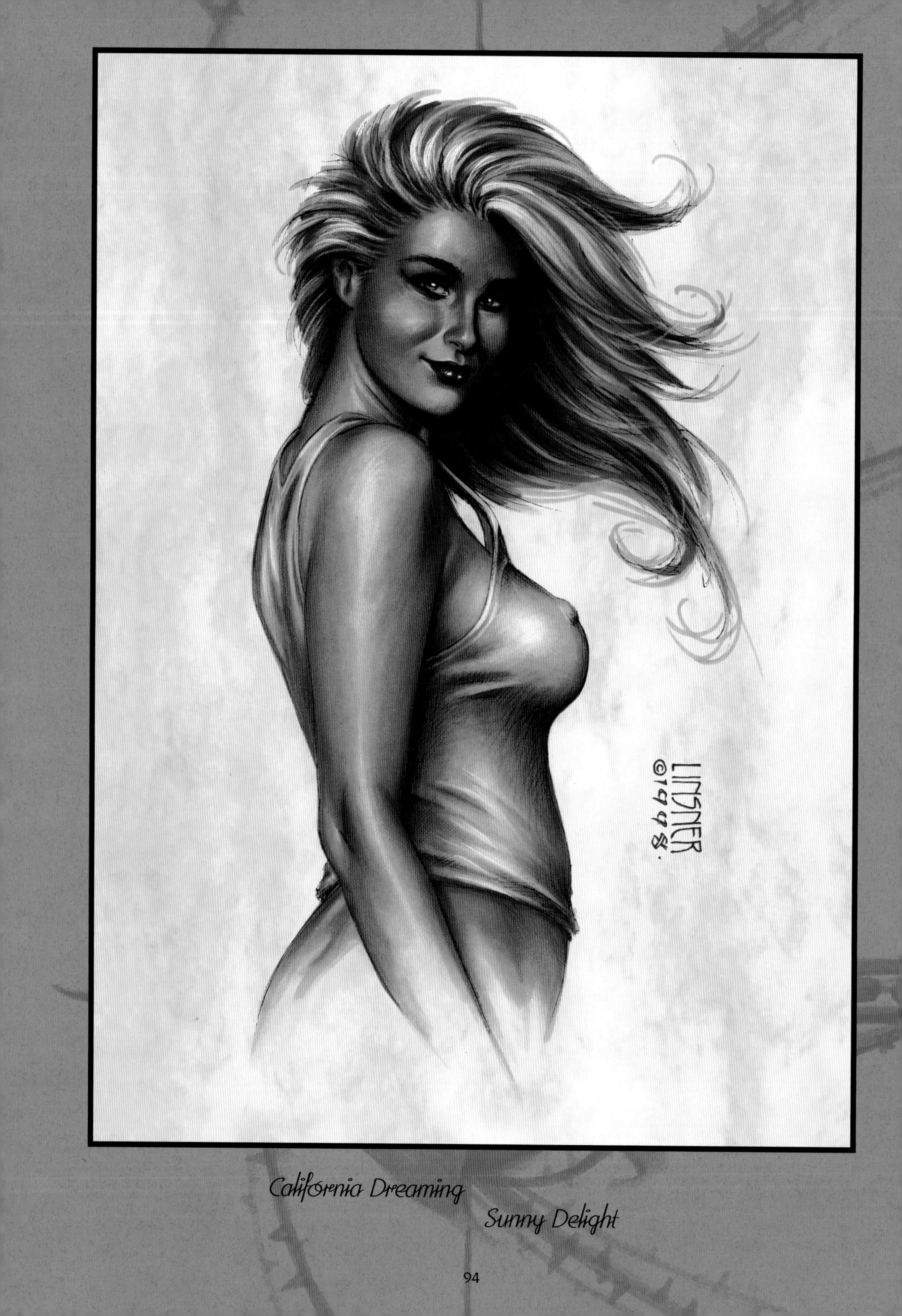
LINSNER
©1998.

California Dreaming

Sunny Delight

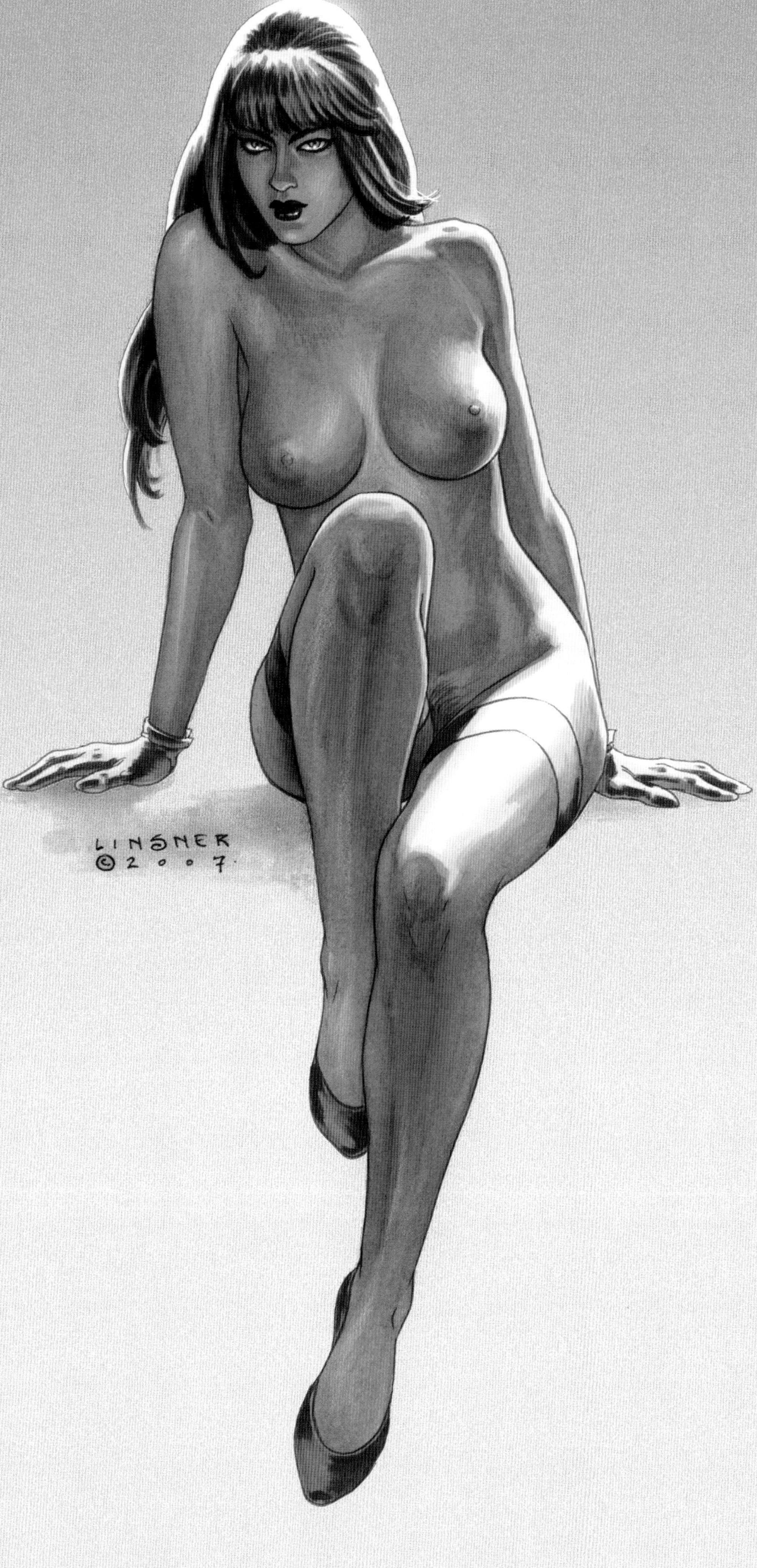
LINSNER
©2007

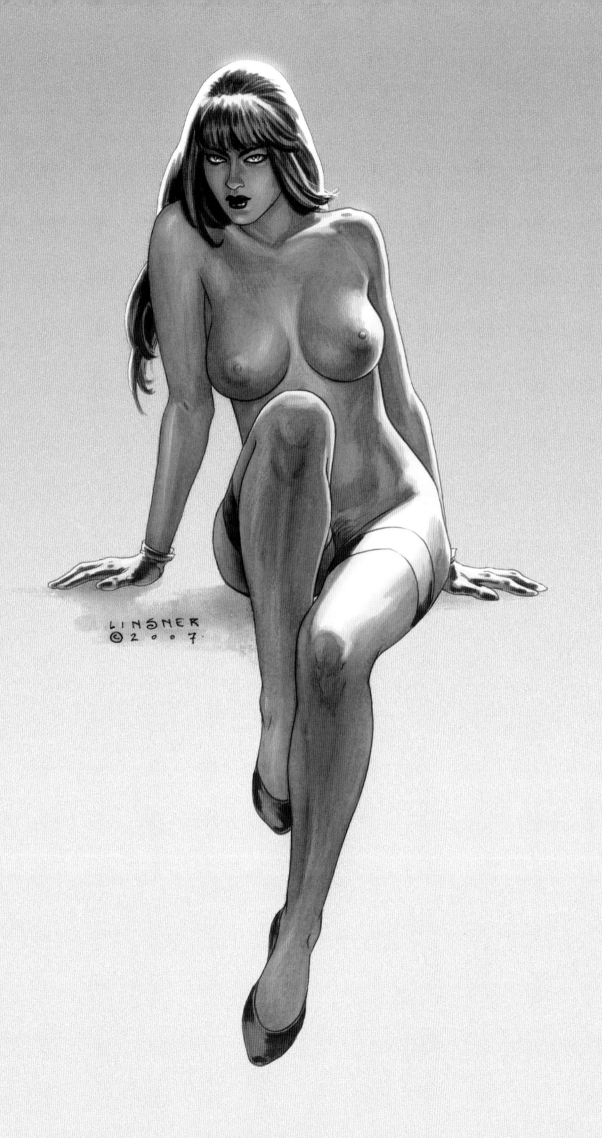

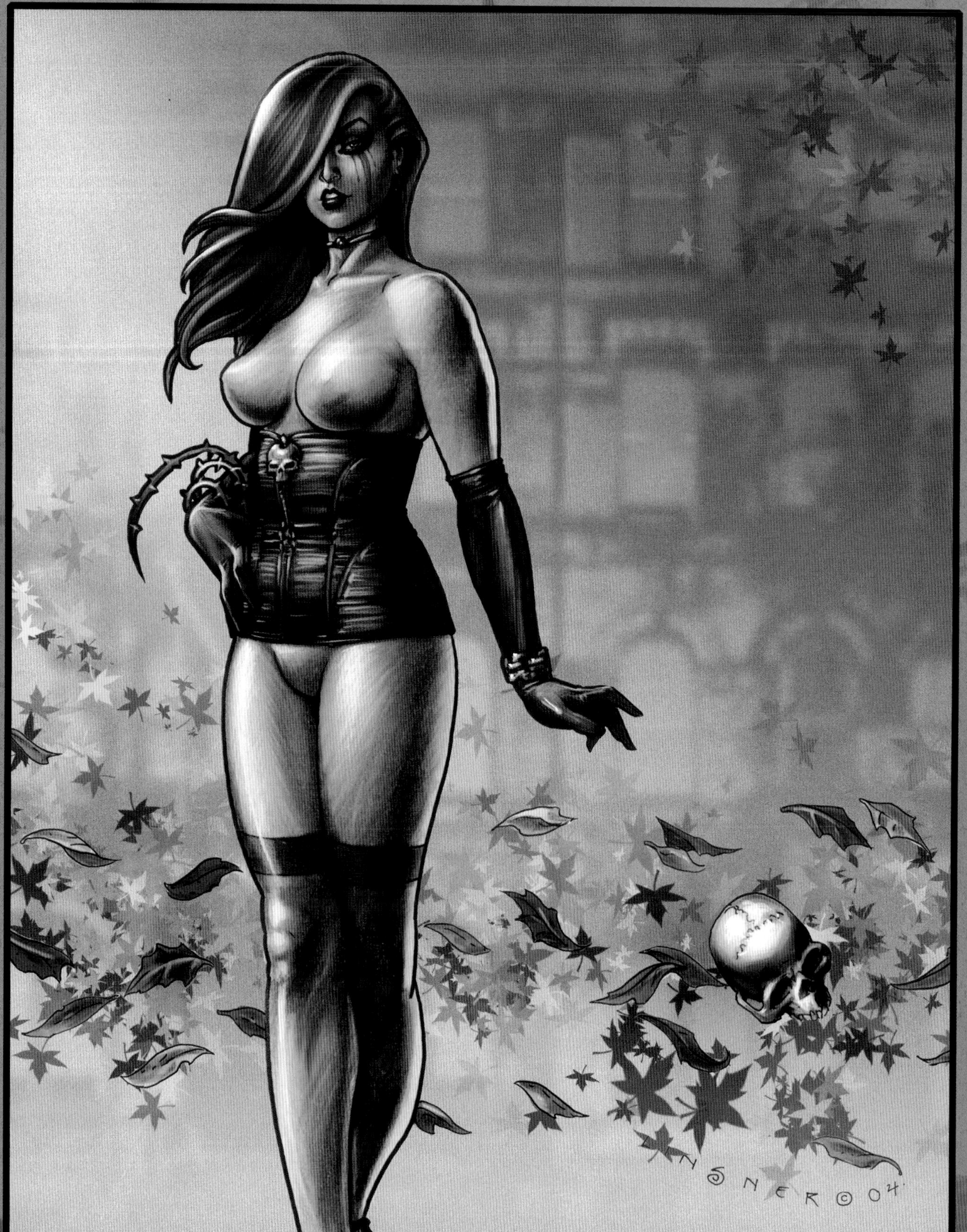

Fall Leaves

Red & Black

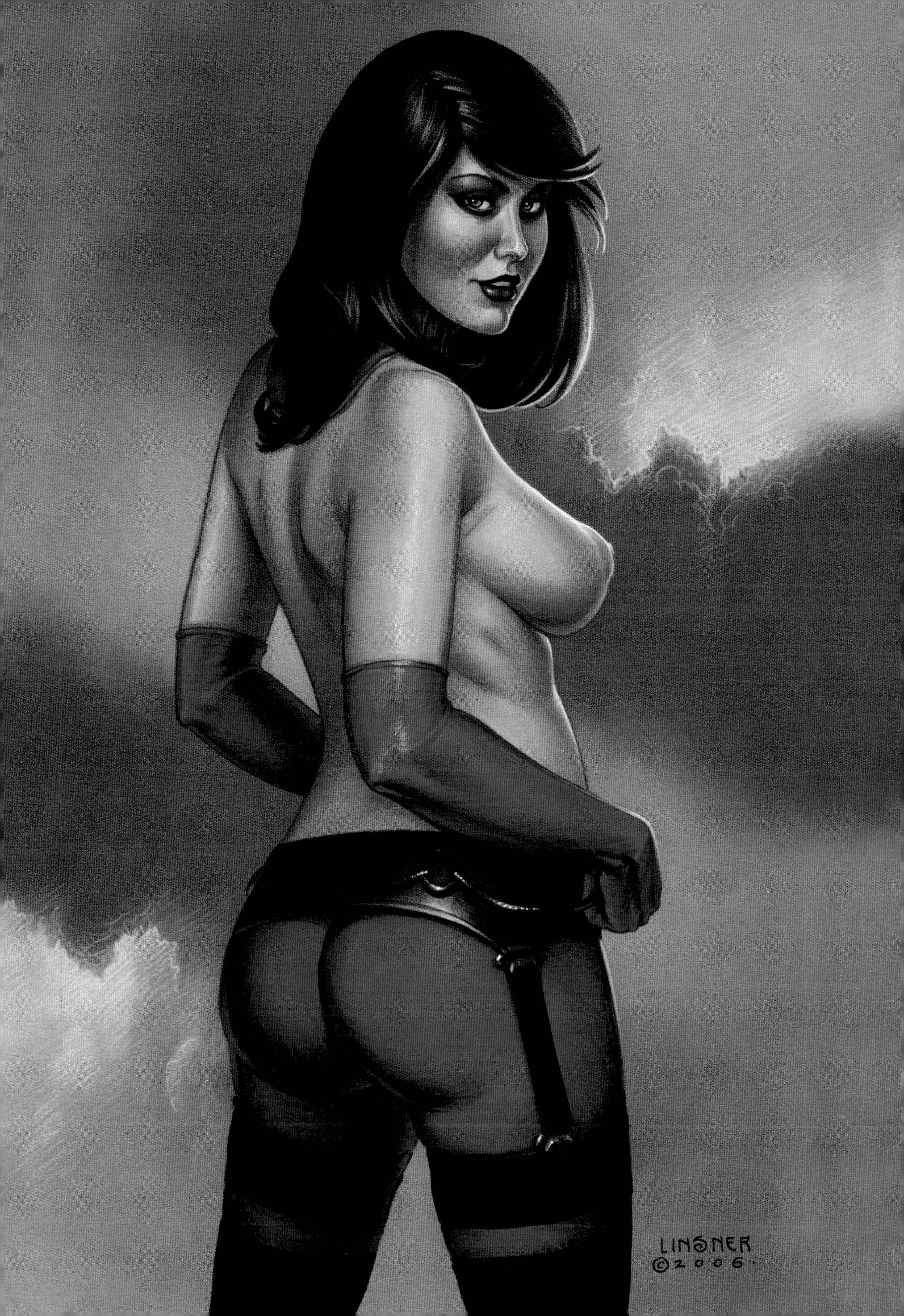
LINSNER
©2006.

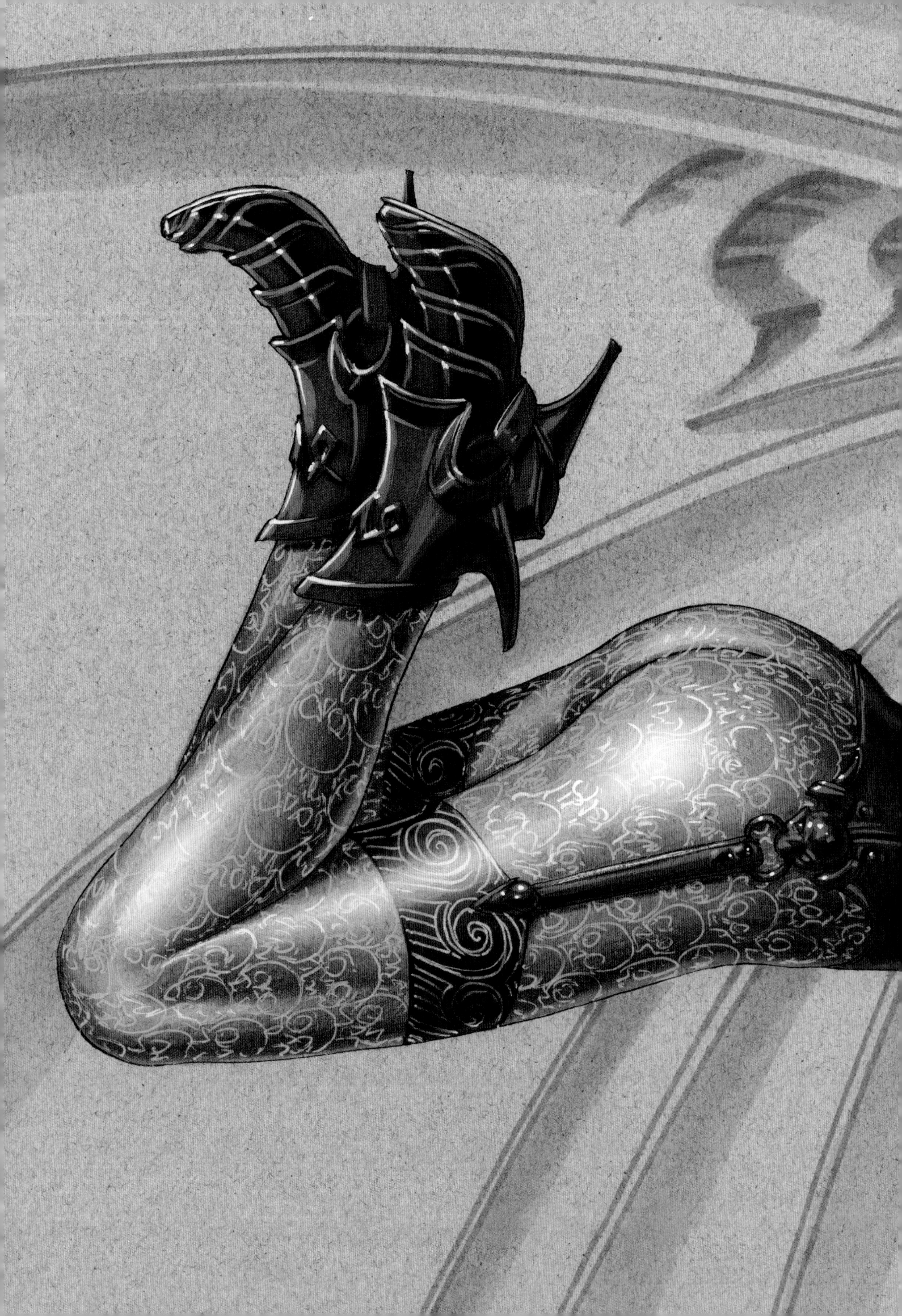

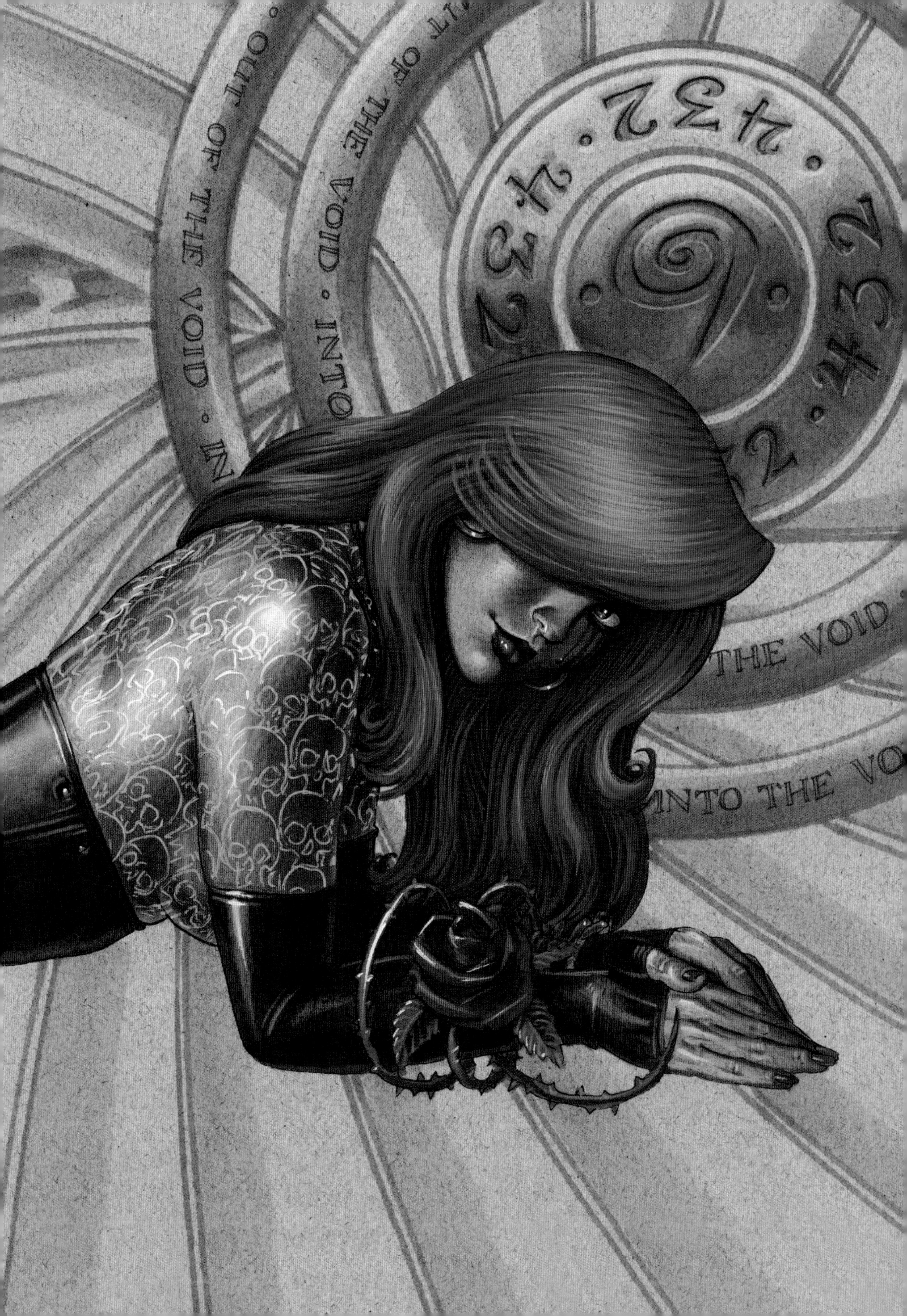

OUT OF THE VOID • IN
OF THE VOID • INTO
THE VOID
INTO THE VO

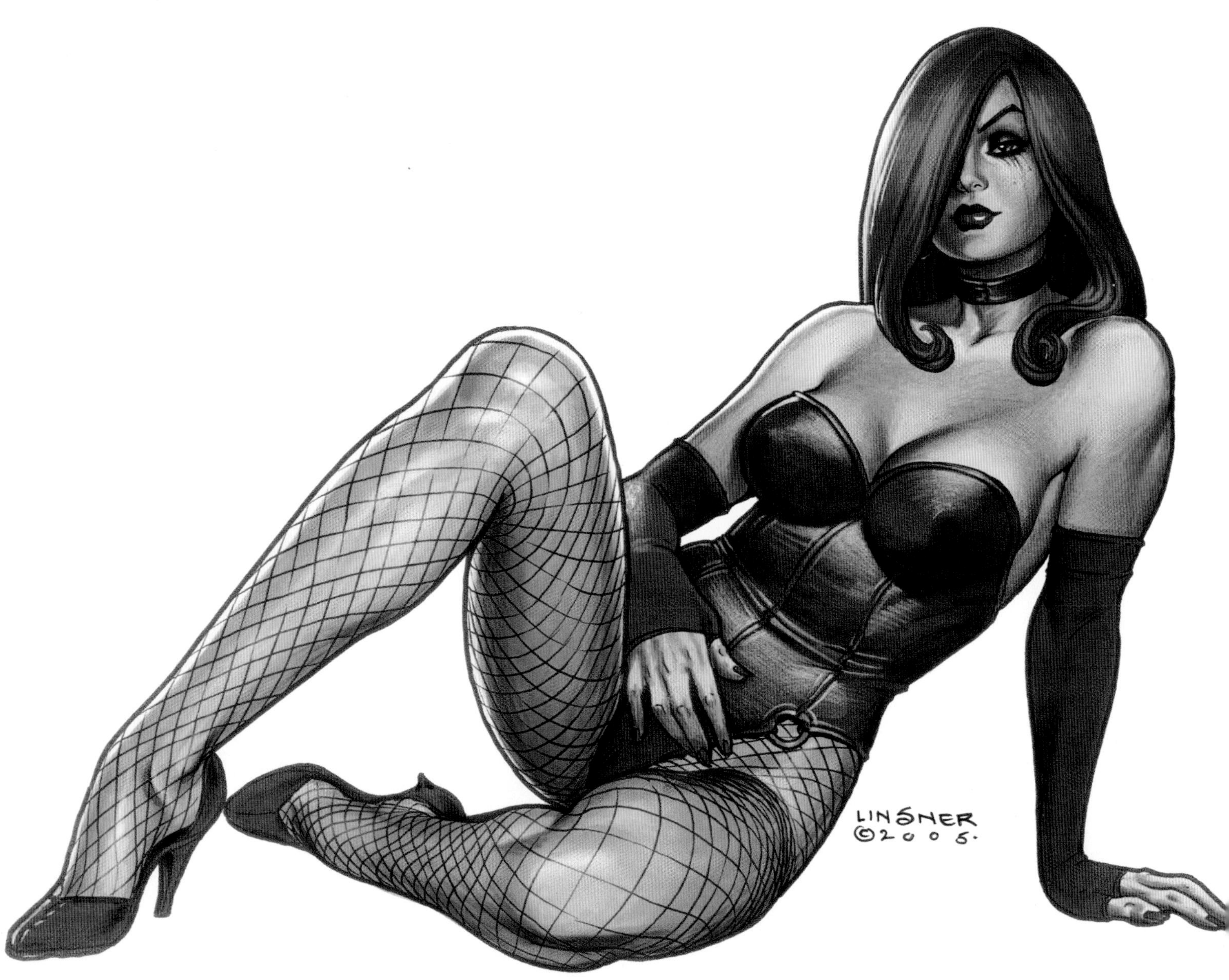
LINSNER
©2005.

Fishnets

Nine, the Number Of the Goddess
(Pages 98-99)

Pitchfork

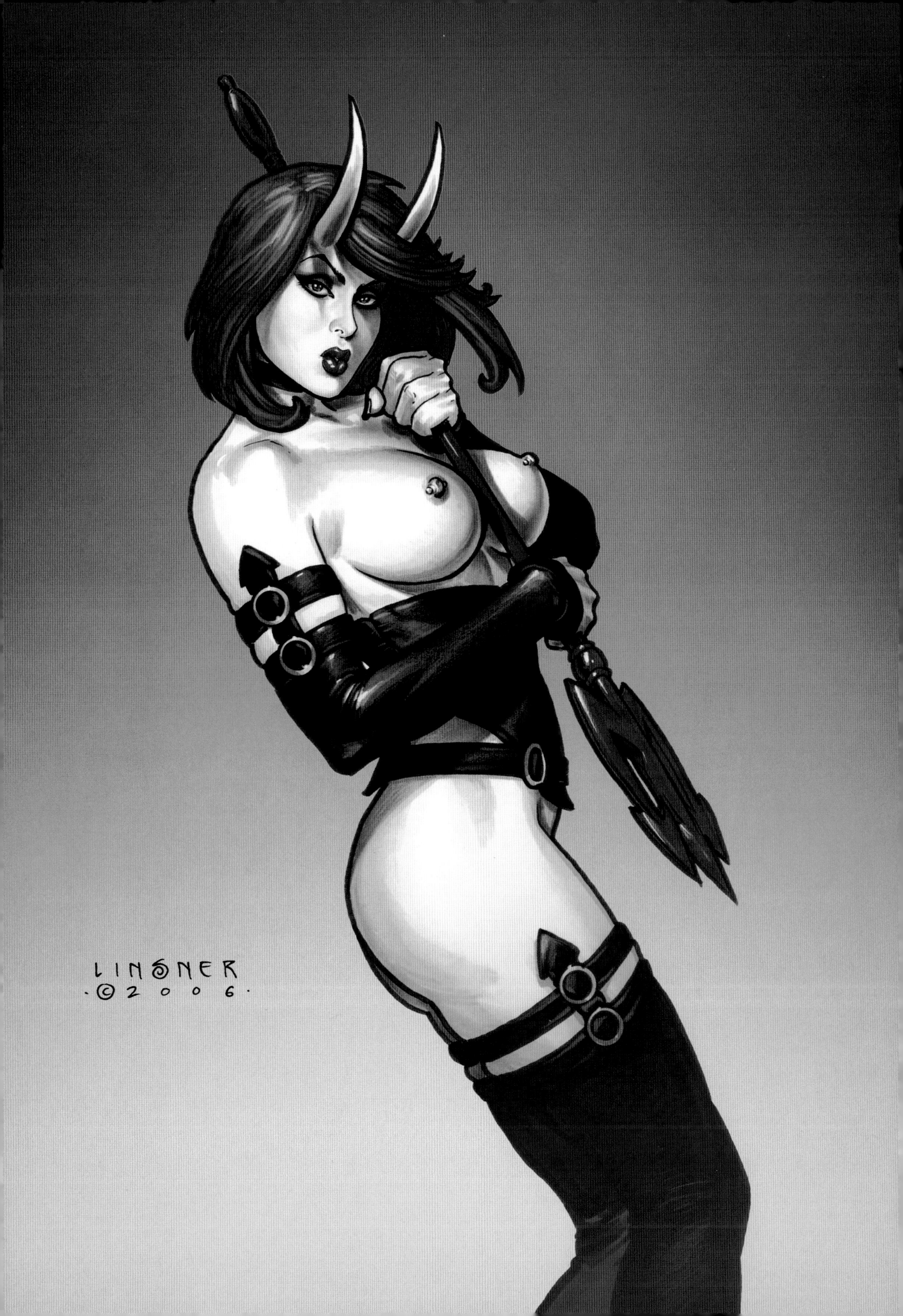
LINSNER
·©2006·

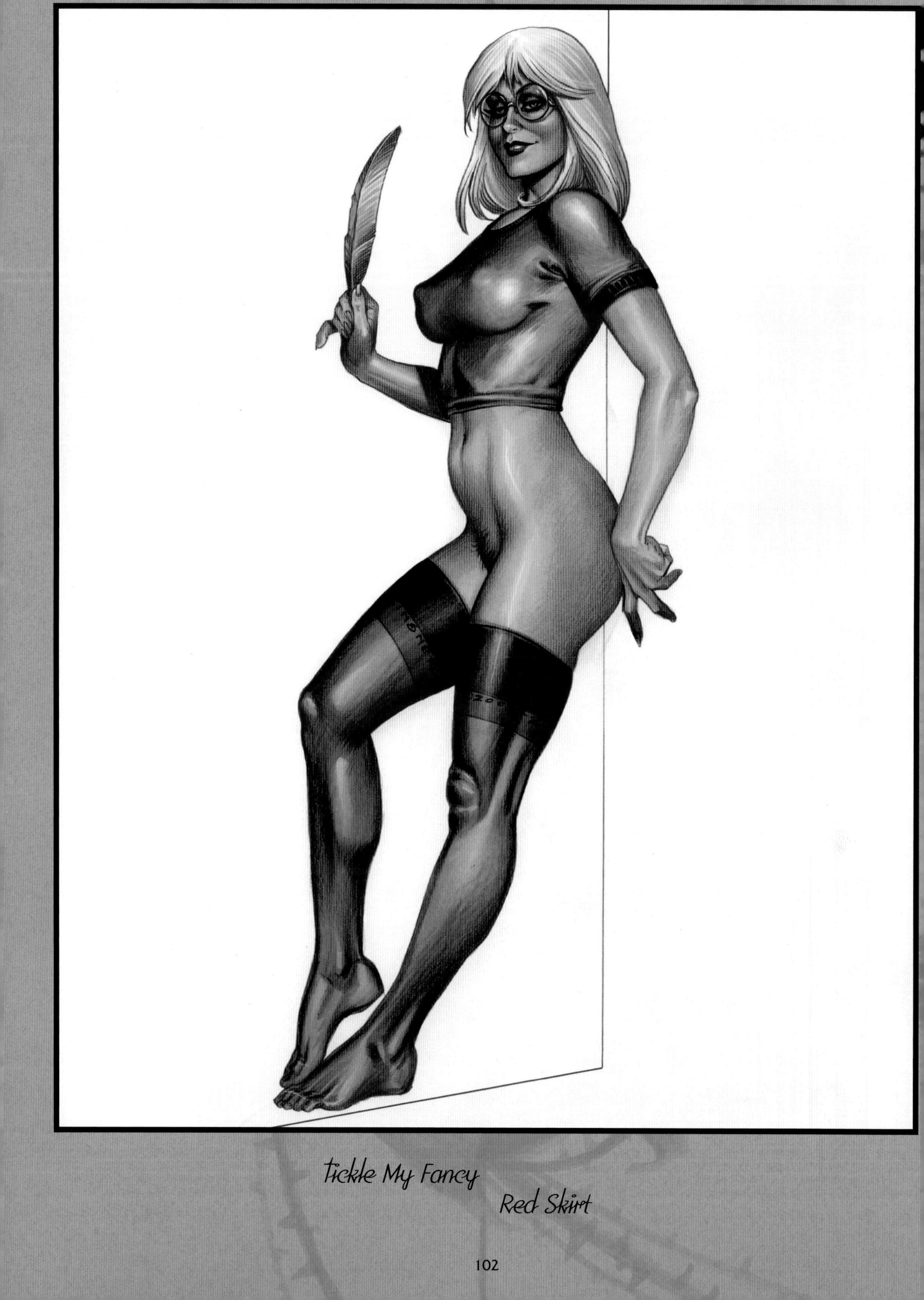

Tickle My Fancy

Red Skirt

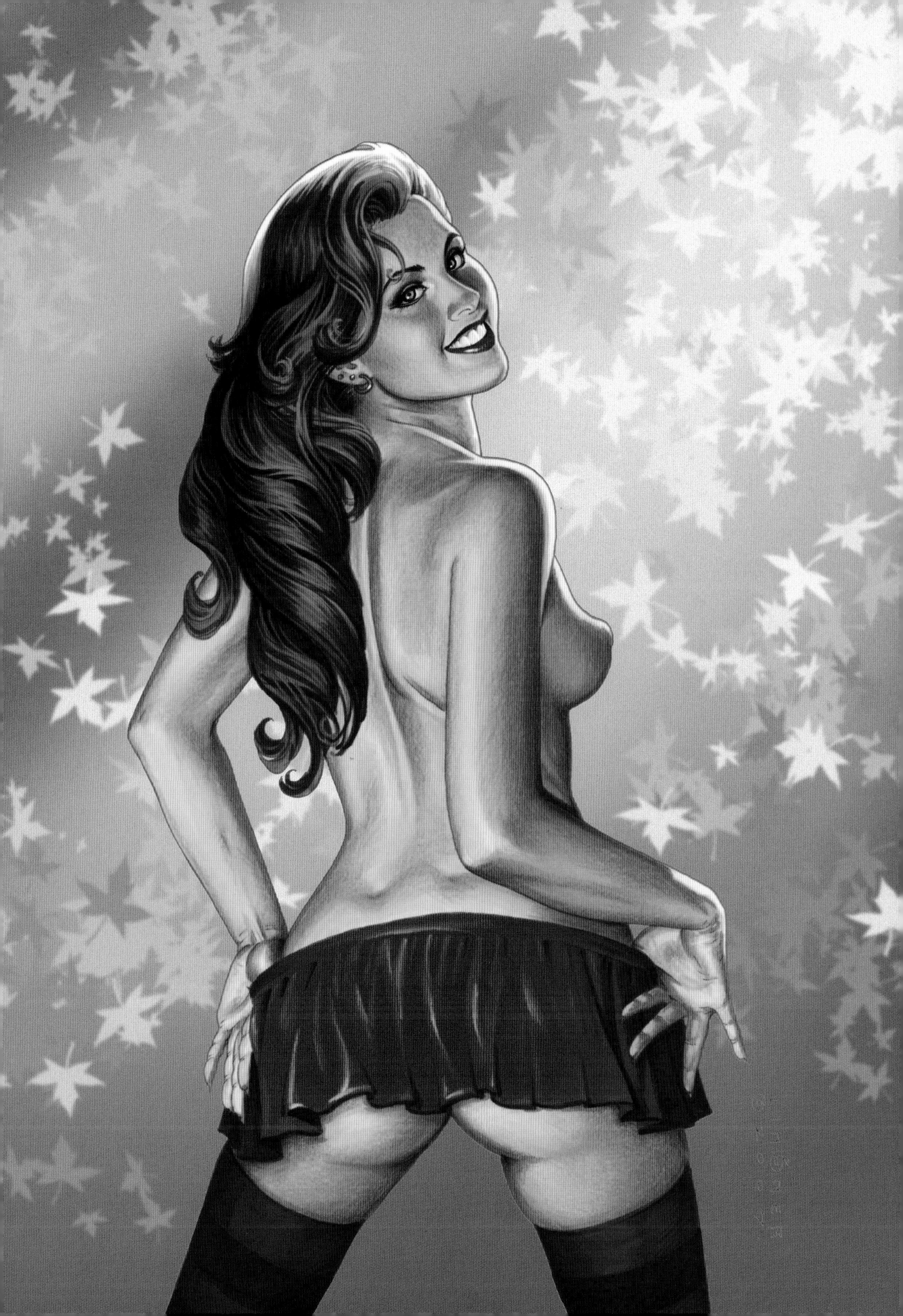

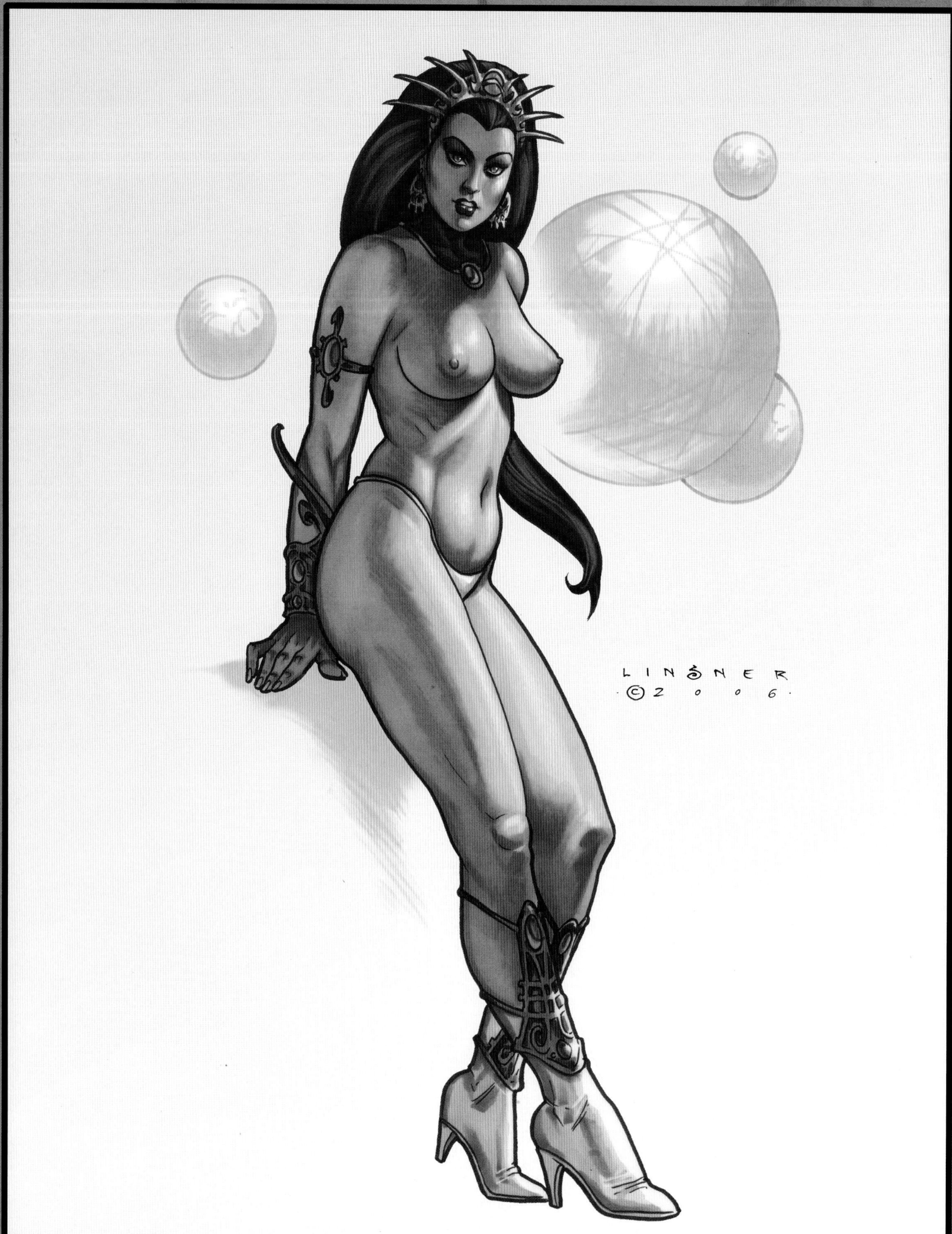
LINSNER
©2006

Dejah

Red Shoes

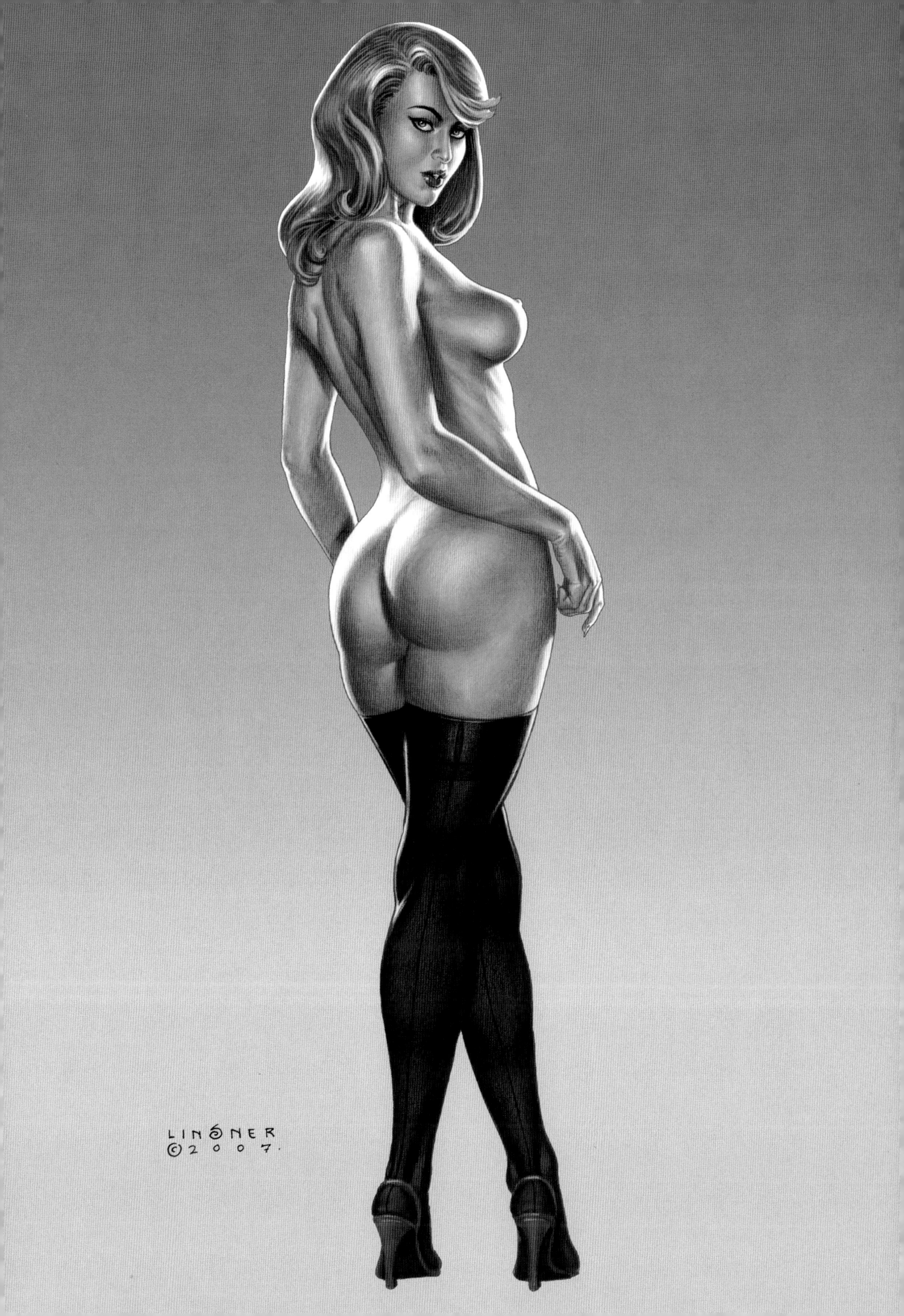
LINDNER
©2007.

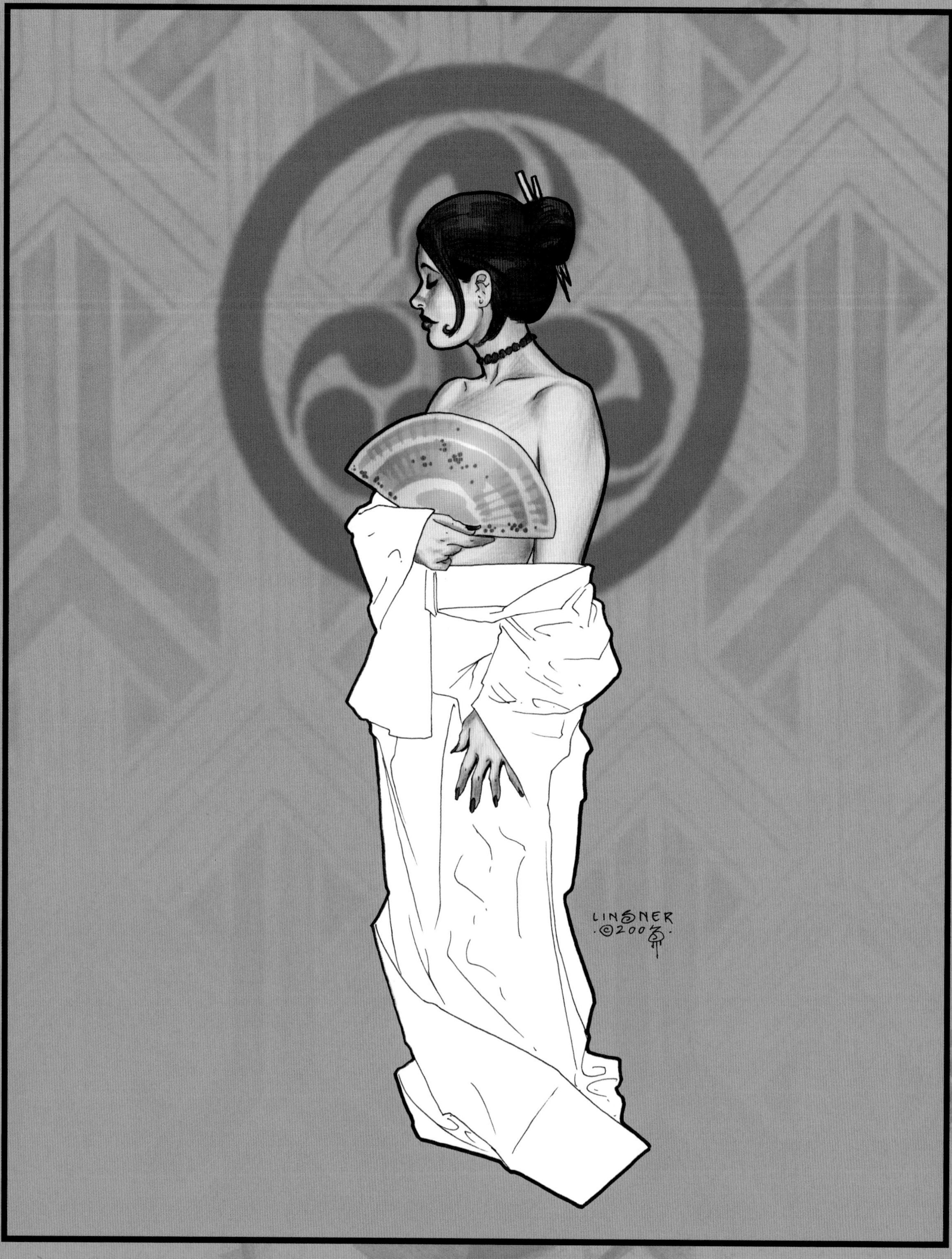
LINSNER
©2003

Carlye

Little Red

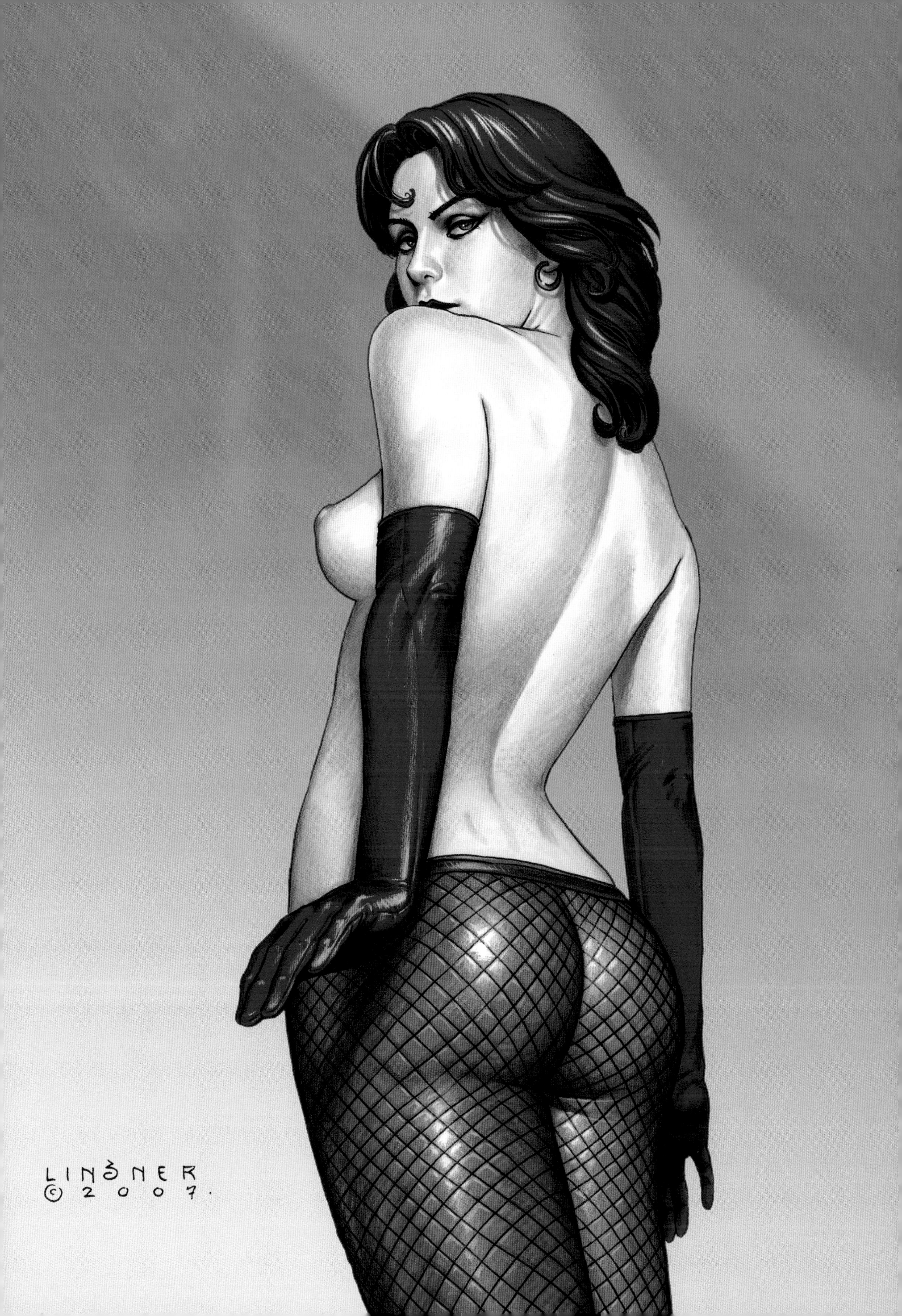
LINSNER
©2007.

Blue Angel
Purple Rose

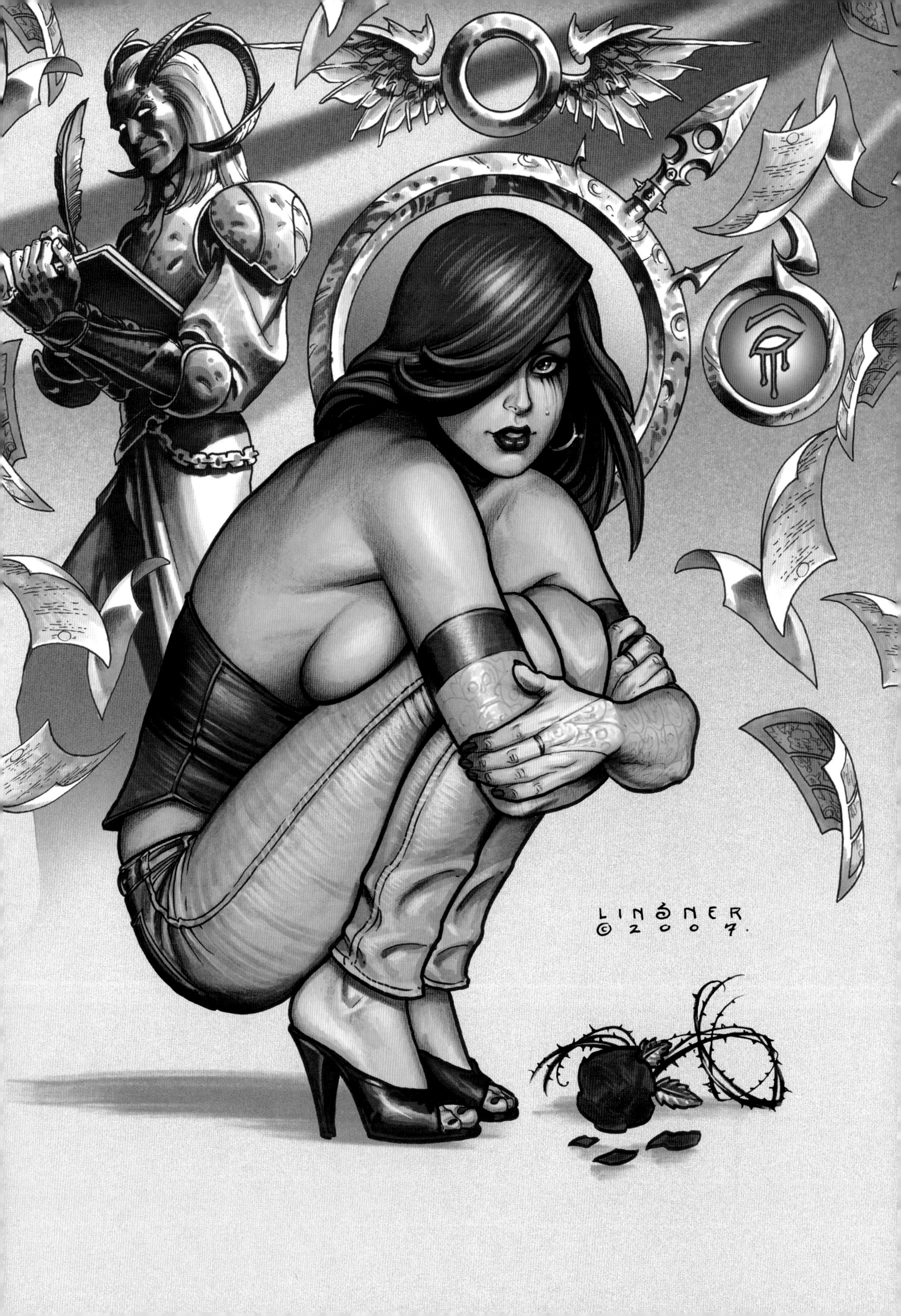
LINSNER
©2007.

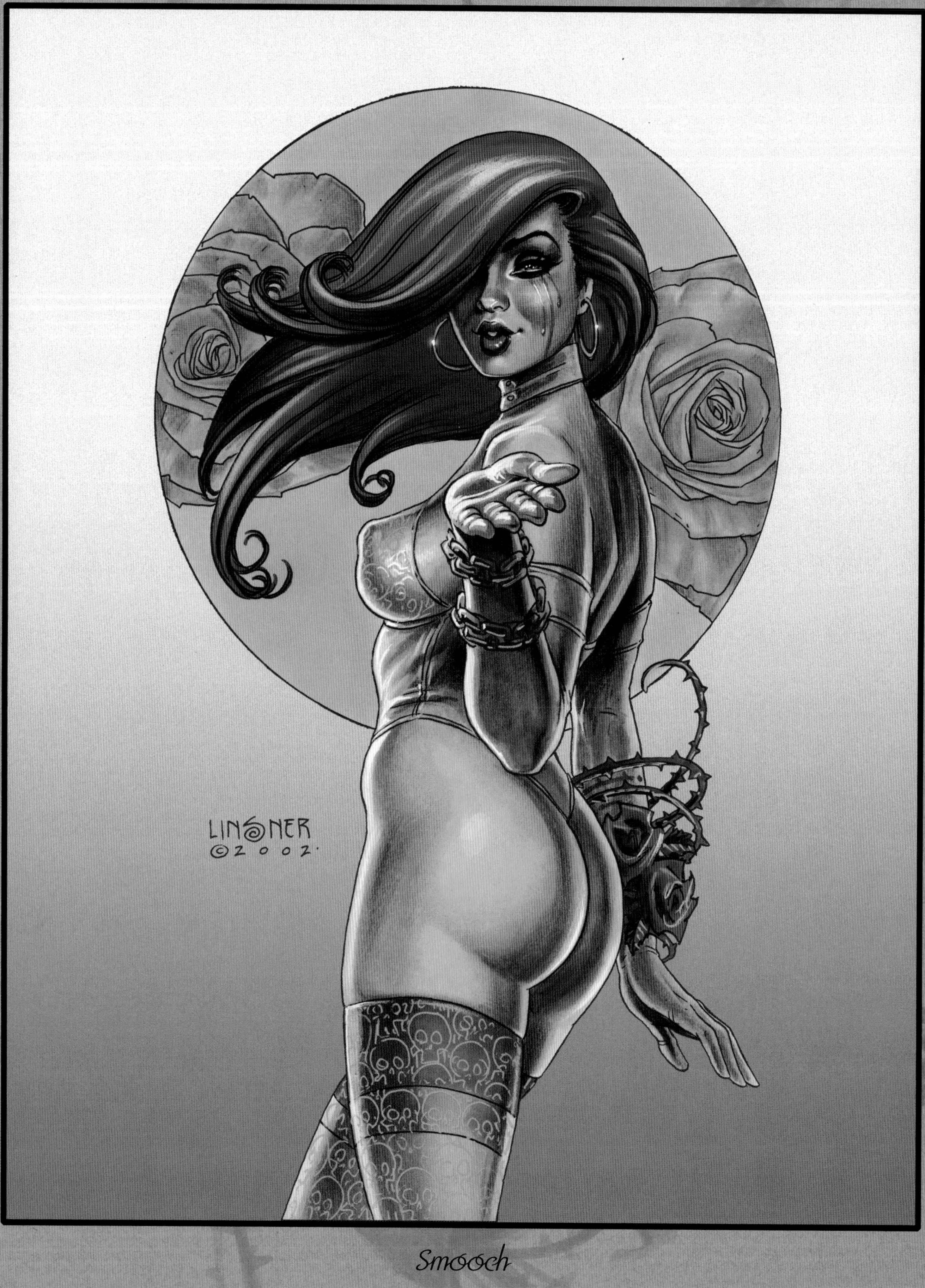
LINSNER
©2002

Smooch

Afterword

by Joe Linsner

y Love for **Pin-Up Art** started before I could read.

grew up in a very small one-bedroom apartment in Flushing ueens, New York. There were only so many places where my father uld hide his Playboys. I remember the golden age before I had to to kindergarten. I was allowed to roam the apartment as my mother d her daily housework. I would always hunt out my father's stash of lie mags. For a while he kept them on a very high shelf in the bath-om. It is a miracle that I didn't break my neck climbing up to get em.

oved the photos of the teasing and taunting girls, but something e really caught my attention. The pin-ups in **Playboy** by **Alberto rgas**. Wow. It was almost like someone had taken the natural beauty the girls and turned the volume up. They were more than sexy. My ur-year-old brain didn't know about sexy. All I knew was what I liked what hit me on a gut level. Vargas blew me away. Was he the first ist whose name I took note of? Maybe. At that same time my ep love for comic books took hold. I remember wondering why I ed certain Batman comics more than others. Could those names in e front of the comic have something to do with its quality? I cognized the visual icon of Vargas's signature before I could actu-y read it. *He had the coolest signature.*

I matured, I took the plunge into the history of Pin-Up art. I rned the difference between 'Varga' and 'Vargas', and all of the rrow involved in that battle. In the early 40's, Esquire magazine ed him to paint "Varga Girls". They were an instant hit. When he nted to leave the magazine, it turned out that Esquire owned the demark to the name "Varga". After an ugly legal battle, Vargas t the right to the name which his art had made famous. After a y lean 50's, Hugh Hefner gave a home to "The Vargas Girl" in pages of Playboy, starting in the early 60's.

ill love Vargas the most. After becoming a professional artist, and tting some real idea about what is good and bad, I am now well are of his faults. A lot of that Playboy work was not very good. His was definitely catching up to him, and his best work was sadly nd him by the early 70's. But I gotta tell ya, the cover to **NDY-O** by ***The Cars***, done in 1979, *is a blessed **masterpiece***. s not a perfect painting -- one could quibble about some of the tomy, but it is still an **awesome** piece of pin-up art.

Elvgren, among many others, may have painted better, and may e been better 'nuts and bolts' draughtsmen, but no one else in the le field of pin-up art has ever possessed Vargas's sense of ***Grace***.

d to me, that is what **Pin-Up** art is all about.

ace.

That one word, **Grace**, might very well sum up my feelings for the females of this planet. **Women** have a delicacy and an elusive *'poetry in motion'* about them that is lacking in the males of the species. Women are connected to something more. Hell, *women are in tune with the cycles of the moon.* All us men can do is *sit back, stare, admire, & **worship***.

Vargas is my hero. I have been looking at his art for over 35 years, and I still get a thrill out of it.

My personal favorite *Vargas* is his portrait of **Marilyn Monroe**. It boils everything down to the essential, and is simply an angelic face, laughing -- *mysteriously* -- with a wicked joy. Held up to her face are dangerous, razor-sharp, blood-red fingernails. *"What is she laughing at? And why does her apparent 'joy' strike such deep cords within me?"* **Genius**. That to me is the distilled essence of pin-up art. When asked what is my favorite body part ('breast-man', 'leg-man' etc...) I always confess that I am a face-man. I am a sucker for a pretty face. If a girl has the right smile, the right twinkle in her eyes, I am putty in her hands. That painting has a profound hold on me.

My second favorite Vargas is his portrait of **Ava Gardner**. That takes my breath away. Ava Gardner had **"IT"**, and no photo ever captured the magic that she exuded in motion on screen. Vargas went where photography cannot go, and he captured her essence. I have no fear of tomorrow's various technologies, (Photoshop, C.G.I., whatever --) because I know that the real essence of what is 'art' must come from a human heart.

Some of my other "Pin-Up Heroes" include **Robert McGinnis**, and **Rolf Armstrong**. The McGinnis archetype of *'long legs, full hips, shapely breasts, all topped by a gorgeous face'* lines up with my personal tastes. Rolf Armstrong loved a pretty face, a pretty smile. Great sense of light and how it dances upon skin. His work crossed the line between teasing and taunting. *There **is** a difference*.

What can one really say about "PIN-UP ART"? To some, that may be a contradiction in terms -- *high-brow* versus *low-brow* -- but to me pin-ups serve ART's highest function. They visualize and make real what words cannot express. They articulate an aspiration. Quite often the aspiration is on the level of simple lust, but when they are done right, they reach for so much more.

Working away at the feminine mystery. As a man, I will forever be on the outside of that mystery. But maybe by taking a deep bath in pin-up art, I am getting one step closer to the heart of it. I have no interest in just painting the shell -- I want to paint the heart -- the soul -- the essence of girls and goddesses.

JML
February 23, 2007

ABOUT THE ARTIST --

In 1989 Joseph Michael Linsner created Dawn, a modern take on classic earth goddess mythology. Since then, his work has developed a worldwide following, having been translated into Spanish, Greek, Italian and Dutch. Born in Queens, New York, he has recently moved to the north Georgia mountains, where he lives with his two Sphynx cats. His next project is the vampire graphic novel, Dark Ivory, to be co-written with Eva Hopkins. 2007 marks the tenth year of the Dawn Look-A-Like contest, held annually at Atlanta's fantastic Dragon-Con.

THE LINSNER LIBRARY

DAWN: Lucifer's Halo

DAWN: Return of the Goddess

DAWN: Three Tears

The Vampire's Christmas

Angry Christ Comix

The Art Of Joseph Michael Linsner
Volume One

W W W . L I N S N E R . C O M